DAYS OF DECISION

an Oral History of Conscientious Objectors in the military during the Vietnam war

GERALD R. GIOGLIO

THE BROKEN RIFLE PRESS, Trenton, New Jersey

DAYS OF DECISION

an Oral History of Conscientious Objectors in the military during the Vietnam war

Gioglio, Gerald R.
Days of Decision.

1. Vietnamese conflict, 1961–1975—personal narratives.
2. Conscientious objection. Pacifism. Antiwar movement.

  The quote by Stephen Fortunato, Jr. appears in We Won't Go: Personal Accounts of War Objectors, © 1968 Alice Lynd. Reprinted by permission of Beacon Press.
  Quotes by Ernest Hemingway and Schopenhauer appear in Seeds of Peace: a Catalogue of Quotations, © 1986 Jeanne Larson & Madge Micheels-Cyrus. Reprinted by permission of New Society Publishers, 4722 Baltimore Ave., Philadelphia, PA 19143.
  The quotation by Charles A. Maresca, Jr. is reprinted by permission of the National Interreligious Service Board for Conscientious Objectors, Suite 600, 800 Eighteenth Street, NW, Washington, DC 20006.
  The quote by Robert Jay Lifton is from the Preface to the Basic Books Edition of Home From The War: Vietnam Veterans—Neither Victims Nor Executioners, by Robert Jay Lifton. © 1973 Robert Jay Lifton. Preface to the Basic Books Edition, © 1985 Robert Jay Lifton. Reprinted by permission of Basic Books, Inc., Publishers, and by permission of International Creative Management. © 1973, 1985 Robert Jay Lifton.
  The quote by Daniel Lang appears in Patriotism Without Flags, 1974 Daniel Lang. W. W. Norton Company, Inc. Reprinted by permission of Harold Ober Associates, New York, New York.

Printed in the United States of America.

Cover by: Howard V. Koby, Los Angeles.

Library of Congress Catalog Card Number: 88–70891.

ISBN: 0–9620024–0–2 Softcover.

TO:

EVERYONE I HAVE EVER LOVED.

FOR:

THE CHILDREN.

THERE ARE NO WARS WAGED
WITHOUT OUR CONSENT.
JUST SAY NO . . . AND MEAN IT.

ACKNOWLEDGMENTS

This project would not have been completed without the assistance and concern of many individuals. Most especially, it required the commitment and depth of feeling expressed by those who were interviewed for this book. My heartfelt thanks to those whose stories appear here. Thank you for sharing your memories and emotions, for opening up your homes, and for helping me to establish your stories as part of the historical record. Without your enthusiasm, cooperation and support this book could not have been written. I am honored to tell of your struggle for peace and human dignity.

The inspiration for the M–16 broken rifle logo came from the international symbol of the War Resisters League. I am extremely grateful for permission to recast and utilize this potent symbol of nonviolent resistance. Kudos to the artist, Enrique Berdecia, Jr.

The book's title came from a song of the same name written by the late Phil Ochs. Many thanks to Michael Ochs for permission to use this thoughtful and relevant phrase.

Many people contributed mightily to the production of this book. They include Howard Koby who created and photographed the book cover; Marilyn Nelson who transcribed several interviews, Ronald Jacobsen and Cathy Mudrak who critiqued portions of the first draft, and Susan Sternberg who gave the work a comprehensive edit.

Special thanks to my friend, sociologist John C. Leggett of Livingston College, Rutgers University. Always an inspiration, he, more than any other, taught me the trade. I am also obliged to Robert Seeley, of the Central Committee for Conscientious Objectors, and to Charles Clements, MD of the Unitarian Universalist Service Committee.

Then too, I am beholden to friends and relatives who gave me shoulders to lean on and the space I needed to complete this work. Mostly, hugs and kisses to my children, Dawn and Eric, for their love, patience, understanding and support.

CONTENTS

PREFACE

POINT OF DEPARTURE

The war, of course *The War,* sweet dead and dumb Jesus, you had to know the war was going on, that in those days and years it was the premise to everything that was happening everywhere you looked, power chords from the bottom and terminal end of the register came howling back across the Pacific to initiate us on a scale and in a way in which we'd never been before; visions of the national rot grown so bad and become so vivid a part of each day that no amount of anticommunism, nor an infinite number of speeches extolling the justice of the country's enterprise could enable people to blink the thing away; visions of what appeared in those days and nights to be the plateau of the next new stage, war without end, a war whose logic denied an end, the worst prophesies come home to roost, and to crow, crowing in every city, in every ghetto, on every campus in the land.

Because the war also took root exactly here, spreading in every direction, the country splitting like dumb earth at its incursion, hating it, or feeding on it, everyone over the age of twelve finding the delineations of true belief in their relationship to the war's ongoing charge, day after night after day watching it recycled on two hundred million TV screens, the terror still robust for all its having travelled back ten thousand miles of cold blue sea, robust being an overstatement, robust being a blood-soaked irony.

Preface

To imagine being there was for those years the national occupation, no matter what levels of attachment or sacrifice, humility or insanity were revealed, from border to border and coast to coast the information was the same: in Atlanta and downtown Chicago, in Jersey City and the streets of L.A., in the Green Mountains of Vermont and along the sand banks of the Sacramento River, in the river-cut valleys of Western Washington as they broadened from tree line in the Cascade Mountains to become the salt beaches of Puget Sound, late at night you could feel the power everywhere in those years rising out of the American continent, feel its surge from your gut to your brain, and know at that moment that no people on Earth, no matter how far away, could absorb that much American love without giving some part of it back, and what came curving back was the pure scream, an echo that left you deaf to nearly everything else.

Jeffrey Porteous
July 1980

INTRODUCTION

On July 3, 1968 a young, working-class Italian deeply kissed his scarlet-haired, milk-skinned bride of five months, bolted from their car and ran to the arms of the Selective Service System. I was twenty years old, just drafted.

Freshly kissed lips still tingled as I arrived at the draft board, and tears welled in my eyes—tears that lifelong exposure to strict Catholic discipline and "thou shalt not cry" American macho could not quite contain. In the deep recesses of my soul I knew I was doing something I should not do. Nobody told me it would be so hard to render to Caesar and to God while remaining true to myself.

Stepping into the building, I pulled myself together; the government claimed a legal right to my body, but my spirit and emotions they would not share, not that day, not ever. I knew this much, though little else. As it turned out, just knowing and believing that was enough.

I came armed with a five-page treatise explaining why I should not be inducted into the Army, and why prior to this, I had not applied for an exemption as a conscientious objector (CO). "They'll read this," I reasoned, "realize I would not fit into their program, and tell me to go away." Wrong.

Conscientious objection was the legal remedy for draft age men who, by reason of religious training and belief, were opposed to participation in warfare, and would agree to perform noncombatant military service or alternative

1

civilian service. During the late Sixties, conscience and common sense told me I fit the definition of a CO. However, after several agonizing months pondering questions of conscience, masculinity and duty, I came to the conclusion that I did not qualify for conscientious objector status.

There's the rub. Like millions of other young men, I had been playing the Selective Service game by their rules. One of those rules required potential COs to proclaim opposition to "participation in war in any form," which the government took to mean opposition to *all* wars, rather than participation in a particular war in any way, shape, manner or form. At the time, I could not sign such a thing. Vietnam was the only war I knew and it disgusted me. But no matter, the young could not pick and choose their wars, the government decided who we should fight and kill. Somehow, during those difficult days of decision, there was little solace in the premise that Americans always wore the white hats.

When I was a child, one of the good Sisters of Charity assured me that killing in a war was not murder. Luckily, another nun told me about the Nuremberg Principles. I thought the second nun made a lot more sense than the first, although both believed in the concept of a "just war." So I did too, and I even thought I knew of one.

As a young boy, I once found several sepia-tinted, 8 × 10 visions of hell hidden in my father's dresser drawer. Flatbeds stacked high with bodies, cords of white, naked, dead people, heads shorn—even the women—faces frozen in agony, shock and wonder. So I learned about the Nazis and United States involvement in something called World War II. I was proud of our people's involvement, and exactly then came to believe in "just wars." At age twenty, I still believed, though I knew little of U.S. and Vatican acts of omission in the killing of the Jews. Nor had I heard the Gandhian pronouncement: "An eye for an eye only ends up making the whole world blind."

At twenty, I only guessed history could be propaganda, that "the best and the brightest" who ran the government would lie, that organized religion could serve the State.

Introduction

But in my gut I knew Vietnam was wrong; I knew my generation was being deceived; I knew impoverished Asian peoples were being exploited; and I knew the leaders of this country were tearing out the very heart and soul of the nation as they sent their young to slaughter. Intuitively, I knew this, but I refused to believe it. Somebody, somewhere, had to be wearing those white hats.

The officials at the induction center thought my treatise was threatening enough to warrant a psychiatric evaluation. The military psychiatrist admitted I was sane, all right, then wrote on the bottom of his report, "The man will follow this through." Four months later, following basic and advanced infantry training, his prophecy was fulfilled. I had seen too much. I had been changed in ways that both confused and scared me. I did not like the person they were trying to make me become. But most of all, I saw clearly that what I was doing was wrong, and I knew I had to confront it directly. Ultimately, I refused to ship to Vietnam by filing for discharge as a conscientious objector.

Once I made the decision to fight back by proclaiming CO status, I felt strong and patriotic. I was now a foot soldier in the war-against-the-war in Vietnam. I became, as the rock group Jefferson Airplane advocated, a "Volunteer of America." As I look back, I realize I have become something of a "lifer." (See the Glossary for GI slang, technical terms and acronyms).

By the time I received my CO discharge, one year and fourteen days after induction, my major antiwar actions included writing every chaplain at Fort Lewis, Washington asking them to speak out against the war, and taking the Army to federal court on the grounds they illegally refused to discharge me as a conscientious objector. I also counseled many soldiers referred to me by other GIs at Fort Lewis or by the GI-Civilian Alliance for Peace, an antiwar organization located in Tacoma, Washington. The latter effort resulted in the discharge of ten men (including two Vietnam combat veterans) for various administrative reasons including hardship and conscientious objection. I got "on the job training" as an organizer, and my life changed forever.

Introduction

I did not struggle alone. I met many outstanding young men who were fighting the same fight, each in his own special way. Five of those men were in-service conscientious objectors who appear in this book: Abraham "Rudy" Byrd, Thomas Cox, Howard Koby, Richard Lovett and Jeffrey Porteous. Because they were my buddies, because of the things they taught me, and because some seventeen years later they were still on my mind, they became the true inspiration for this book. The more I thought about what we were able to accomplish, and the more I worried about the present generation of young men (and now women) who are being wooed into the military, the more I realized our story must be told.

Then too, the nation has become more receptive to learning about the events of that time. Combat veterans have been publishing their stories in biographies, oral histories and novels. The theater and films of the Eighties have captured the attention of an American public finally ready to take another look at what happened to their soldiers, to the Vietnamese and to our nation.

Vietnam era veterans, especially the combat veterans, have effectively used these media to say, "this is who we are, this is what we did, and this is how we feel about it." The power and raw honesty of this material has helped strip away many myths and stereotypes about the war and the millions of men in uniform during that time. Some of this has led to bravado and flag-waving, but mostly there has been a healing and cleansing process for both the veterans and the nation.

A study conducted for the Veterans Administration by Louis Harris and Associates not only found favorable public attitudes toward members of the Vietnam generation, but that feelings of sympathy for Vietnam era veterans had increased between 1971 and 1980 (Committee on Veterans' Affairs, 1980, pp. 80–89). The Harris study also characterized the public's attitude toward those who demonstrated against the war as "neutral," neither warm nor cold. But then, support for opposition to the war for reasons of conscience was also apparent. According to Harris, 54% of the

Introduction

public and 52% of the Vietnam era veterans surveyed agreed with the statement: "Those who refused induction as a matter of conscience, and were willing to face the consequences, deserve respect" (Committee on Veterans' Affairs, p. 90).

Slowly, the public seems to have accepted the idea that Vietnam was a different sort of a cat, that war generally is an unsavory business, and that their citizen-soldiers, at the very least, were true victims of their leaders' misguided imperial designs. More cleansing can occur if each adult American of that time comes to accept personal responsibility for the conduct of the war, a spiritual awakening not likely to occur outside pockets of Vietnam era veterans, antiwar participants, and the families of both, whose lives have been directly affected.

Public acceptance, indeed recognition, of the antiwar veteran poses another challenge, because our open resistance to the war and things military ran against the grain of the traditional American view of patriotism. That is, when one puts on a military uniform, the public expectation is for such individuals to unquestionably follow the dictum, "My country, right or wrong." Antiwar veterans, however, discovered there were many ways to fight for the country, including conducting an internal struggle against a civilian and military leadership bent on having its way with Third World peoples.

As demonstrated by Cortright (1975) the resistance took many forms, violent and nonviolent, individual and organizational, antimilitary and antiwar. It occurred stateside and in Vietnam. GIs published newspapers, joined GI-civilian organizations, wrote their congresspeople, participated in demonstrations, formed underground networks to counsel and help one another, went AWOL, deserted, refused orders, fragged their superiors, and committed innumerable acts of sabotage against equipment and standard operating procedures. Not infrequently, participants were returned combat veterans who had become disillusioned and angry over what they had been sent to do, and what they had seen and done.

Introduction

This book focuses on a select group within the resistance, in-service conscientious objectors, men who either entered the service after receiving noncombatant status (1–A–O) from their draft boards or who applied for CO status after serving some time in the military. Baskir and Strauss (1978) reported that during the Vietnam era, approximately 172,000 men received "1–O" conscientious objector status from their local draft boards. Like other registrants, those with 1–O status were subject to the draft. If drafted, however, they were usually assigned to two years alternative civilian service, often in hospitals, government agencies or nonprofit organizations. These alternative service COs are not included in this book. The focus is entirely on conscientious objectors within the military.

Men wishing to obtain either 1–O or 1–A–O conscientious objector status had to request and complete the "Special Form for Conscientious Objectors," SSS Form 150 (see Appendix). The form asked for descriptive information about the registrant, details on the nature and sources of his beliefs, circumstances where he believed in the use of force, and descriptions of activities which demonstrated the depth of the applicant's convictions. The local board then decided to approve or deny CO status. Personal appearances could be requested to support a claim or to appeal a negative decision.

Although conscientious objector status was a legal exemption from either military service (classification 1–O) or combatant military service (1–A–O), it was not easy to obtain. Local board members often considered those who applied for CO status as cast from the same mold as nonregistrants or draft evaders. The fact remains, however, that COs were drafted, either into the military or into the civilian service; plus, as has been well-documented, there were easier ways for young men to dodge the draft (Baskir and Strauss, chap. 2; MacPherson, 1985). Some local boards were more lenient with 1–A–O requests, because unlike 1–O civilian inductees, the induction of noncombatants counted toward fulfillment of their military manpower quotas.

Introduction

For years, aspiring COs had to tie their objection to religious training and to belief in a Supreme Being. Therefore, men who were not members of traditional pacifist sects, like the Quakers or the Mennonites, had a difficult time convincing local boards of their sincerity. Local boards tended to be extremely narrow in their interpretation of those terms, until a series of court decisions removed the Supreme Being limitation and broadened the definition of what could be construed as religion in a person's life (Rohr, 1971). In addition to these hurdles, CO applicants had to have good writing skills, as well as fairly well-developed positions on issues of war, peace and pacifism. A tall order for the average eighteen year old.

Incredibly, the Selective Service System has never published accurate statistics on the number of young men who received 1-A-O conscientious objector status during the Vietnam era. For whatever practical or political reasons, classification 1-A-O and classification 1-A were combined and published as a category called, "available for military service." Therefore, in order to determine the number of men drafted as 1-A-Os, one would have to wade through the archives of approximately 4,100 local boards, records now stored by the Federal Records Center of the General Services Administration.

Once inducted, most of these 1-A-O conscientious objectors were trained as medics. Other noncombatant assignments included cooks or truck drivers. According to the draft counseling literature of the time, a young man entering the military as a 1-A-O was more likely than draftees in general to be sent into combat; indeed, upon becoming a medic, one was virtually assured of going to Vietnam (Tatum and Tuchinsky, 1969).

Data on in-service CO applications is not complete prior to 1965; however, an estimated 17,000–18,000 applications for discharge or noncombatant status were processed by the various branches of military between 1965 and 1973 (Cortright, p. 16). While questions on the military's CO forms were similar to those used by the Selective Service System, the approval process was more elaborate. Decisions by Selective Service were, for the most part, made on the local level. In-service claims, however, were reviewed by the applicant's company and base commanders before being forwarded to the Department of Defense for final review. In-service applicants had to be interviewed by an officer, usually their company commander, a chaplain and a psychiatrist. The chaplain and the officer had to attest to the CO's sincerity; all three had to recommend approval or disapproval.

This process often took several months. In the meantime, COs were usually placed in holding status and were exempt from military training or activity that involved the handling or use of weapons. The interpretation of what constituted military training, or even weapons handling, led to some interesting, often humorous, confrontations between the military and the COs. Several of the these events are detailed in Chapters 2–4.

Between 1965 and 1969, only 19% of the CO applications filed by active Army personnel were approved. Toward the end of the war, as the Army cleaned house of its detractors and malcontents, over 80% of all applications were approved. Approval rates for the services as a whole were comparable: 28% approved in 1967, 77% in 1972 (Cortright, p. 17).

If a CO application was returned disapproved, applicants were expected to return to duty. No longer protected by restrictions on training or weapons handling, these young men had to decide whether to cooperate or to disobey orders. Those who refused to obey orders were often court-martialed and sentenced to military stockades or to the United States Disciplinary Barracks at Fort Leavenworth, Kansas. Four of the men featured in this book, David Brown, Rudy Byrd, Tom Cox and Jeffrey Porteous, disobeyed orders and were incarcerated for activities related to their conscientious objection.

The men presented below were located through a number of classified advertisements placed in a variety of liberal and progressive journals, and through correspondence with several of the major veterans organizations and peace groups listed in the Appendix of this book. Individuals who contacted me were asked to complete a comprehensive questionnaire that was subsequently used to structure individualized questions for the actual interview. The men were asked to discuss their lives prior to entering military service, and to identify important influences that affected their decision to become COs. They were asked to describe the reaction of family and friends to their position and to provide detail on the treatment accorded them by draft board members and military personnel. Those sent overseas were questioned on their experiences as conscientious objectors in Southeast Asia. All were asked about personal involvement in peace or antiwar activities. Several reported on their attempts to be discharged, and/or their experience of court-martial and imprisonment. The men were also asked to discuss the effect that being both a conscientious objector and a veteran has had on their lives. Finally, all were asked to describe additional past, or any current, involvement in peace-related activities or other social causes.

The data were collected and the interviews conducted between 1985–1987. I traversed the nation to hold in-person interviews with most of these respondents. In a few cases, however, telephone interviews were conducted. Most interviews were one-on-one; however, four COs asked that wives and/or children be allowed to listen. In each case family members reported they had never heard the entire story before.

Several of these men retraced steps through a virtual minefield of savage memories that left emotions unhinged. Sometimes we stopped to regain our composure. I felt like I was dragging some of them through hell, that I had no right to stir up these painful memories. But those who had been to hell—Vietnam or prison—were willing to endure the psychic trip back, fully realizing their perspective on the war needed to be made part of the historical record. Several men were grateful that someone was interested in

Introduction

both their peace stories and their military experiences. Many assured me that our talking was therapeutic—still—after all these years.

Although the mailed questionnaire and the interview process were products of sociological inquiry, this book does not necessarily represent the experiences of all in-service conscientious objectors. Military personnel and draft counselor records are confidential, so there are no lists of COs from which to draw a random sample. These men had to be found. More, a determined effort was made to find several COs that I had met, between 1968–1969, at Fort Lewis, Washington. In addition to this obvious bias, nonwhites and COs who were members of traditional peace churches did not respond to my advertisements. Therefore, this book is not a fully comprehensive analysis of in-service conscientious objection; rather, it seeks to present a distinctive range of perspectives on the war. These perspectives, and this kind of analytic work, have been missing from the record of that time.

As you will see, Vietnam era COs were a heterogeneous group. For the purposes of this book, they have been clustered into three main categories: in-service, imprisoned COs, those who were jailed for reasons of conscientious objection; noncombatant service COs, those who entered the military as 1–A–Os and served without weapons; and in-service, discharged COs, those who were discharged for reasons of conscientious objection usually without serving in Vietnam or being imprisoned. Although many COs had similar experiences, especially related to training, these groupings do help differentiate them and governs the organization of this book.

The book features three men whose narratives best depict one of these groupings. Their narrations begin appropriate chapters, and each of their stories is presented in its entirety. The main narrators are: Jeffrey Porteous, representing the in-service, imprisoned COs; John Lawrence, characterizing the noncombatant service COs; and Mike Ferner, representing the in-service, discharged COs.

Introduction

Jeffrey Porteous filed for discharge after completing basic and advanced infantry training. When the Army rejected his application Jeff refused to obey orders. He was court-martialed and confined to the United States Disciplinary Barracks at Fort Leavenworth. Jeff's insightful and eloquent story shows how the individual, against massive odds, can struggle to maintain personal freedom and human dignity.

In 1968, John Lawrence applied for and received 1–A–O noncombatant status from his draft board. John was drafted into the U.S. Army and spent a year in Vietnam as a medic. If it is possible to grasp the nefarious nature of war from words on the printed page, then John Lawrence presents it in italics.

Mike Ferner joined the U.S. Navy in 1969 and was trained as a hospital corpsman. Mike became increasingly involved in antiwar activity during his time in the military. After two years he applied for, and received, a discharge for reasons of conscientious objection. Mike recounts a powerful tale of personal and collective resistance to the military and the war.

The reader may follow each of these men, from beginning to end, by proceeding from chapter to chapter. Or, one can follow them by reading an entire chapter in tandem with vignettes from the other COs. These latter stories cluster around the three main narratives, providing additional insight into the in-service CO experience.

These narratives were chosen to more completely reveal the powerful sociological factors and historical events that were occurring at the time. For example, Stephan Gubar, Jim Kraus and others provide important details about the consciousness raising aspects of the youth culture and the civil rights movement. John Vail takes us inside the GI-civilian movement with his account of activists involved in the GI press; and Rudy Byrd's transcript chronicles the deep divisions that occurred between officers and servicemen over issues related to duty, discipline and involvement in the Vietnam war.

Introduction

Some of the men, like in-service CO James Willingham, appear only once; others, such as Harold O., a noncombatant service CO, and David Brown, an in-service, imprisoned objector, appear in two or more chapters. In most cases this format allows the reader to follow individual COs chronologically, from draft age to post-military experiences.

Chapter 1 details the development of a personal belief system that led these men to oppose war. Chapter 2 presents memories from basic and advanced military training. Chapter 3 captures visions of Vietnam from the unique perspective of the conscientious objector. Chapter 4 reports on resistance and antiwar activity, including court-martial and imprisonment. Chapter 5 discusses life after the military, including adjustment problems and current attitudes on issues of war, peace and conscientious objection.

Chapter 6 features the stories of two men who did not quite meet the "operational definition" of a conscientious objector used for this book. That is, they either did not formally file for CO status, or after doing so, found other ways to express their opposition to the war. Their stories help us to understand the feelings of confusion and desperation felt by many servicemen of that era; further, they offer insight into the more generalized resistance that occurred in the military during that time. The Afterword outlines some common themes presented by the COs, and briefly discusses some of the other forms of GI resistance to the war.

What follows is an oral history recounting the experiences of twenty-four in-service conscientious objectors. A "Record of Trial" (the transcript of Rudy Byrd's court-martial) and the Afterword are the only exceptions to the narrative format. Two respondents asked that their names not be published. The pseudonyms, "Harold O." and "Robert D." are used to satisfy these requests for anonymity.

The accounts presented here are from men who come from mainstream religions and fairly typical social environments. These are remarkably ordinary men, neither saints nor soldiers, who accomplished extraordinary deeds while part of an organization in which they were an anath-

Introduction

ema. I am grateful to have been chosen to tell their stories, and thankful that as a younger man, I found the strength to be counted among those you are about to meet. May the young men and women who will follow in our footsteps find strength in our humble witness.

CHAPTER 1

Coming to Consciousness, Heading for War.

All truth passes through three stages.
First, it is ridiculed.
Second, it is violently opposed.
Third, it is accepted as being self-evident.

Schopenhauer

Jeffrey Porteous

**In-service, imprisoned CO
U.S. Army 1969–1972
Veteran U.S. Disciplinary Barracks, Fort
Leavenworth**

*Hell, I think we are all conscientious objectors until we are
swindled out of it.*

* * * *

How do I begin? I don't know ... the first seven, eight
years of my life everything they told me to do, I did. But
somehow, somewhere in there, I stopped listening. Suddenly I was the kid who got into trouble. I don't remember
looking for it, it was just where I was most of the time. By
the eighth grade I'd been thrown out of the school's whole
offering of accelerated classes, and the entire city-wide
school system. I was a disciplinary problem, that was my
description. It was very hard for me to get along in ways
other children found easy.

I grew up in the 1960s, went to the local high school, and
graduated by the skin of my teeth in 1966. I played football, I played the flute, I played first base on my little
league baseball team; I was lousy at all three. I also read a
lot, anything I could get my hands on, and all the time.

There were things going on in those years, the end of my
high school years, with which I deeply identified, a sort of
wave spreading out across the entire nation. It was tens of
millions of us that were reaching a common consciousness—all of us—all at the same time. Consciousness. The
word may seem milked of all human meaning, but it got
used a lot back then. It was my intuition in those days that
the national consciousness changed through the sheer fact
of our great numbers, literally—baby boomers reaching
critical mass in the mid-sixties, igniting the explosion that

blew the whole roof off the place. We were all eighteen, all listening to the same music, all experiencing the effects of the same drugs, all keeping time to the same beat, all falling in love—love, love, love—as far as we understood it, and maybe freedom, and even, perhaps, God. And, of course, the pain and confusion and horror of being eighteen.

I got turned on to weed the day I graduated from high school. By the time I was drafted, a year later, I'd sampled much of the chemical cornucopia. I grew up in a country club, for Christ's sake. God help me if I hadn't been allowed to get some sort of perspective on that. I was reading Hesse and Huxley and Tim Leary, listening to the Beatles and Dylan and the Doors. I thought they were prophets of the new age then, maybe I still do, and it came as a revelation that there could be such a thing as a spiritual life, that there could be an end goal such as wisdom, that the ultimate aim of life actually could be something other than making mortgage payments on a house and car.

But, here's how goofy and naive I was: you know the phrase "withering away of the state?" I thought there would be a withering away of our culture. I thought there would be a change of consciousness that was so profound that the accoutrements of our culture would suddenly become meaningless, and lie about us like rubble; we'd simply walk away from it. I thought the young had a lock on morality, had been chosen, were "the good," that we were smarter and better, and that we were right. I believed in Jimmy Morrison of the Doors when he sang about "breaking on through to the other side." God knows what the other side was. I didn't know. But I felt it—felt something was ready to happen—and I wanted it. It was in the air, patterns visible everywhere you looked, and I had a notion where you found pattern, you found meaning; so there was the feeling that existence was meaningful, that there was some kind of consciousness at work in the universe, that it wasn't all just the dead clockworks of the nineteenth century philosophers, that perhaps things were even holy.

My parents took me to an Episcopalian Church for about three years beginning when I was ten or eleven. This was a church where some of the old money in the city gathered to pray for more money. It was like being dead for a few hours each Sunday, and Sundays were bad enough. Walk out the doors and you're resurrected. Religion had no impact, not if you're talking about being a Catholic or Baptist or Jew.

I think I was an unconscious patriot, like most of the kids I grew up with. I mean, in the Fifties, something would have been amiss if classes hadn't started with the "Pledge of Allegiance." I suppose as a boy I thought of America the way I had been trained to think of America, as the city on a hill, a light in the darkness of the world. America . . . to say the word was to light up all those moral centers in your soul. I was sarcastic, and antagonistic, of course, but at bottom, I was probably that sort of patriot. I was made in America.

By graduation from high school, the war had been in the papers for years. It seemed the type of insanity in which you pried up one layer of horror, only to find a further level of madness beneath it. It was a constant ugliness in the popular magazines and on TV. Some people I knew began to go, started to be disappearing to that. I knew I was against it without having to ask myself why. I don't think you could have gotten high, really high, and believed in the music, and the art, the literature, the kinds of noises the Sixties were making in the world and still have thought about going to Vietnam to defend the "sanctity" of the South Vietnamese political system. If one, then not the other. I know they've called Vietnam the first "rock'n'roll war," but I don't think you could have been a true volunteer for the music, and not have known something stunk pretty bad in Vietnam.

I was eighteen, angry, hurt, confused. I tried college for a time, but was unable to focus. I think that I had read about conscientious objection a bit. I knew there was something called "conscientious objection," a wonderful phrase; I conscientiously objected to a lot of things. I told my parents that I wanted to talk to someone about it. They arranged a visit with a child psychologist. "I know I'm about to be drafted," I told him, "and I'm thinking about conscientious objection." I think I wanted to know if I was sincere. I wanted him to tell me that. He asked me a few questions, if I ate red meat, as I remember, then he advised me to let the Army know about my feelings.

Vietnam was the single clearest symbol of all that was then insane in the country. Everyone I respected believed that, and I believed it too—with all of my heart, and all of my mind, and all of my soul—and I went down to my draft board and volunteered for the war. Why? I don't know. I knew I was going to be drafted, that my own life, in some ways, had just never come together, so I hurried things up. I talked to a recruiter beforehand and told him I wanted to be a medic. He said to go ahead and make my wishes known at my duty station, at boot camp. The proviso, my proviso, was that I be a 1–A–0 conscientious objector, a medic, and not carry a weapon. I never applied for the 1–A–0 from the draft board.

The next month, November 1967, I went down to the Induction Center, a huge, square, unpainted cement building on the city docks; I went through a battery of tests and that evening got on a Greyhound bus. It was just dusk when the driver pulled out, there must have been about fifty of us, more, every seat taken, our destinations being Fort Lewis, Washington, and the recruit barracks there. They were just words to me then.

John Lawrence

Noncombatant service CO
U.S. Army 1968–1970
Vietnam veteran

Not only am I a walking war memorial, I am a walking contradiction.

* * * *

I was raised by my grandparents in a very traditional, very Republican, conservative family. We had a military tradition in the family; my granddad was a Marine during World War I; however, he didn't go overseas. My dad was a civilian who worked for the Air Force in World War II. After the war, and until his death in 1952, he worked as an instructor of electrical engineering for the Air Force. That's when my grandparents started helping to raise me. My granddad was an extremely military person and we lived on a kind of military time schedule. We had inspections in the morning, and we voted for Nixon in 1960.

I went to religious school where no fighting was allowed; however, boxing was one of the athletic activities, and I got into that. My family was very religious, we belonged to the Church of Christ, Fundamentalist and spent a great deal of time reading and memorizing verses in the Bible. Of course, there was this constant reference to the "Prince of Peace," and that we lived our lives nonviolently through peace, and by loving our enemies. Those are ingrained principles in me. At the same time my family was very military, a contradiction I don't think they even saw.

When I was a kid, in the mid-fifties, there was a John Wayne mania going on. I was crazy about John Wayne. I didn't want him to ever die. It was crazy. I really believed America was a fantastic country that could do no wrong. I believed it with all my heart. I thought this was the best country ever created. Of course, as a child you hear that from the adult world—how America saved the world from Hitler and all the bad guys; you want to believe it. You want to believe in the best, in the good, and I did. God and country were one and the same.

In school, I was Senior Class President. I was editor of the school newspaper. I was on the state track team and was voted "one of the most popular," you know, the real catchall things that were important back then. I was building toward a career in psychology and counseling. I really saw myself as a psychologist. I was going to figure out the world.

I started reading philosophy in college and I began to pick up on some of the pacifist readings, like Bertrand Russell. It was just a gradual exposure and, of course, I would debate ideas with students and it felt good. Pacifism always felt good, for whatever reason. The uglier people would get about their defense of violence, the clearer it became to me where I stood. It wasn't something I deliberately did. It wasn't something I sat down and decided to stick to, declaring myself different. It just came out of the process of learning, and I think, from the kinds of materials I was exposing myself to. Reading the great thinkers of philosophy, who were pacifists, became something of an avocation with me, and I slowly became aware that I was coming to a decision point in my life.

In 1963 I registered for the draft, not even thinking anything of it. It was just something you did after your birthday. It wasn't even a matter of conscience at the time. I went down, filled out the card and walked out the door. There was nothing going on in the world to even make me aware that there was any risk involved in confronting my own values. I didn't know anything about conscientious objection, that wasn't something that was advertised by the Selective Service System.

I graduated from a two year religious college in 1965 and went to Abilene Christian College in Abilene, Texas. At that time the Selective Service System was getting onto me about continuing school. Vietnam wasn't exactly hot and active, but the draft was picking up, and I was becoming very aware of the Selective Service. So, on my own, I wrote the draft board and essentially said, "Based on my understanding of philosophy and the scriptures, I'd like to declare myself a conscientious objector, but I'd be willing to serve in the military." You see, I wanted the best of both worlds. I was willing to meet my obligations as a citizen of this country, at the same time not going so far as killing somebody. I had been raised on the diet that you do serve your country and it was my full intent to serve my country in a noncombatant position. I didn't know what position they would put me in; I'd heard there were medics and people like that, so I knew I could serve my country without having to take up arms. I felt strongly about it at the time.

So, they sent the forms and I filled them out, stating my position and quoting my sources. They accepted them, I never had a hearing, and I knew they would not reject my claim. When they sent back saying I'd be classified a 1–A–O conscientious objector I saw how the system worked. I was convinced it was going to work, and it worked! I was still into, "If America says it's okay to follow your conscience, it's okay to follow your conscience," and I did. Morally, I saw myself as out of a dilemma, willing to serve my country, but at the same time not willing to kill for it. This was three or four years before I was drafted.

The people in Abilene were very promilitary, very much behind the war effort. I was definitely the odd one out and I was receiving a great deal of flack from my peers; like, "Why are you taking that position?" I was kind of the preacher on a soap box going my own way, but they tolerated me. I was "Mr. Clean," a straight-arrow guy. It was like, "John's a little eccentric, you know, but he's nice and popular." I was accepted, but they'd look at me askance and wonder what was wrong with me. However, my teachers never wanted to debate me in class. There was just grim tolerance. The only time we had arguments was in the hallways and in the dormitory rooms, places like that.

John Lawrence

I was pretty radical for that environment. While most of the country, in '66 and '67, was demonstrating against the war, Abilene was having demonstrations for the war. Divinity students would rally in the cafeteria and give homage to fallen soldiers in Vietnam. But, I felt very strongly about where I was coming from. At that time I felt very satisfied with being a conscientious objector. I learned though.

I got into a real go-around with a minister of my church. He was arguing the hypotheticals—"What would you do if Russia came over and dropped an atomic bomb?" Or, "If a man was breaking into your house and was going to rape your wife, mother or sister, what would you do?" So, we'd argue hypotheticals. It came down to either/or's. Either you're going to carry a weapon or not at all, but none of this in-between stuff. It got down to those "well if," "maybe not" arguments that tend to take the either/or twist. It got to be these ridiculous go-arounds and I began to realize that the ministers were for the war, for war! Meanwhile, I was becoming more and more the pacifist. The more I had to argue my position, the stronger I became.

I graduated from college and started my first job as a child welfare worker. In September 1968, I received my draft notice. Of course, in the upper right hand corner of the draft notice was this little box checked "1–A–O, Conscientious Objector." Well, I took the paper down to the induction center in Abilene, and it turns out the clerks didn't see that little box, and they processed me through as a regular.

Out of the fifty that went to the induction center, twenty-five of us were chosen for the military. They pulled us out of the ranks and put us into this little ceremonial room. It was a small room with chairs along the walls, the center area was empty. There was posh, beautiful carpeting—purple, and there was a platform with a podium and the flags of Texas and the United States behind it. We were all grouped in the center of this room and this very stern, serious captain walked in and stood at the podium. Out of routine he said, "I'm going to swear you into the military, you are going to take the oath that will induct you into the military, are there any questions?" I was in the back and I raised my hand. He said, "Yes, you, what do you want?" He's very annoyed because I am breaking protocol here—you don't ask questions, that's rhetorical, but dummy me! I said, "I'm a conscientious objector, what do I do?" And he froze. I mean, we're talking captain-going-major and he's got this rebel in his ranks. He says, "You, take three steps back and do not raise your hand!" That's all he could figure out to do with me. He was angry.

So, he gets up there and says, "Now the rest of you raise your right hand." He says, "Do you swear, you know, blah, blah, blah." Then he says, "Dismissed, except you, go over there." He pointed to a chair on the wall, I sat down and he stormed out of the room, slammed the door and went down the hallway. I'm sitting there, all by myself, and a few minutes later he comes ripping back into the room, slams the door and walks formally up to the podium. He said, "Do you know what you are doing?" I said, "Yes." I'm thinking, my papers are in order, I saw that little box checked there. And he said, "You are hereby charged with treason against the United States government." And he read me my rights. I'm sitting there, thinking this was the way you're supposed to do it; like it was part of the system. So, I thought, "This is interesting." It didn't even phase me.

He storms back out of the room and slams the door. I've just been read the treason act. Then, the door flies open and I hear a voice, "Conscientious objector coming down the hall!" I get up and this sergeant comes in and he says, "You, follow me." I notice everybody is standing in the hallway, they've got to see the CO. We're talking Abilene, Texas now and I'm walking down the hall and everybody is going, "Conscientious objector! Conscientious objector!" They set me down in this chair and all the civilians in the office gather around, and they're just firing questions at me left and right. I'm being interrogated by civilians in the induction center. Suddenly, this woman comes up to me, squared off nose-to-nose and it looks like when you look into a Christmas tree bulb, kind of distorted. Her face comes at me like that and she goes, "I'm a member of the Church of Christ and I believe in killing, why don't you?" I'm getting those kinds of questions and everybody is just taking all this in. For Abilene, Texas this is just an unheard of, incredible experience.

Finally, this sergeant whips out a goldenrod piece of paper and its got **"TREASON"** right across the top in thirty-six point type, you can't miss it. He's cussing me out royally. He says, "Do you know what kind of paperwork you're causing me?" And he stuffs it in this old clunker, manual typewriter, bang, bang, bang, hit and peck. He says, "Why are you doing this? Why are you doing this to me?" He finally gets done and he pulls the paper out and puts it on the very top of the inside of my "201" personnel file. He slams it shut and puts it in this manila folder, putting it on top of everyone elses. Then, they sent us out of the building and told us to report back at five o'clock, and I thought, "Boy, am I in trouble!"

I could have walked out the door and kept going, but no, not me. I believed, so I came back at five o'clock. The same sergeant who cussed me out walked up to me and handed me the stack of everyones' 201 files; then he said, "You're in command now." I looked on the top of all these personnel files and everyones' name was listed. Mine had an asterisk; so I said, "Why is my name asterisked?" He said, "You're the leader, you are the only one with a college degree and you're going to lead this bunch to the reception center at Fort Bliss." I said, "I'm in command of all these guys? I just got charged with treason and I'm in charge of them?" So, I took command, and you know, I still haven't quite figured that out.

Mike Ferner

In-service, discharged CO
U.S. Navy 1969–1972

I see myself as part of a long line of activists that fight for social justice.

* * * *

I came from a family of eight kids, and for some reason, I'm kind of an oddball in terms of how we turned out. I grew up in a very small farming village just west of Toledo; we had, I think, fourteen kids in our eighth grade graduating class. So, it was very small. Being a traditional Catholic, in the early and mid-Sixties, I got a strong dose of rabid anticommunism. We were taught by over-the-hill Franciscan nuns who'd tell us jibberish horror stories about communists and how they had dominated Red China, and one thing and another. We got several Catholic publications at our house. And, in the mid-to-late Sixties when the Vietnam war was building up, there was a steady dose of things like the communists were the "bad guys" and the U.S. government was there trying to keep the peace.

In grade school I remember visiting migrant labor camps with my mom. There were a lot of migrant farmworkers in the area when I was growing up. My mom wanted to learn Spanish so she went to the camps. I went with her and saw the conditions that people lived in. I can remember writing our local Congressman telling him that something had to be done about those camps. They were terrible. I think that was the first activist sort of thing I did. Just little things like that. I'm a union organizer now, so organizing and activism have been a recurrent theme for me.

I didn't really fit in at school; I felt more like I stood out like a sore thumb—only because I was from a little farm town. There I was, at a Jesuit high school in Toledo, with city kids from families with higher-than-average incomes; I just never quite fit in. But, I was in the band for a few years and on the track team. I felt a need to excel for some reason. I was the president of the band, the Student Council, things like that. To my classmates, I was known to be outspoken and quick with an opinion, even if those opinions changed every week.

Through grade school and high school I was taught two really different views of the world: the conservative, anticommunist, flag-waving view, and that which appealed to higher moral values, like "Thou shalt not kill," and concern for one's fellow man. At that point I thought the U.S. Marines were great; so, in speech class I gave a speech on how wonderful the Marines were, but then the next week I'd talk about the horrors of war.

This kind of stuff kept bouncing back and forth inside my head. I didn't know how I was going to come out of this. I was approaching high school graduation knowing I did not want to go to college, and knowing if you didn't go to college, you got drafted. I did not know, from one week to the next, whether or not I was going to enlist in the Marines, or go to Canada. I bounced back and forth between those two things all the time. I thought about this every day, all day long, some days.

At the time, I was kind of a hawk; I had full-color pictures of battleships stuck all over my wall. The only thing I knew about current events was what was reported in the mass media. My family didn't take popular magazines, although I did see *Life* magazine occasionally. But obviously, there were things from a variety of sources that made an impression on me. Also, my English teacher, a priest, talked about what was going on at the 1968 Democratic Convention and about the riots in the cities. It all seemed completely foreign to me. It really opened my eyes to think that somebody in Toledo would be concerned about what was happening in other parts of the country.

I knew there were a lot of people getting killed in Indochina. They were being blown up by ships like those I had plastered on the wall of my room. To a seventeen year old kid it looked kind of neat to see a cruiser belching orange flames out at the enemy. I would think about what it was like; but the difference was I carried it a bit further at times. I imagined what it was like when the shells exploded in a village. I don't know how or why I thought about those things, but I did.

So, I was raised a real traditional Catholic, and there has to be some correlation between being raised Catholic and turning out a hell-raiser. I can't believe the number of people in the various movements that I've been involved in who are ex-Catholics, an amazing correlation. But anyway, somehow in my upbringing, from Catholic school and from my parents, I learned obedience to authority; and at the same time, I learned about individual responsibility for not just following what's handed down as "the thing to do." I was taught that an individual's conscience was very important. I can't really articulate how I came to internalize these values; it was just something that happened over the years.

When I was in grade school, my dad took me on a destroyer escort that pulled into Toledo harbor. Then later, when I was really "into" the Marines, I thought, "This is something you should do and you have to do." It came through hot and heavy. Being in the Marines, involved in the most intense combat, seemed to be the best place for those trying to fulfill their duty to fight communists.

As I bounced from one position to the other I thought, "Well, maybe I should go into the Marines, maybe I should go into the Navy, maybe I should go to Canada." Kind of a compromise was to be a Navy Hospital Corpsman. This seemed to be the kind of work that would be okay to do; it would calm my questioning conscience, and I could still go into the service. Just before I went in, I learned the Marines got their corpsmen from the Navy, and that many guys who became Navy corpsmen were surprised to find themselves stationed with a Marine unit.

I enlisted, I wasn't drafted. I figured, as soon as I graduated I was probably going to get drafted. So, I never even went down to the draft board. That was one experience I didn't have to go through; I never had the draft physical, or anything.

I did file for CO status from Selective Service, but the draft board turned me down. I remember quoting part of *The Universal Soldier,* a song by Buffy Sainte-Marie, as part of my reason for being opposed to war. The draft board didn't even give me a hearing, just a letter stating my CO claim was rejected. They said I wasn't one of the standard religions—Quakers or other groups—that they gave CO status to. At the time, I just didn't know my own mind or what I wanted to do. Later, when I applied for discharge from the Navy, I knew what I wanted to do. It took me awhile, it took almost three-and-a-half years, but things finally became clear to me. If the Navy told me "tough luck kid, you're not a Quaker, you can't get a CO," I wouldn't have bought it. But the draft board knew what it was doing, and I wasn't sure.

Anyhow, when I graduated from high school, I was eighteen-and-a-half, and from what I knew about the Army, getting drafted wasn't something I particularly wanted to do. So, I chose something closer to what I wanted, which was the Navy. I enlisted in October 1969.

Stephan Gubar

Noncombatant service CO
U.S. Army 1969–1971
Vietnam veteran

I was like an indentured servant, forced to go and do these things against my will.

* * * *

I grew up in the age of Sputnik, during the race for space and the building of nuclear power plants. I was impressed and excited about this and had a keen interest in the science of the 1950's. Jack Kerouac and hitchhiking were also really important to me. I felt like I was part of the beat generation.

I went to a rather liberal school, the Horace Mann School in the Bronx. There were a lot of leftists and liberals there. My math teacher was Bob Moses, an organizer for the freedom rides who eventually surfaced in the Student Nonviolent Coordinating Committee. He developed an awareness among many of us. Part of the reading there included the *Communist Manifesto.* But, I also had a really repressive history teacher who used to say, "If you think communism is so great, I'll personally get you a one-way ticket to Russia!" So, there was a balance, certainly, between the extreme right and the liberal left; but, there was a broader exposure to liberal politics.

I wouldn't say I was radicalized there, but I was impressed by what I found. I learned what the government was telling me was wrong, that there were problems with the manufacture of nuclear power and there were problems with the storage and strategy of nuclear weapons. I learned it was necessary for me to find out what was going on and to say something about it.

Stephan Gubar

The first demonstration that I attended was in 1959, in front of New York City Hall, a "ban the bomb" demonstration. After this demonstration my father sat me down and explained to me the "evils of communism" and how this could affect me for the rest of my life. He had been in the Second World War. He graduated from high school, enlisted, went to Officer Candidate School and was sent to Europe under General Patton. He was extremely bitter at the end of the war, but still felt "My country, right or wrong." He believed in what was going on, but in many ways had allowed me a liberal head.

From there I became involved with the civil rights movement and the American Friends Service Committee. I was involved in building renovations in East Harlem and I went to Alabama, for the second Selma march. So, I started with civil rights and grew into the antiwar movement.

I was into the counterculture and spent a lot of time in New York City hanging out at certain bars. I was into the music scene. I played the banjo and the guitar, but I wasn't impressed politically by music. I looked strange and I dressed strangely. I wore bracelets, cut-off dungarees, had relatively long hair and a scraggly beard. Again, I was much more a part of the beat generation, and I came into social protest through the beat generation's concern with nuclear weapons.

Originally, I had a student deferment; I didn't apply for CO status until my senior year in college. The only person I knew who was doing draft counseling at the time was a reverend in Jersey City. There was nothing on campus; as a matter of fact, in 1967 and '68, the military recruiters were on campus.

After college I got a teaching job, and in 1968, I applied for CO status through my local draft board. I had no religious convictions and refused to admit any. I had a moral objection to our involvement in the war. I had ethical and political objections based on the nature of our interference with Third World and emerging countries. I also had a moral objection to taking of human life, but that was not my primary reason for filing as a conscientious objector.

When I filled out the CO papers, I attempted to be as straight as I possibly could. I didn't want to appear too deviant, because it became obvious to me that if I antagonized the people who were doing the reviews, then they had a very easy way of getting even. So, basically, I had a sense of caution in that being young and being "different" certainly would not work in my behalf. I didn't have the sense that, individually, I had any power.

I had the hearing on my CO appeal in Hoboken, New Jersey. It was in a dank, dark office building that still stands on Washington Street. A group of old men, I wouldn't even say old now as I picture them, questioned me about my ethics and my morals. It was a sleazy situation at best—horrendous, horrendous. It reminded me of being—"backroom, down and dirty"; just the appearance of the office, the appearance of the room, the fact that it was dimly lit. I knew shortly after I entered that I had no chance of getting alternative service as a civilian. I was told they would be willing to grant a 1–A–O status, but that I didn't qualify for a 1–O. The board was very specific in saying I was qualified for noncombatant military duty. I assumed I would get some kind of medical detail, but in the back of my mind I always hoped there would be some other kind of thing that I could do. I guess I always knew that if I was drafted, I was probably going to Vietnam.

In 1969 we moved and I went to the draft board to notify them, but they couldn't find my file. I waited around for about an hour; finally, I said, "I'm leaving." The secretary at the draft board said, "You can't leave, I can't find your file." I said, "Look, I came here to report my change of address; whether you can find the file or not is your problem." So, I left and this woman was screaming at me as I left the office. It wasn't more than two weeks later that I got my draft notice. I've always assumed this was a punitive action taken by the draft board because they got pissed that I refused to help them and just walked out.

I was just stunned when I got the "Greetings" letter, my induction notice. My wife and I began to talk about the options. Expatriation didn't seem like a viable alternative at the time. I didn't see expatriation as being bad. I didn't think of expatriation as draft dodging. I didn't think of it as cowardice or as not fulfilling the "male image." Actually, I realized it took a certain amount of courage in order to leave everything, to cut all ties. I mean, that's a really frightening thing to do, to know you can never go back; to know you've effectively lost your family, your friends, to know that you've got to start your life in a foreign country.

I knew I couldn't go to jail. There was no way I could handle that. It was not something I wanted to face, so that was excluded immediately. It was much more a decision not to go to jail. I had been arrested for other things I thought were right, but I knew this was not something that I could handle. Regardless of what my convictions were I knew I couldn't or wouldn't survive jail.

So, the only thing left was to be drafted. That was the easiest route to take and that's the thing I regret. I regret I didn't have more strength at the time, because ultimately, by being a 1–A–O, I was able to salve my own conscience. The easiest thing to do was to be drafted, because it took the responsibility for bad decisions out of my hands.

Induction day was really strange. I got on a bus with very few white people, mostly black people. We were driven to the Federal Building in Newark, New Jersey. There was a tremendous amount of tension on the bus because we were told they were drafting Marines. This was really strange because I always believed the bullshit that the Marines were a volunteer unit. So, the anxiety and tension was raised to a fever pitch by the possibility of being drafted into the Marines. The word passed that every fourth man was being drafted as a Marine and I was chosen as a fourth man. I walked out of the room and went to a phone, called my wife and said, "I'm not going to take the step forward." There would be no way I could be drafted as a Marine. But, the captain who was interviewing at the time read my packet and rejected me. There are no COs in the Marines! So, when that didn't occur, it was almost a relief taking the step forward. Otherwise, I wasn't treated particularly differently; I got on the bus and went to Fort Dix, New Jersey.

Tom Cox

In-service, discharged CO
U.S. Army 1967–1970

Once you are exposed to injustice, and you try to do something about it, you just can't turn that off.

* * * *

There are no college graduates in my family, probably still to this day. My dad worked with his hands, pipefitting, a little construction. My mom worked when he was in the service, but mostly she was a housewife taking care of us. They were just working class people, and most of the neighborhoods I lived in were Irish or Italian working class.

I guess I was a junior in high school when I first became aware of the conflict in Southeast Asia, or that there was such a place as Vietnam. I didn't know what was going on out there in the real world. The whole thing, the war, the draft, the military, none of it was real to me at the time. However, by the time I was a senior I realized there was a possibility that I could get sent to Vietnam. But, I still really didn't know what was going on. I didn't know a lot about politics. I was a naive kid. I didn't think so at the time, but I guess I had a pretty sheltered life.

I knew I had to register for the draft, but it was something I didn't take too seriously. To me, it was just something the government wanted you to do. It was just a matter of filling out a form or two and you were done. Nobody I knew even questioned the draft; it just was. You're eighteen, you sign up for the draft. It's like today, you see a lot of kids doing the same thing and you wonder how they could be so naive about it; but I was, I really was.

Awareness started creeping in. There was a war on and young people were going over there. I mean, you couldn't hide from it; it was on TV, it was in the papers, and it was taking on more serious complexions. You were forced to stop and think about what was going on. You couldn't start life off the way you wanted to. One way or another you had to deal with military obligations first, then you could get your life back.

At that time I didn't even know what a conscientious objector was. There was no resistance per se, there was no draft counseling, nothing like that. Of course, I was aware of different religions that backed pacifists, like the Quakers. But, I just didn't know there was a special status, or category, set aside for people who didn't believe in war.

The first time I ever heard about any type of resistance was when Mohammed Ali refused to go into the service. This happened about the same time I was supposed to be drafted. As far as I knew, he wasn't even a conscientious objector. He just said he wasn't going. I thought that was good, I thought he made sense. The media gave him a lot of negative coverage, talking about this man who was obviously big and strong and able to fight, so why should he be excluded from serving his country?

Well, I got a draft notice in the mail. I was supposed to be drafted in May 1967. So, okay, I went down to see this recruiter with my friend, 'cause I didn't want to be drafted, and I didn't know what my options were. So, this recruiter says, "You got your draft notice already, huh?" He said, "Well, you're going to have to go in the service. You don't want to go to Vietnam, do you?" I said, "Well no, I really don't." And he said, "You'd like to learn a trade, wouldn't you? If you're going to be in there anyway, you might as well learn something." So, I agreed that sounded pretty good. He convinced me that what I should do is enlist in the Army, get this "guaranteed" training at a school of my choice, not have to go to Vietnam, and come out of there with a skill that could be transferred to civilian life. So, I went for it. I signed the papers to get into radar school, my skill was to be electronics. I took the summer off, and on August 22, 1967 I headed for basic training at Fort Dix, New Jersey.

Jeff Engel

Noncombatant service CO
U.S. Army 1969–1971
Vietnam veteran

This question of conscience is part of the working-out of human history, part of the evolution of mankind.

* * * *

I imagine it would be safe to characterize me as pretty much an all American kid. Both my parents were Marines, and while I wasn't a John Wayne type, I did want to be a cowboy. I gave patriotic speeches in high school, heartrending speeches about the flag, but I didn't perceive myself as a zealot. I was just a pretty conventional kid and I felt like these were just appropriate things. I didn't really even think about them, I just did them.

My family was affiliated with an organization called "The Church of God," headquartered in Anderson, Indiana. It's a mainstream evangelical organization. I was involved in the youth organization and went to the church's colleges on the west coast and in the Midwest.

I was an athlete. During those days I was going to be a teacher and a coach. I remember writing a paper entitled "My Mission as a Coach" in a college class called "Christian Education." My life was pretty much viewed from a spiritual perspective. But, I was pretty conventional in my spiritual beliefs, "mainstream" may be the way to characterize it.

Accidentally almost, I had started reading about conscientious objection. I was about seventeen years old when I started reading about it, before I even registered for the draft. Actually, I don't think I knew the word "draft" early in 1963. I graduated from high school that year, and had no idea which way I was headed regarding the draft. Anyway, I remember reading a biography of Ghandi, reading about Civil War conscientious objectors, and I also discovered the Quaker Church.

By 1965, in college in Indiana, I had become a longhaired hippie, and I wasn't the only longhaired kid in town. I wore the typical stuff, had a beard, and everybody knew I was some sort of weird crossover from California. By 1969, I'd stop traffic when I walked downtown, there'd be these gaping mouths and stuff. Still, it wasn't a political statement.

I did get involved with politics and the civil rights movement in college. Getting involved in civil rights seemed morally and legally appropriate. My family had been in Georgia in 1955 when I was in the fifth grade. This shaped my consciousness about the issue of equality. For me, the issue was simple. If we were a Christian nation, then racism was wrong. By participating in the civil rights movement, I felt I was broadening the scope of my spiritual involvement that was part of my life.

I had kind of lost interest in athletic competition at that point, it had phased out. I'd gotten really turned off by what I'd seen athletics become. I had encounters with militant right-wingers, fascists, racists, to throw out some labels. I encountered a lot of racism in conversations and in the smoky rooms of the Midwest. Racist comments, a lot of "nigger" jokes and other people of color jokes. Also, a "salt and pepper" couple I knew was confronted by shotgun wielding toughs in East Chicago and told to separate.

A lot of anomalies of belief versus practice also came to my attention then, even in the context of the church college I was attending. A man who was on the board of the church was gouging rents and owned the bar downtown. There was racism and greed among the people I was told to admire, because of their "upright" church stand. Also, I was in Gary, Indiana the night Robert Kennedy was killed. We watched the news on a big, six-foot screen. At the point where he was shot, and was just lying on the floor, about 150 people, men and women cheered... A lot of this shocked me and pushed me to a politicization of my belief system.

I got the information to register for conscientious objector status in the summer of 1963. I read it and decided that I was opposed to killing because my religious training and beliefs said that I shouldn't. So, no big political position, it was just based on my religious training. I discussed this with the minister of the church, with a friend and with my mother; everyone was supportive. In retrospect, I don't think they understood the implications.

I don't remember the entire CO registration event except the uncomfortable sense about it. Helen "somebody" was the woman I met working in the Redding, California local office of the Selective Service. She was very brusque, very short with me when I notified her that I wanted to register as a "1–O," a conscientious objector that would perform alternative civilian service. She said, "Okay, I'll take care of it." I didn't sign anything. I thanked her and I left.

In 1969, six years of college later, things started to heat up a bit. I was substitute teaching in Red Bluff, California. A minister friend of mine was running for a school board position. One of the issues was a voluntary sex education program—hot stuff! He supported the introduction of a voluntary program in the schools because he was seeing a lot of pregnant young girls. So, I worked with him on his campaign. Pamphleteering, that kind of stuff. It just happened that the town was a center for the John Birch Society. The state president of the Society, a physician, was a local resident. We got veiled threats, threatening letters and phone calls saying either God, or one of them, was going to get us. But, my friend was elected to the board and the program was adopted by the school district.

A couple of days after the election I received my "Notice to Report for Induction." Not from my local board, but from the local board in Red Bluff! Four days later, I got a notice that I was to respond to the Notice to Report for Induction or face prosecution because I had failed to register. So, I called dear, old Helen, who was still working in Redding. I

said, "Helen, there's been some error! I registered as a 1–
O, as I was supposed to, in 1963. Now I get this order to
report for induction." She said she'd check into it. Meanwhile, I got some counseling from a guy at a Methodist
Church. He helped me to institute an appeal according to
Selective Service codes and guidelines. I was not really concerned about the situation, because I *knew* the system
would vindicate me.

One day, soon after receiving all this communication
from Selective Service, I was walking in a local supermar-
ket. This little old, dried-up prune of a man comes walking
down one of the aisles toward me. I'd never seen him before
in my life. He made this series of incomprehensible comments to me, something about: "If you mess with the big
boys, you get into trouble." I thought he was a wino, I kind
of laughed at him and walked on down the aisle. Going
down another aisle, he comes towards me again and he
makes another comment like, "A couple of years in the
military will straighten you out." Again, I make no connection at all! You know, I thought, maybe in a small town,
he's heard about this; I didn't realize I was such a well-
known guy.

Probably a week later, I was riding with my minister
friend and went past one of the local watering holes. A
bunch of these old guys were sitting on a bench out front
and I saw this same old fellow. I said, "Who is that guy?"
He gave a name and asked, "Why?" I mentioned our little
encounter and he pulls over to the curb and says, "He's on
the local draft board!" The drama thickened a bit, but I
still couldn't have imagined—I just had no inkling that
they were operating illegally or conspiratorily; and still, to
this day I have no evidence that they were. Well, I went
back to my own local draft board and talked again with
Helen, that was the extent of it. I never had a hearing. I
never talked to anyone but good, old Helen. I went through
the whole appeal process and finally, in June 1969, I received a 1–A–O, a noncombatant military service classification.

I reported to Oakland, California for my pre-induction

physical. My father implied that he was ready to send me to Canada. He thought it was madness—this was from an ex-Marine! After that I went around in a haze. Less than thirty days later I reported for induction, the same day Prince Charles became the Prince of Wales, I always like to share that. On July 7, 1969 I became a member of the United States Army.

Jim Kraus

In-service, discharged CO
U.S. Navy 1967–1970
Vietnam veteran

Just knowing I had the power to refuse gave me a funny kind of reinforcement, a sense that the individual had the power to alter things.

* * * *

I grew up in a military family. My father was a career Army helicopter pilot, so we lived here and there during the Fifties. We moved just about every three years when I was growing up.

I emulated my dad and the military, as most Army kids did. I was a Boy Scout who had dreams of going to a military academy and ending up an officer. It was pretty extreme, actually, though looking back on things, I'd say those ideas were beginning to erode by the time I was thirteen, by around 1960.

Perhaps the start of the erosion had something to do with the civil rights movement. We were living in St. Augustine, Florida, the year before the first major civil rights demonstration had taken place there. At that time the civil rights movement in Florida was still submerged. Feelings were submerged, even among whites who cared and were trying to think things through. For example, I remember taking the bus to my all-white school. The tourist trade in St. Augustine was a big deal, and there used to be horse drawn carriages lined up along the waterfront early in the morning. For the most part elderly black men drove them. We would go by in the bus and almost all of the white kids would taunt them as we drove by, for absolutely no reason at all, except that the old men were black. That didn't seem at all normal to me; it disturbed me and I know it disturbed some of my friends. But, there was no organized way for us to deal with our feelings, so we did our best to hide them.

The closest I got to rebellion was when a couple of fellows and I formed a little jazz combo. We'd go down to St. George Street to an off beat—emphasis on "beat"—coffeehouse. We'd go down to listen to music and to play chess, but on another level, I knew the place stood for something that went against the grain of my upbringing.

At the heart of my upbringing was the constant reminder that I was the grandson of a Presbyterian minister. I went to Sunday School every week from kindergarten through ninth grade. What I got was pretty much a Methodist and Presbyterian presentation of the Ten Commandments and the Beatitudes. But by the time we left Florida for Hawaii, I wasn't a regular at church. Usually, I would go surfing. That was my religion! It wasn't until years later that I looked inside and linked up religious elements to my uneasy concerns about the way blacks had been treated in Florida.

But there were also racial problems in Hawaii. The high school I went to was famous for having race riots. My friends and I talked about these problems between classes or when we went to church. For me, there was strong concern with what was fair and just in the world.

Nevertheless, I was in Junior ROTC all the way through high school. It was required at our school, as it was in all the public high schools in Hawaii back then. And I was enthusiastic about it, actually; I was in the Color Guard, I was the captain of the rifle team, I spit-shined boots and all that stuff. And I still wanted to go to a military academy. I knew I wasn't on my way to Annapolis or West Point, but I had a chance to get into the Coast Guard Academy; eventually I got turned down.

As second best, I decided to go to the University of Hawaii to major in engineering. That didn't go so well, and after my third semester of school I flunked out. Of course, by now we were well into the Vietnam war; and lots of rumors circulated that would-be engineers were being forced out of college, because the military was really hurting for people with technical skills. They were desperate for people who had a couple of semesters of calculus and physics and could learn basic electronics. My God, I'd say half of my friends from high school were engineering students and we were all flunking out, even the valedictorian of my high school class who ended up going to Vietnam as a sergeant.

Yet, when I got into the military I realized how much training I'd really gotten in college, because I was at the top of my class in their technical schools. But, I'd flunked out of college, and I didn't know what to blame—perhaps myself, perhaps the "system"—perhaps something inside myself I was still trying to understand.

There were antiwar activities happening on the University of Hawaii campus; although, for the most part, I wasn't willing to engage in any of them. At this point, I really didn't know anything about conscientious objection. There was one fellow from my high school class who went before the draft board and was successfully classified a CO. But, in those days, there wasn't a lot of talk about it. I mean, except for my girlfriend, all my close friends were from military families. These things just weren't talked about.

What was talked about—at least in my family—was surfing. In those days, surfing was still a relatively unpopular thing; it was just different. You were an oddball if you were a surfer. I was criticized all the time, by my mother and father especially, because I refused to get involved in mainstream sports. But, I wasn't about to put that kind of energy and athletic talent to work on a football field. It just seemed senseless to me. I began to realize there was a conflict inside between what I was setting up for myself and what I was being steered toward by my friends and family. There was tension between conformity and a part of me that demanded breaking away to be very different.

Some of that tension was certainly coming from campus antiwar activity. There was a guy named Noel who was the first I knew to do overt protest action there. He burned an

American flag and it was front page news. At the time I didn't know him, but I knew who he was. I saw him as a kind of ragged, antisocial type. I really didn't think through the consequences of what he was doing. At some level, though, things were beginning to come together— Noel's protest, the fact that a guy from our high school had just been killed in Vietnam—and one other thing. The president of the surfing association I belonged to made a speech resigning the presidency; he said he wanted to put all of his time into fighting against the war in Vietnam. He told us we were all going to be cannon fodder, and that there were people in the room who were going to die. That hadn't occurred to me, you know, it really hadn't.

Anyhow, by that point I knew I wasn't going into the Army. I knew I wasn't going to Vietnam, and I was really scared about getting drafted. I thought a lot about it, "Is it two years with a risk of being sent off to Vietnam or four years with another level of risk?"

I got the hard sell from a Navy recruiter who put it to me this way, "You can sign up for six years and be guaranteed you're not going to get shot." That's exactly how he said it. This was the line most seventeen and eighteen year olds were getting in 1966–67. You know, it was a major marketing ploy. Anyhow, I signed up for a technical enlistment in nuclear power and in March 1967 I left for boot camp. I flew first class, for the first and only time in my life, from Hawaii to San Diego, California.

CHAPTER 2

Neither Saints nor Soldiers:
Basic and Advanced Military Training.

A deafening chant began: "Kill! Kill! Kill!..." Clerks, mechanics, teachers, college students, a few professional men, were all screaming, "Kill!" Very few of these men are inherently cruel, depraved, or deranged. But fear, power and hatred are the order of the day, and it is to these forces, so constantly presented to us both by demagogues and by those who should know better, that men submit without question. Good men do bad things because they are too benumbed to ask "Why?" or say "No!"

Stephen Fortunato, Jr.

Jeffrey Porteous

When we arrived at the base we were herded into a large gravel compound and shuttled in and out of various buildings around this square. Our heads were shaved, we were given fatigue uniforms, bedding, and more tests; it was three o'clock in the morning before we were allowed to sleep. In those first few days I began to tell whoever would listen that I wanted medic's school, that I didn't want to carry a weapon. They told me they'd take it under advisement. They said, "We know what your wishes are; in the meantime, you have to go through boot camp, to learn to march and to obey orders." So, I was to be a medic, but meanwhile, they were teaching me weapons handling.

I was ready to be a medic, to go overseas, to go to Vietnam, at least I thought I was—knowing absolutely nothing at all. I thought, "Well, I have to go through this first in order to do that." And, I tried to do what they wanted, I tried very hard.

Look, there were parts of boot camp I enjoyed. I liked the rigorousness of it. But I couldn't escape the fact that it focused upon an end I thought was nuts, and I told people that. I told people right from the start, and I kept it up. So I got a reputation. I was the CO, the guy against the war. Some people wanted to talk about it, some people wanted to listen, and I never got any heat from recruits in boot camp.

But boot camp *was* a revelation; I knew nothing about the Army before I went in. The smallness and stupidity of a great many of the people that ran it struck me immediately—the absolute meanness of them. I don't mean they were cruel, but that they were little men. And I watched the way they treated each other, the way officers treated enlisted people and the way noncommissioned officers (NCOs) treated recruits. It was ugly. But, I mean, the enlisted men were being forced to do what they did by the NCOs, who were being forced to act by the officers, who were being forced to do what they did by the power of the United States government, by tradition, by the sheer weight of custom and conformity. Everyone was warped by it, and I hated it, man. I could not help it, I had an attitude. They knew I did not respect them, I did not believe in them and it was hard for me to hide that. One time, during an inspection, a young second lieutenant, stood directly in front of me as I stood at attention. "Porteous," he told me, "I ought to slap your face." And he meant it. I hadn't said a word, but he knew.

I remember thinking we were all on a gigantic slide, like a playground slide, boot camp and AIT being steps up to the top, to the cusp which was the Overseas Replacement Center, where you boarded the planes—after that, forget it, it was out of your control. I felt if I didn't do something, if I waited, nothing could be done. I began to feel a futility, things began to feel altogether unreal. It was one more thing you had to fight. Basic training is a well-known mindfuck, they pretty much try to turn you entirely into something else. I was not the sort of person they were going to be too successful with. But I was very confused, like, "What in hell is going on here?"

It got to the point where the fundamental fact of boot camp became more and more apparent, more and more precisely insane. One evening, while the rest of the company was watching a movie, I snuck back to my barracks, put on my dress greens and hitch hiked off the base. I was absent without leave (AWOL) for about a month. I picked up my girl and went to Canada for a week. We thought about staying, about just leaving it all, and becoming Canadian citizens. But we drove back after a week. Then my girlfriend and I took off up into the mountains, hiking along the Cascade Trail. By the time we'd come off the mountain, I'd decided I would not go to Canada, I would go to prison. I was no longer willing to be a 1-A-O medic, the whole thing was fucked at the root, and I would not be part of it.

So, I found a lawyer, and I remember exactly what I said to him. I asked, "What is the most eloquent way in which I can register my objection to the war in Vietnam?" He said, "File for a discharge as a conscientious objector." I took his advice, but first I married my girl, then I returned myself from AWOL, married all of 45 minutes, with my first CO application.

Essentially, the questions on the CO form asked you what you believed to be the meaning of life. I was eighteen, intellectually arrogant, confused, inarticulate, and up against the United States Army. I had no framework of formal religious training, I didn't have Thomas Aquinas on tap to fill in the blanks. But I thought about it. I told them I was a pantheist. I told them that the totality of existence was God itself—I'm some part of God, as are you, that tree, that bush—all in relationship with the rest of the universe. And relationship is what is fundamentally important. How we act, how we treat each other, is of the essence. And that to see this was to accept the responsibility of moral obligation; like, you don't cause pain, you try not to do damage, you don't hurt people, you don't kill Vietnamese. Suffice it to say, this wasn't an answer acceptable to the Army.

I received an Article 15 (non-judicial punishment) for being AWOL, a ninety-day suspended sentence. Then, I was sent to another barracks to finish boot camp. Upon graduation I was issued orders for NCO Leadership Preparation School in Fort Polk, Louisiana. They never processed my CO claim. I was told that the best place to begin my paperwork would be at my next duty station, Advanced Infantry Training. They looked me right in the eye and said, "If this is what you want, then this is how you do it." So, I went. But before I did, I told them I wouldn't go to any leadership school and I never got orders to be a medic.

At Fort Polk, I took my paperwork to my new commanding officer, a captain. I can remember standing in front of his door and taking about ten deep breaths. I was about to tell this fellow that I was a conscientious objector, right? So, I was nervous. I knocked on his door, he told me to come in; I walked in, came to attention, saluted him and I said, "Sir, I'm here to tell you that I want to file my paperwork as a conscientious objector." His first words to me were, "Oh, another pseudo-intellectual." It got worse from there.

I can remember a colonel getting up in front of the thousands of us in AIT, after we'd jumped to our feet on command, roaring like tigers (AIT in Fort Polk was designated "Tigerland") saying, "Gentlemen, 45,000 men have trained at Fort Polk and shipped to Vietnam. You will put aside individual morality, and ignore the broader issues, because you *will* be going to Vietnam as combat infantrymen." Looking back on it, I suppose the fact that he spoke of the issue at all, shows how rattled they'd become. And, as it turned out, there were other guys in my company thinking about filing for CO status. My company commander soon began singling us out at company formations. We were made to step forward and pointed out as individuals who did not want to go to Vietnam as infantry soldiers. That we were some kind of strange breed known as "conscientious objectors." One of the sergeants called us communist observers. Which was funny, really, what the hell. He was just trying to fuck with us.

People began coming up to ask me what conscientious objector status was. "What is it? What's going on? What are you about?" I mean, good, long conversations so that real strong kinds of relationships developed. People looked to me for help. There was an older fellow from New Jersey who was crying all the time. There was a tough little guy from southern California who'd come up through reform schools and just didn't want to take any more shit; there was a kid from Missouri who had bitten his fingernails down to the blood, and there was a big, raw-boned farmer from the South somewhere, couldn't read or write, but in some deep hillbilly wisdom, knew this was nuts. He just wanted to get back to his farm and his wife and kids. All I could do was to tell them what I was doing and try to encourage them.

I had a good relationship with my squad leader, an E–5 sergeant from Texas. He was a "Shake and Bake," you know, they made him a quick E–5 to shoot him over to 'Nam. I admired him, though he was a racist, and dead fucking wrong about the war. We would talk, and it finally got down to this, "Porteous," he said, "Don't you understand that Vietnam is the *only* game you'll ever be able to play in your *entire* life, where you'll get to put your life on the line?" That was from his Texas heart. What could I say? I told him, "Hey man, it's not a game, people are dying in Vietnam."

And I heard other things. People would say, "I know what you are saying, I hear you, but I have to go. I cannot not go." I don't think there were enlisted men who fought in Vietnam for reasons of patriotism, or for all the grand abstractions. It was more personal than that. I knew some fine people that didn't want to go to Vietnam. I mean really didn't want to go, and went. They couldn't do otherwise, though they wished to. I'll bet there were a lot of unregistered COs in Vietnam.

So, I continued to train as an infantryman, but I told them that I wasn't going anywhere. I said, "You can train me, but I'm not going to Vietnam, I'm going to prison." It's funny, it didn't ever register that I might actually be discharged as a conscientious objector; even then, I had made the conscious decision to go to prison.

I remember the first time we got the M–16, this ugly, black plastic thing. I thought, "This thing stinks of evil. This thing reeks of bad shit." I mean, if someone had wanted to make a weapon that somehow, in all its parts, personified just what the war in Vietnam was all about, they would have come up with the M–16. It is a real potent symbol of that war.

There was a chapel we would march past on our comings and goings out of Tigerland. It was built on a grassy knoll, made of clapboard, and it seemed extraordinarily white, though that may have been the blue spring skies we saw it against. It had a steeple at one end, with a loud speaker in it, over which someone played recordings of Bach and Mozart and Brahms. The incongruity of this chapel's nostalgic symmetry, its outpouring of angelic music, and our constant armed marches through Tigerland was bad enough, but one day it got even better. One day a small billboard appeared at the foot of the knoll, placed so that we would be forced to see it each day as we marched by. On it was an official portrait of a Vietnamese peasant, the Army's sign painter having equipped the figure with slabbed, purplish lips, a flattened nose, and hooded, slit eyes. This fellow wore a conical straw hat, a black shirt, and was standing chest deep in long yellow grass. And in his hand, he held a large, unsheathed knife. Above the picture, printed neatly, was the word, "ENEMY," while underneath, in red, were the words, "VIET CONG." The wood was new, the paint fresh, the nailheads glistened in the hard Louisiana sun. And all the while, the chapel kept spiriting Bach and Mozart out over our steel-potted heads. I marched by in full field gear, my black plastic M–16 in hand, and I thought about time. That's what the sign tripped in me. There was something about its newness, about its existence in time that made me think forward to the time of signs to come, of manufactured enemies even poorer and more fanciful, and of the next young men forced to suffocate, to slog through this world of shit.

I finished AIT with orders to report to the Overseas Replacement Center back at Fort Lewis. They hadn't processed my CO claim; I was told that my paperwork shouldn't be filed until I arrived at Lewis, my next duty station. And I believed them. But it didn't matter anymore.

John Lawrence

At two o'clock in the morning we arrived at this huge, armored command center at Fort Bliss, Texas. There were 1,500 of us being processed in, a three-day processing deal.

The first day was testing. They took us into this big warehouse and packed as many as they could in there. I have no idea how many guys were in there, but it was wall-to-wall GIs—all with bald heads. During the testing process they ranked everybody according to their scores. The first group was tested and they took the top 50% and segregated them out while the bottom 50% continued to process in, getting their uniforms and stuff like that. Then they tested the top 50% from the first group and they kept going until they came to the last twelve men. Well, I was in the last twelve, and they gave us a blank, yellow 3×5 card to carry around. Those of us with the yellow cards were considered the "officer class," so we got to go through processing first, right to the front of the line. We got the royal treatment. It was, "You guys, would you like to come in here?" You know, that sort of deal, the top twelve! And, that line went on forever, you know, I looked back there and I thought, "The last guy is going to take forever."

About noon they took the twelve of us into a building to start briefing us on OCS, Officer Candidate School. A sergeant came in and was addressing us as "gentlemen" and all that, and he finished off saying, "Any questions?" I raised my hand. He said, "Yes, you, what do you want?" And I said, "I'm a conscientious objector, what do I do?" So he froze and he thought it over for a second. I had ruined his whole spiel. He yelled, "The rest of you, clear out of here; I got a bad apple in the bunch!" Then he screamed, "You, sit over there!" The eleven others cleared out of the room, then he left.

I'm sitting there all by myself when the door flies open, and this time I'm greeted with a yell down the stairs, "Conscientious objector, come out!" It's like a hostage situation. So, I start this long gruelling process up the stairwell; and, of course, I'm looking up at all these people looking down at me. They couldn't believe what was happening to their well-oiled system. They call me out to the parade ground and in front of the whole shebang I was "field court-martialed." Of course, they couldn't demote me. I was E-slick-sleeve zero status. So, this sergeant says, "This, gentlemen, is a conscientious objector." He took my little yellow card, tore it up and says, "You are now at the back of the line!" And I went all the way back to the last guy on the line.

Okay, that's around noon. I'm the last guy going through this whole process, getting fingerprinted, getting the uniform and stuff. Finally, I come to personnel. It's near quitting time and everybody is real tired and edgy. I came up the stairs and waited in the last line to get my 201 file processed. I'll never forget it. I walked through the door into a big open office area on the third floor of this personnel building. The clerk at the desk is sighing, "Last guy." Of course, I'm supposed to have really low mental ability, so it's direct orders this time, "Give me your file!" I hand him the file, he opens it up and there's that goldenrod sheet with **"TREASON"** across the top. He just looked at it. Then he looked up at me and he says, "What the hell are you doing here?" I said, "I'm just doing what they tell me to do." The clerk yells over to the station on the other side of the room, "This guy is being charged with treason!" It was like a gun went off in that building. It went stone quiet. All the machines and everything just seemed to quiet at once. And they looked at me, standing in front of this desk, at a quarter-to-five, with treason written all over my file. They had not seen it during that whole time.

Suddenly this civilian, who I assume was something on the order of the CIA, or military intelligence, jumps up out of his desk. He points to a second lieutenant with a .45 strapped to him and he says, "Go to that guy!" I was immediately put under house arrest.

They called me over to the civilian's desk and this amazing system began. It was a kangaroo court, set up immediately. It became a "Mutt and Jeff" routine. The civilian guy was the "bad guy" and the sergeant that was standing there was a "good guy." The civilian said, "Did you say this?" And, "Did you say that?" And, "Did you refuse to take the oath?" I said, "I just did what they told me to do!" And the sergeant is going, "Now it's okay, this guy is just doing his job, don't worry about it." Of course, I'm looking at the sergeant like, hey, protect me. I mean, this civilian was good. He came across just as cold as steel and he'd interject things like, "We're going to take care of you, fella. We're going to get rid of you in Vietnam." And the sergeant is going, "Don't listen to this guy, he's just angry and upset because you messed up his day." Meanwhile, the second lieutenant who's guarding me says word nothing, he just stands there. They called the Abilene induction center and talked to the captain over the phone. Then the civilian slammed down the phone and he says, "we're sentencing you to Vietnam!"

The second phase of their interrogation process began when they lined the whole company up on bleachers; then the lieutenant walked me in front of this company. They started jeering at me, you know, "You coward"—obscenities—everything was just pouring down on me, it was like, "We're going to get you, fella, we're going to take care of you," and "You won't be able to sleep very well to-night!" All these threats and innuendos. It was meant to alienate me or ostracize me from the group. I was getting scared. I started to get the impact of this whole treatment. I started seeing the guard as my bodyguard, protecting me from these guys. I mean, there was intense anger coming out of those bleachers. These guys saw me as nothing more than the enemy. The Army was essentially telling hundreds of men that this was okay, that I was fair game. And there I am getting the impact of all that energy coming down on me.

The third part of my interrogation began in the main office building. They called the Commanding General of the base who was in contact with Washington, DC. There was a kind of conference call going on, you know, what to do with me. Now, the only two people in the waiting area were the second lieutenant and me. I could hear sergeants yelling out, "What'll we do with this guy? In a war we'd execute him! He can ruin the whole base." Remember, my guard never said a word during this whole thing. He observed. He was with me from beginning to end. And, he understood the system well enough. So, he turned to me and he said, "I want your 201 file." I handed it to him, and he ripped out the goldenrod piece of paper, wadded it up and threw it in the trash can. He gave me my 201 file and he said, "Now get out of here." Then he said, "I'm really sorry for the way they treated you, I'm really sorry for what they've done." Now, I don't know if that second lieutenant is breaking rocks at some federal prison or not. I don't know what happened to him. I never looked back. I walked out of the door with my 201 file and I kept going, and gladly too, because I felt my life was in real serious danger at that time. Also, I was never officially sworn into the Army. But of the 1,500 guys there, only my orders had been cut. They were already in the machine. I was to report to Company E at Fort Sam Houston, Texas, the conscientious objector camp at that time. They actually flew me and one other guy, who was declared a CO, out on Continental Airlines that same day.

I did basic training at Class 13–B, Company E, Fort Sam Houston. We trained off-post; there was a training area they put us in. We were all conscientious objectors, and you know, it was fantastic, because now I was with my comrades. We were coming in with horror stories from all over the country. Guys were coming in from Fort Ord and Fort Dix and Fort Lewis and we were all telling the stories of how we survived the reception centers. A lot of them came in terrified; the system had done a very good job on them. And so, we gave each other a great deal of support. There was an intensity of relationship there that the Army could never understand. It didn't matter if you were ugly or dumb or smelled bad or what. We knew how important we were to each other, so there was an esprit-de-corps that would have made the Army envious beyond degree. We were all there and we knew why; but the military had a great deal of contempt for us, we were hated and despised.

John Lawrence

The Army was used to COs being at Fort Sam. They'd transport classes of about fifty COs to the base and inject us into the program for medics. In a battalion of about 2,000 men, fifty or so could easily be dispersed and not have that great an impact. There were four platoons in my company. One platoon of regular enlistees; one platoon of Army Reserves, one platoon of National Guards and one platoon of conscientious objectors. The regular Army went to Germany, the Reserves and the National Guard went home, all the COs went to Vietnam. It was that clean-cut; we were the cannon fodder.

There were two types of COs, religious and political. Some of these guys were super brilliant; my test scores were not that good compared to some of those that were coming in. In our class, the average educational level was seventeen years, which meant a goodly number of them had Masters degrees, at least. A lot of us were married, older guys in the mid-twenties. These were highly educated, career-oriented people. These were the cream of the crop, truly, in all respects. Some of them were coming in as lawyers, professors, pharmacists, and they all had well thought-out positions. They weren't there because of some whim. They knew where they stood, and I was very proud to be a part of them.

There wasn't that much antiwar or antimilitary stuff going on in my class. But, I think that Class 11 organized an underground newspaper and started distributing it. The military intelligence descended on them; I mean, it was swift and very effective. Of course, what could they do to us, send us to Vietnam? At some point you got very cynical about it.

Life at Fort Sam was interesting. They had a problem with COs because we didn't pull guard duty. We did other things like KP and we could do light guard duty, you know, like in the barracks. We couldn't carry a weapon. Now, they would put us on regular guard, but they had a problem with that because what do you do with a pacifist? So, it was funny, they gave us a flashlight and a whistle. And they said, "Now when you get into trouble blow the whistle and run." You can have a lot of fun being a pacifist in a military compound; like, when a commanding officer finds out that half his command is conscientious objectors, he freaks out. The guard roster gets all messed up. He has to go through all kinds of gyrations to figure out what to do with his command.

One captain, who didn't like COs, taught us how to give each other shots and IVs. He said, "I don't want any crybabies in this outfit, nobody is going to get squeamish on me." So, they set up some chairs and I happened to pick a guy who didn't know how to insert an IV. He drives it straight in my arm and told the captain, "I'm not getting any blood." He said, "go deeper," meaning up into the vein. And this guy goes straight in, all the way to my elbow. Straight pain. The captain walks over and goes, "What the hell are you doing!" The needle is imbedded into my joint, they pull it out and he said to me, "You don't have to do anymore duty from here on." So, I was duty free. I didn't yell, I was close to fainting, but I didn't yell. Guys would miss, then hit weird, and you'd come out of there feeling like you'd been punched through quite a bit. It was quite an experience, and we learned how to give shots very quickly.

During AIT I began to see the reality of my situation. I was scared a lot, but I knew I was really into it now. I did the best I could on the tests and in learning the material, not knowing how deficient it really was. You know, I assumed I was getting the best training that the Army could give on combat situations. I thought everything they gave me was the best technology, the state-of-the-art. That's what I assumed; I learned differently later.

After AIT I got my orders to go to Vietnam. I was really scared. You see, there is a myth about medics in this country, that because we're noncombatants we are, therefore, not going to get hurt. No, that's a misnomer. Medics don't survive. I heard, that in Vietnam, the life expectancy of a medic in a firefight was fifteen seconds. Medics are part of the command structure and very vulnerable; we are the targets. So, at that point I began to weigh who I was; I mean, a real life and death struggle began to take place. When you are twenty-three years old you don't feel mortal. You don't think of death; it's way off in the future, but that was when I started dealing with the real issue of my own mortality.

They gave me a two and one-half week leave, so I visited my family in Portland. During that time I came to appreciate an execution scenario. I had to go down and fill out my last will and testament, all the married men had to. That really drove it home—just this constant consciousness that I was going to Vietnam and the real fear of going as a medic.

I reported to the Overseas Replacement Center in Oakland, California. I remember my first night there. Two guys were talking in the corner. One guy said, "Hey listen, if I lose a leg, I'll get to come home;" and the other guy said, "Wait listen, let's not go for the leg, let's go for the arm. If we just lose an arm, it'll be the same thing and you can still walk." This is the kind of conversation these two guys are carrying on, and I'm going, "Where am I? What is happening?" I felt like my whole universe was collapsing in on my ego, on who I was. I remember kind of walking around the parade ground, just kind of in a daze.

We were housed in this giant warehouse, under armed guard. I'm going, "What's happening?" Well, people said there was rioting going on up at Berkeley. Ronald Reagan sent in the National Guard to try to snuff it out. The Army was afraid some of that would spill over to Oakland, because there were a lot of anti-Vietnam feelings among the soldiers, especially among the draftees; so, they kept us in this big warehouse. Whenever we were called out for chow, they'd block us up into rows of ten and ten—a hundred of us—and on each corner would be an armed guard, and they'd march us to the chow hall. We'd eat under guard, they'd march us back to the warehouse, slam this big door shut, and that was the only way out; we were under real close control.

When the time came for us to go to the airport for Vietnam, these antipersonnel buses, the ones with the iron mesh windows, rolled up. They put us on the buses and drove us to Travis Air Force Base, just outside San Francisco. They loaded us onto a plane, and in flight, they handed out our orders. I was a "91–Alpha–10," medic, the rest were infantry. I realized then why they handed out orders in the air, because you were not going to go anywhere. This plane full of guys went totally still during that sixteen-hour flight. That's when I started giving up my career, my wife, my money, anything of value just started going out the window. I began to go through the dying process—I realize that now—a process of letting go of everything. What became really important to me was existence itself. I felt like I was going into the jaws of death.

Mike Ferner

My first impression of the military as a screwed-up organization concerned the method they used to ship us to Chicago. First, they put us on a bus to Cleveland; twelve hours later we're waiting for a plane to Chicago. I thought, "There's got to be a better way to run an outfit than to send you east to go west!" So, my first day in, I started thinking that these guys weren't all together. Then, when we got to Great Lakes Naval Base, I got stuck in what they called a "holding company." There weren't enough of us to make up a company, so they stuck us in a barracks which must have been condemned twenty years before that, and we waited for about two weeks until there were enough recruits to make up a company.

They called the hospital recruits "HRs." Supposedly, when guys enlisted, you were "guaranteed" whatever job you wanted. Very few people got the guaranteed job—except the hospital recruits—because they were chewing them up in Vietnam. Little did I know, when first talking with a recruiter, that a lot of guys wound up being hospital recruits who didn't enlist to be HRs, and who didn't want anything to do with it. But, I wanted to be an HR. I remember, I said to the Navy recruiter, "Please let me be a hospital recruit."

My brain was really churning that first day in the military, just like it was in high school. I still felt faced with, and almost overwhelmed by, those same moral dilemmas; but now I'd taken the plunge, I was in. Adding to this confusion was that every day lots of things happened that made no sense at all. In fact, some of the people in authority—the "lifers" we quickly learned to call them— did things that not only didn't make sense, they were downright cruel. For example, one Sunday, the only day of the week you could kind of relax, a lifer who wasn't even in authority over our company brought his girlfriend through the barracks. Just to impress her, I guess, he had us all down doing push-ups as he barked commands.

There were times when various lifers would come

through, and for no apparent reason, decide to torment some recruits. They'd usually pick someone small or sickly who looked like an easy mark. They'd get the person's name, call us to attention, and publicly ridicule the victim's appearance, his name or his mannerisms. Some of the recruits they picked on were such innocents and were so shy that I felt rage building up in me. I wanted to break ranks and go strangle the lifer who was tormenting them. This kind of thing happened all too often; and if this wasn't bad enough, it also made it easier for the recruit-bullies to behave in a similar fashion when the lifers weren't around. It made for a real cruel, ugly atmosphere.

Guys got pneumonia and died so regularly that finally the federal government placed a limit on the amount of time people could spend outdoors in the winter. So, they would march us in the drill halls in full uniform, stand us at attention—and guys would fall over. Two guys collapsed right in front of me. One fell over backwards, and bounced on his head a couple of times. The next thing I know, another guy fell forward, face-first and lost some of his teeth. I was the one who ran to the dispensary to bring a corpsman to take care of him. The nonchalant attitude of the corpsmen on duty was really distressing. I wondered if they had been people who cared at first, and this was what being in the Navy did to them. Every goddamn day we had this crap. Every day in boot camp something like this occurred.

I got very, very sick, as did everybody else. One friend of mine had to have had walking pneumonia; I tried to get him sent to the hospital, but he wasn't allowed to go. I got so sick I prayed I could go to the hospital, just to get out of there for awhile. I finally passed out one day and they had to give me a sick day. I found out later that our company was in competition with other basic training units, competing to keep reported sick time down, trying to be "the best." But, everybody was sick, sick, very sick. It was a combination of the weather, and the stress, I suspect. It was a very bad time.

I said before that I often wanted to be out front, to excel; so, the first day in boot camp they named a "recruit petty officer." Since I had been in a marching band and knew about walking in cadence, I was seen as having quite a skill. When they asked, I raised my hand. Of course, I became the guy who called cadence and marched seventy guys down to the mess hall. The first time I tried to march them we wound up wandering around on the grass—I couldn't figure out what the command was to get them to turn left! The brass said, "That's enough." So, I got back in line and decided that for the rest of my time in the Navy, I would just follow the guy in front of me. That got me through a lot of shit.

Early on in boot camp we had to drill with our "pieces," rifles that didn't work; but we still had to drill with them, learn the "Manual of Arms" and so forth. I was thinking, you know, "Why am I doing this bullshit. What is the purpose of this nonfunctional rifle?" It just angered me. I knew I was going to be a hospital corpsman and I didn't have to know what those things were about, but yet, I had to drill. And I started thinking, "What would happen if I refused to drill with the pieces?" It wasn't until later that I realized how closely connected the hospital corps was in spirit, and in function, to the combat troops.

Hospital corpsman training was at Great Lakes, too. We got our training manuals on the first day, and there, in the introduction to the book, it said something that smacked me right in the face: "The purpose of the Naval Hospital Corps is to keep as many men at as many guns for as many days as possible." That was the first day! In the introduction to the book! I said, "Boy, I'm going to have problems with this. I'm not going to be able to salve my conscience doing this." Things progressed from there.

The fourteen week training to become a corpsman was roughly equivalent to an LPN's course, which takes about a year. I worked at it. It was the hardest I ever studied; but I wanted to challenge myself, I wanted to prove that I could do it. I graduated third or fourth in a class of about sixty. I busted my ass, but I did it. It was good training, it really was. But, to go from there to combat you'd be up a creek. They didn't really have enough combat-oriented training. Other than that, it was very good.

Stephan Gubar

At Fort Dix, New Jersey they started issuing things. I said, "Wait a minute, hold it, I'm a 1–A–O, I'm not going to pick up a weapon." And they said, "Oh, you've got to go to Texas." So, they issued me a plane ticket and put me on a bus to Philadelphia. I didn't know which end was up! I flew to San Antonio. When I got to Fort Sam Houston it was nighttime. I remember being alone in the barracks, just like, alone.

In basic training COs had the same training everyone else went through, except there was no weaponry. The drill sergeants rode the hell out of you, you ran miles in the morning and you didn't walk to the mess hall, you ran. You did all that and you went to classes. A lot of the drill sergeants resented being there; they didn't look at it as a real basic training unit. They'd shout and they'd scream and they did all kinds of shit, because to them, we were pansies who weren't going to pick up guns.

The COs at Fort Sam weren't necessarily political, but there were some political COs. That was really neat, because I got to team up with some people and we were able to organize. One of the guys belonged to one of the GI coffeehouses, and had done some draft counseling. He had actually enlisted as an attempt to organize the military from the inside. I was freaked out, that was crazy! He was a good person.

Also, there was a guy who arrived at Fort Sam with a collapsed lung, so they sent him to the hospital and put him on light duty. He showed up at the beginning of my basic training cycle. He was a crazy son-of-a-bitch, he'd take a cigarette, put it in the tube in his chest and smoke directly through the tube. Anyway, he told them, "I have a collapsed lung and I'm not going to do this shit." So, the drill sergeants used a lot of group pressure on us saying, "If he doesn't do it, you guys are going to get punished." A group of us got together, sat down and talked to this guy, not in the sense of trying to convince him to do anything, but to figure out how we, as a group, could get through this. So, the organization was based on survival.

I think the guys who wound up in medical training, for the most part, were gentler kinds of people—even Regular Army people who enlisted; I mean, when the guys came around to talk about going to the Airborne Rangers, people just laughed! Even though they were Regular Army people. Nobody wanted to be an Airborne medic, people just wanted to get through.

The majority of people who were at Fort Sam Houston were Seventh Day Adventists and members of the Baha'i World Faith. The Baha'is didn't object to the war, they objected to killing. They believed there was a "rightness" to what the United States was doing in Vietnam, but there was a "wrongness" for them to personally pull the trigger. Because I had no idea what the Baha'i World Faith was about, I sat down and talked to one of these guys. I remember having a long discussion. He was talking about organizing the world under this one faith; and I said, "Suppose there are a whole bunch of us that do not want to do this?" "Well," he said, "then the World Council gets to send out its army." And I said, "Shit, this is just as bad as now!" It was really strange to be mixed in with that group.

A lot of military shit was lax at Fort Sam Houston. They were used to dealing with COs. They were used to having very strange dietary regulations. A lot of the Seventh Day Adventists would not eat meat, they were vegetarians. The cooks would have vegetarian meals prepared—except on bivouac, when you had to eat C-rations, then it was a mess! I always thought the Army not only tested people physically, but they also tested people's convictions, so they didn't provide anything for these guys on bivouac. A lot of guys just scrambled for whatever else was in the C-rations pack—sweet rolls, crackers or peanut butter and jelly, stuff like that.

There was one drill sergeant, a Chicano, who I thought was somewhat more human than the other DIs. He asked me why I was a CO. I told him and he said, "I was in Korea, and I believed in Korea." And he said, "I believe we should be in Vietnam," and he had this whole military and patriotic thing about defense of the country and the Domino Theory. After he explained his side and I explained my side, it became obvious there was no meeting place. He said, "I know where you're coming from. I can respect the decisions that you made, if you know where I'm coming from and can respect the decisions I made." He was intelligent, and I had a sense that he wasn't so sure anymore. If you see enough people questioning your life, you have to begin to question it too.

Advanced Individual Training was relatively uneventful, but really scary. I suddenly realized there was a possibility that if I did go to Vietnam, somebody's life was going to depend on me; so, AIT was a time when I stayed awake. I actively participated in the courses and learned my lessons well. I was always afraid I didn't learn enough, and was aware that with this minimal amount of training somebody's life could depend on what I might do or not do.

The thing that stands out most was the end of AIT, the cutting of orders, being really scared, being in formation and listening to the names and assignments being called. The majority of COs I knew had orders cut for Vietnam. And even though I could hear that happening, even though I could hear that every time a CO's name came up, the orders were cut for Vietnam, I still thought there was a possibility I might not go. Then, when they called my name and said, "Vietnam" I broke ranks, I left. Nobody stopped me. I went to a phone and I called my wife. It was a tremendous shock.

Tom Cox

As soon as we got to Fort Dix, they started in with their intimidation. I knew I could handle the physical part of the training, but I just didn't like their meanness, the screaming and the intimidation. The way they tried to train people was so obvious and so silly. They were trying to break people down and then build them back up in their image of a man, or a soldier, or whatever. The mentality and the consciousness of some of the old-timers was just so pathetic—it had as much to do with the evolution of my consciousness as anything. These were people who we were supposed to look up to, and they always talked about war and killing as if it was nothing.

There were a few people, probably a half dozen in my platoon, that rejected this stuff. We sort of gravitated toward one another right away. I would say these were the people who would resist later on—maybe not as conscientious objectors, but they were people who would definitely not buy into the whole program. A couple of these guys had a year or two of college, some were from the bigger cities and probably had more information available to them. For some reason our mind-set was a little bit different and we didn't break down when the sergeants put pressure on us. A lot of people were so scared they would jump as soon as the DIs said a word. Well, we would too, externally, but there was always something inside that was resisting, so you knew you weren't buying into what they were doing. These few people were my support group; I was able to express ideas and relate to them and that helped me a lot.

After graduation from basic I got whisked away to Arizona for an eight week course in ground surveillance and radar repair. They teach you to go out into the field to do first and second echelon maintenance on mobile radar screens. It turns out that this radar was obsolete and rarely used in Vietnam. It was not very functional for guerrilla or jungle warfare. Plus, I was starting to be aware that the promises made by recruiters were not necessarily guarantees. Other people had been lied to and were being sent to

Vietnam. When we graduated from AIT, twenty-one of the twenty-three guys went to Vietnam as part of the signal corps. One guy was sent to Spain and there were no orders whatsoever for me. Eventually, I was sent to Fort Monmouth, New Jersey, the home of the signal corps. I thought that was pretty amazing.

John Vail

In-service, discharged CO
U.S. Army 1968–1970

Look at what they are doing to you, look at what they are doing to all of us.

[AUTHOR'S NOTE]

John Vail's father, and the training John received from the Episcopal Church, were important in the development of his social consciousness. His father was a clergyman interested in social issues; and at the time their diocese was headed by a bishop who was a social activist. John also studied religion in college during a time when many in organized religion felt that faith required involvement in social, political and economic issues. Consequently, he came to expect the church to be involved in political and social issues.

John followed through by working on a church project that brought white, suburban students into the inner cities to rehabilitate housing for ghetto families. He walked picket lines in an attempt to desegregate a private school in Philadelphia; and he also participated in a project that attempted to increase church involvement in neighborhood community organizations.

At this point John was not yet opposed to the war in Vietnam. He described his thinking this way:

I was a patriotic sort; I actually supported the war, in a way. I believed that our country wouldn't be involved in a war unless it made some sense. Like most people in 1965–66, I hadn't really questioned the war.

Politically, John Vail saw the antiwar movement as a

distraction from important civil rights work that was going on at the time.

John enlisted into the Marine Corps' Platoon Leaders Class during his sophomore year in college. He completed the ten weeks of intensive training in Quantico and stayed in the program for two years. However, John became disillusioned with the program and decided to resign prior to being commissioned. He said:

> I thought being an officer would be more comfortable and interesting, but I was really turned off by their operation. I didn't like the way they harassed and intimidated the trainees. It was really enlightening to see how critical it was to the military to defeat and shame people. It was demeaning, and I was becoming more opposed to the war.

Three months after resigning from the Marine Corps, John was drafted into the Army. During his first week of basic training he began to speak out against the military and the war. John Vail's story begins here and continues in Chapter 4.

* * * *

I hated the intimidation that was going on in basic training, so I started talking to other trainees about it. We'd sit around the barracks, some people would talk and some would just listen. First, it was political, theoretical and ideological sorts of stuff. Later, I decided to talk more on what basic training was about. So, I'd say, "Hey man, look at how they treat you, look at what they are doing to you, look at what they are doing to all of us." One guy called me a communist and threatened to kill me. But another time, a redneck from North Carolina came up to me and said, "You know, man, I think you are kind of right about this." This was after the drill sergeants had been dumping on him all day.

About the third week of training the company commander, who was a real jerk, heard about the things I'd been saying. This guy was a real shitty commander who was into lots of punitive kinds of things. Nobody liked him.

Anyway, I got called into his office. He had three or four others with him, a couple of lieutenants and the first sergeant. He pointed a finger at me and said, "You know, you are creating a morale problem in my unit with the things you've been talking about. I don't like the things you are saying and doing. Do you understand what I'm getting at?" I said something like, "Well, I hear what you're saying, but I don't understand what you want me to do or not do." That sort of made him back off, and he said, "Now, wait a minute, I'm not telling you that you can't say stuff." He said something like, "I'm not trying to take away your First Amendment rights or anything." He was being real careful, and I wasn't even well-informed enough to know that I stood on firm ground. It ended up with him telling me that since I spent some time in the Marine Corps, he expected me to set a good example. It was really ridiculous.

After that it became fun to fuck with this guy. Once he stopped me and said, "I notice that when you speak to officers you don't say 'sir' very much. It seems that you don't really have much respect for the officers. What's the deal, Vail?" I said, "Well, I really don't think saying 'sir' is a sign of respect, because I feel that I'm being forced to say this; it's demeaning. So, when I say 'sir' what I'm really thinking is that the people I'm talking to are jerks, because they need this adulation or deference made to them." And then, for the rest of our conversation, I littered our conversation with "sirs," I "sir'd" him up and down. I could see he didn't appreciate this very much.

At some point, during basic training, I found out that you could apply for conscientious objector status. I had already gotten to the point where I didn't want to participate in Vietnam; so, once I found out about it, I made up my mind that I was going to apply as a noncombatant. I didn't apply for discharge because I didn't think I met the criteria. I couldn't say that I was opposed to war in any form, but I knew I was opposed to carrying arms.

I started asking the first sergeant what I had to do to apply. He said he'd find out, but he was just putting me off. So, I just kept asking and asking. Nobody really knew how to go about it; they said they didn't know the regulations or what process to follow.

One day, when my company was to do guard duty, we had this big inspection. The sergeants went through the ranks and picked the most together looking trainee to be the colonel's orderly for the day. Well, due to my prior Marine training, I knew what the deal was; I knew how to shine boots and make a uniform look presentable. So, I got picked as the colonel's orderly.

Because of the run-ins we had, my company commander was not too thrilled about me being picked, but I stayed the choice. It cracked me up, because usually the one they pick is the gung-ho, patriotic sort of guy. The NCOs picked the orderly solely on the basis of who had the best looking uniform, the best looking boots and the cleanest rifle.

So, the colonel got to meet me. He asked me how things were going and I said, "Well, I'm trying to apply as a conscientious objector, but it seems that nobody really knows how to do it." It turns out that even though he was a career military man, he was also a fair and reasonable guy; so this didn't freak him out. We talked a little bit about it. I told him I was opposed to what was going on and that I wanted to apply for noncombatant status. So, he gets on the phone and told some people to get me the papers.

I filled out the forms and brought the document to the company clerk. He goes, "Oh God, I have to type all this shit?" He was pissed off, the first sergeant was pissed off. It was such a headache for them to do my application; they really got fed up with it. I didn't get harassed, it just bugged them.

After I turned in the paperwork, I had to go for an interview with a chaplain. I'm sitting outside the chaplain's office and I hear him talking to this guy who was in there crying. The kid's telling him that he can't take the harassment anymore. So, here's this chaplain, who you think would be sympathetic and helpful, lambasting the poor kid. He sounded just like one of the sergeants, he says, "You're a fuckin' pussy. What's the matter, are you a wimp?" That just made the kid cry more. I was so mad. I couldn't believe this guy was a chaplain. God, it was so bizarre.

The chaplains, as well as other officers who reviewed CO applications, would argue with you. They had these logical, point-counterpoint kinds of arguments. So, if you didn't have that kind of skill, it was very easy for them to intimidate you intellectually. Like, I knew some COs who came from poor backgrounds, uneducated people who were fundamentalists. They were devout and so forth, but very ignorant. If you asked them why they opposed war, they simply said, "Because Jesus said it was wrong." Filling out the CO application was a very demanding thing, and to be successful you had to be relatively articulate.

It took the Army about nine months to process my application. They didn't seem to know what they had to do with it, or who to send it to for review. They had given me orders for Advanced Infantry Training at Fort Polk, Louisiana, but the orders were cancelled, pending a decision on my application. So, I was placed in holding status and was used as a clerk in the basic training unit. Eventually, the application was approved. Since I was doing such a good job in the orderly room, I was actually assigned as the company clerk for that unit.

As the next cycles of trainees came in, I would rap with the new guys and tell them about their options. I'd explain conscientious objection, compassionate reassignment, hardship discharge and stuff like that. It got to the point where during the first week of training, the sergeants would get up before the whole company and tell them to see me if they thought they were conscientious objectors. In every cycle there were three or four guys who would put in an application.

Bill Burke

Noncombatant service CO
U.S. Army 1972–1974

I'm not going, period.

[AUTHOR'S NOTE]

Bill Burke received a very low number (25) from the Selective Service lottery drawn for 1972. He received a draft notice during final exam week of his freshman year of college and was drafted immediately after the school year ended. He was nineteen years old when he was inducted into the Army. Bill had serious doubts about participating in military service. He was taught to "do good" as part of his Roman Catholic upbringing, and lived his life based on the commandments of the Church. However, at the time of his induction he was not completely sure that he could apply for conscientious objector status.

Bill reportedly ignored initial correspondence he received from Selective Service. However, his father, a World War II combat veteran, finally took him to register for the draft.

Although openly opposed to the war, Bill did not participate in student demonstrations. He considered people in Students for a Democratic Society (SDS) and other radicals to be "kind of violent themselves." On the other hand, he admits that they "did make some sense" by drawing attention to the seriousness of the war in Vietnam.

Describing himself as "always kind of different," Bill knew before he was drafted that he "wasn't going to be just another soldier." As he put it, being in the military was "contradictory to everything I believed in. I really felt that if I killed somebody, I was basically killing myself." By the second week of military training Bill became "100% convinced" that what he was doing was wrong. He details two critical consciousness raising events here and discusses his quest for noncombatant status in Chapter 4.

* * * *

During basic training we had a demonstration of the M–16 rifle. It was a beautiful morning, early, the sun had just come up. We're there with this sergeant, a real hard guy, a real "RA"—a Regular Army type. He says, "I'm going to show you a demonstration of the magnificent power of this machine." They had cinder blocks lined up and he fired a clip of twenty rounds into them. It was unbelievable, one of the most violent things I had ever seen. In seconds the blocks just disintegrated; they went all over the place. It was impressive, and a lot of guys were cheering. I knew that if people got hit with a clip like that, limbs would be flying off. I should have stopped right then and there—to this day I don't know why I didn't.

Shortly after that we had to fire the M–16. This was the only time I saw a chaplain in the field with us. I went over to him and said, "I want to put this gun down and walk the hell out of here." He was very nice, but not supportive at all. He said, "Don't worry about it, just shoot the gun; it'll be over before you know it."

I thought that was bunk, and I really resented it. He was only there to tell people it was alright to shoot the weapons. He was RA all the way, a Catholic chaplain and a captain in the military. He was very detrimental to guys who had questions about this. Words of encouragement might have changed a lot of things, but he offered nothing, zero. I met some real crumbs in the military, people I thought were pretty lousy; but that guy was one of the lowest. He sold out 100%. How many people did he send to Vietnam with those words of wisdom? I knew then that this was not where I belonged.

Michael Rosenfield

In-service, discharged CO
U.S. Army 1969–1970

*Making waves made me realize you can overcome adversity,
and you don't have to knuckle under to the powers that be.*

[AUTHOR'S NOTE]

Michael Rosenfield had a dream of becoming a lawyer
to "help people," and to "save the world." This attitude
made him something of an anomaly at the conservative, central Pennsylvania law school which he attended. When draft deferments were eliminated for
second-year law students, Mike filed suit in federal
court to allow law students the same rights of delayed
military service that were granted to medical students.
The case was not successful. Mike was accepted by the
Peace Corps; however, the three year leave of absence
for Peace Corps duty would have forced him to repeat
three semesters of law school. Mike then opted for the
military as a way to get back into law school without
academic penalty. While attending law school, Mike
had discussions with a professor who had been a conscientious objector during World War II. However, at that
time Mike considered himself an atheist, and, given his
understanding of Selective Service regulations, felt
that he didn't have the grounds to apply for CO status.
Mike was drafted into the Army in 1969 at age 22. His
vivid memories of basic training and his developing resistance to warmaking provide a cogent and often humorous picture of one person's rise to consciousness in a
military environment. Mike's testimony appears here
and in Chapters 4 and 5.

* * * *

Going into the military was a totally alien experience. I

79

was petrified. I had no idea what to do. It was like sending someone from the black ghetto to a lily-white preparatory school. I was just completely out of my element. I couldn't believe that for two years I had no control over my life, that somebody would be telling me what to do, what to wear, what to eat, when to go here, when to go there. I felt like I was in a penitentiary without bars.

They give you a battery of tests when you first get in, aptitude and attitude tests. I scored real well on the aptitude tests and they called me in to interview for Officer Candidate School. I didn't want to be an officer, so I purposely didn't score well on the attitude test they gave. They had questions like, a doctor in my community is (a) highly respected (b) somewhat respected (c) not respected at all. Then they'd ask similar questions about military people. Well, I checked lawyers and doctors as "well respected" and checked all the worst categories for the military people. They didn't invite me to a second interview. Actually, I didn't want another interview, because I didn't want to blurt out how antimilitary I felt at that point.

I remember boot camp like it was yesterday. At boot camp you learned how to act like a robot; you learned how not to think. The sergeants who ran the place were morons who didn't know they only had a little bit of power. They were idiots. You had to chuckle about it except you knew those idiots were in charge of training people to be soldiers, and those idiots might lead people into battle. It was very scary to picture these people as responsible for training us how to survive.

I was a hopeless case in basic. Once I screwed up in hand-to-hand combat training and the drill sergeant says, "Boy, have you ever been in a fight in your life?" I said, "No, I never have." He says, "You're a real fuck up! What are we doing with you in here?" I said, "That's a good question." In their eyes, I was the dummy of the class.

My best friend in boot camp was a fellow who had been one of the leaders of the Students for a Democratic Society (SDS) at Kent State. We got to be good friends and he politicized me. He really radicalized me; he got me to express my antiwar feelings. I couldn't believe this guy was there, he was actually doing political work inside the Army.

He was a good talker, kind of low-key, trying to recruit people, including the Puerto Ricans and the kids from Harlem. So, he and I would talk to kids from the South and from Harlem in real down-to-earth terms. He'd say, "Why should you go over and kill somebody in Vietnam?" And they'd say, "Oh, the government wants us to." And he'd say, "Why should you accept what the government is going to do? Do you feel good about going there?" They'd say, "No." He'd say, "Well, if you don't feel good about it, why do you want to do that?" He really would have these people questioning what they were doing.

See, every day the military was trying to get people to act like lemmings, to do what they were told, not to think, just to react and to accept orders. My friend kind of broke this down for these people, he got them to question whether they should really be accepting orders. Once in awhile, someone would say to us, "You're anti-American" and want to fight with us. We were kind of low-key and nonviolent and said, "Look, everybody has the right to their own opinions. If you want to go over and kill somebody, go kill them. We don't want to do that, it doesn't make any sense to us." We didn't challenge anybody. We just tried to get them to think and to question things they were being told not to question.

The Army took these raw recruits, eighteen and nineteen years old, and sent them places to kill people. These kids didn't know shit from shinola about the real world. Lots of them saw the military as an escape from the ghetto, a way of learning a trade or maybe as a way of getting some money for college after discharge. But, if you asked them to write an essay before they entered the military about what they expected their role would be as soldiers, I'd venture to say that very few would see their role as shooting and killing people.

The young kids I served with in basic training really didn't know what they were getting themselves into. In fact, if you sat down with them and were able to get them to tell you what their true feelings were, you'd find that most people were conscientious objectors—they may have been ignorant of that term or turned off by the term, but if you asked them how they felt, a very large number of people would say they identified most with those of us who called ourselves conscientious objectors.

Taking bayonet training and watching a movie on escape also turned me toward conscientious objection. In the film American soldiers were being marched through the jungle by Oriental people who were beating and torturing them. The message in the film was you were not allowed to be captured, you had an obligation to escape. You must do everything you can to escape or it was presumed that you were cooperating with the enemy. If you were a prisoner of war you had to risk your life to get out of the situation. At that point I realized I was being led by a bunch of maniacs. It just came to me that these people had no conception at all of human life. To them you were just a little pawn on the chess board in that war. You were not a human being, you were just a "grunt." You grunted and carried a rifle and tried to kill other people.

The other thing was bayonet training. They'd give you a rifle with a bayonet and they'd say, "What is the spirit of the bayonet?" And you had to yell, "To kill!" And, I'll never forget, I'd pantomime. I wouldn't say it. So, to make us say it louder, the sergeant would yell, "I can't hear you!" People would scream "To kill!" And again, I was pantomiming. Once, they said, "If you don't say it louder, we're not going to give you people lemonade." And, I'll never forget, at one point I yelled that the purpose of the bayonet was to kill— the first time I ever did that—and it was to get some lemonade because I was so exhausted and dehydrated. I felt so embarrassed after I did that—I knew then I had to get out of there. I realized they got me to the point where they could control me, they could make me admit I would kill somebody with a bayonet. At that point I knew I just couldn't continue any longer.

I thought, "How could they make murderers out of people? How could we train people to go and kill?" I realized this was just insanity and anyone who was part of it was also insane. So, it wasn't just what they were doing to the Vietnamese people, but also what they were doing to those of us who were going to be sent over there.

Robert D. (Pseudonym)

Noncombatant service CO
U.S. Army 1970–1972

My ambulance was my territory . . . under no circumstances were weapons allowed in my vehicle.

[AUTHOR'S NOTE]

Robert grew up in a strict Mormon family. His father was not in the military, and reportedly never handled a gun. He even refused to buy toy guns for his son, although he never stopped Robert from playing with them.

Religious training in the Church of the Latter Day Saints required members to live by the law of the land. Therefore, when Robert came to a position of conscientious objection, he did not receive much support from members of the church.

As a youth Robert considered himself to be an individualist, "a loner in my beliefs," he said. He felt strongly about being able to figure out his own situation. He told me, "Nobody else could be smarter than me in controlling my destiny." When he was sixteen years old, Robert left both school and home, moving heavily into the counterculture of the Sixties. He described this experience as being "carried along with the current of the times, especially the hippie culture."

At age eighteen, Robert had developed serious questions about participating in the Vietnam War. He came to the conclusion that, "I didn't want to kill people and I didn't want anyone innocent to die by my hand." At the same time, Robert said he believed in personal self-defense and war in defense of the country, "If there was a war that jeopardized the country directly." On the other hand, he thought, "It was stupid to go out and kill people for territorial or political gain." For Robert:

> learning how to kill people, going to war and purposefully putting yourself in a position where you might take an innocent life is different than defending yourself.

When Robert registered for the draft he also applied for, and received, 1–A–O noncombatant status. The clerk at the draft board actually misrepresented conscientious objector status by not telling him about alternative service. She told him 1–Os did not believe in serving the country, but that 1–A–Os did. Robert was not opposed to serving as a noncombatant; however, had he been told about alternative service, he would have applied for that status.

Robert was drafted into the Army in April 1970, and trained as a medic. His narrative begins here and concludes in Chapter 4.

* * * *

Upon arrival at Fort Lewis, Washington I was pulled aside, and the sergeant told the group, "See this guy right here? He's not going to have to go through the hell you guys are going to go through for eight weeks. We're going to send him down to a little country club in Texas for awhile. He won't carry a weapon. He doesn't have to yell 'kill;' he's going to take it easy, because he's a conscientious chicken-shit."

It was an uneasy situation, but I wasn't scared. What this drill instructor didn't know was I had dropped a couple of hits of LSD for the journey to the base. This was probably not a real good idea, but then again, I smiled during that whole situation, I was a smilin' fool. There wasn't any way he could get the best of me at that point.

Later, when they shaved our heads, the barber shaved a couple of furrows right down the middle of my head. Then, he dry-shaved off my moustache and had me sit in the middle of the room. They told the other trainees, "This is the guy who's going to the country club."

I made it through, but this put a bee in a couple of guys' bonnets. They were really gung-ho, like, "We joined the Army to go kill Vietnamese" and on and on. So, several nights later, I had a slight encounter with two or three of them in the barracks. They cornered me and told me they didn't like my beliefs. They were mad because they had to go through basic training and I didn't. So, they decided to take it out on me. I told them, "If you think that just because I don't believe in killing innocent people means I'm not going to defend myself, you are dead wrong." And, just as one of them jumped me, and the other put his foot in my back, about half the barracks went after them.

Frankly, I was surprised. But, the people who stood up for me were very good guys. They were intelligent kids who had been jerked out of college and were adverse to being there in the first place. These guys figured that anyone who had the guts to stand up for what he believed, even against three guys, deserved to be backed up. A few of the guys became friendly; they told me, "Whatever you believe is fine, this is America, you can believe whatever you want."

The next night the MPs came for me. They turned on the lights, got me out of bed and put me in a barred holding barracks. I was locked in there, by myself, with guards at both doors. They said it was routine, they had to check me out as a security risk. To the Army, being a CO and not believing in killing for your country, meant you were either a communist or crazy. I spent a couple of days incarcerated while waiting for a security clearance. Finally, they shipped me and another CO out to Fort Sam Houston for basic training.

Basic training was the strangest experience I ever had in my life, because it wasn't really what I expected from the Army. The drill instructors had a lot of respect for us; no one there called you a "shithead" or degraded you in any way.

Robert D. (Pseudonym)

All of the seventy or so trainees were either politically or religiously against the war or against killing. There were only two or three people who didn't belong there, people who lied to get in, thinking it was an easy way out. Basically, the COs were very good, sound, honest people. Like, after lights went out, guys would be kneeling next to their bunks praying. If you didn't watch out, you'd trip over them.

We drilled, learned the code of honor, and did physical training. We did survival training, first aid and radio communications. There was no weapons training, but we practiced hand-to-hand combat, which I refused to do. So, they made me do two hours of laps and push-ups. Later, when I found out what a joke hand-to-hand combat training was, I wished I had agreed to participate.

The drill sergeants talked a lot about people who had completed this program and became fantastic medics in Vietnam. The drill instructors had a lot of respect for those medics, and considered them more dedicated than anybody over there who served with a gun. They also talked about some COs who went to Vietnam, and out of fear, picked up guns. But, we heard more stories about the COs who didn't go against their beliefs.

After AIT one-half of my class was sent to Vietnam. I lucked out. I got sent to Germany.

Jeff Engel

I reported for induction at Oakland, California. There were demonstrations going on outside, so I talked with some of the people. It was a pretty "loosey-goosey" situation. The military had learned not to confront the issue. They usually had blacks or other people of color dealing with the demonstrators, or maybe GIs with a little longer hair and a moustache or something. They'd give the protesters the "high-five" or a "bro" handshake, whatever. But then, it was Oakland, California, the summer of '69, and everybody was going to San Francisco to wear flowers in their hair. Anyway, we were either bussed or flown to Fort Lewis, Washington; I don't remember because I had ingested substantial quantities of alcohol over the previous few days.

At Fort Lewis I was put into a barracks with a sergeant of Puerto Rican descent who was trying to divide us into National Guard, Enlisted Reserve and so forth. Well finally, I was the only one left. I hadn't fit into any of his categories. He was at the other end of the barracks being a *sergeant* to us. So, he screams, "and you?" And I said, "Well, I'm registered as a 1–A–O, a conscientious objector." Well! He stopped with this long pause, pulls a knife out of his pocket, and he starts cleaning his fingernails as he walks towards me. He has this real stony kind of stare, walking this considerable distance of barracks and says, "Conscientious objector?" I was trying not to panic or anything, and he broke into this big grin and said, "Ballsy position." Then he said, "You're in the wrong spot though. You're to go down South, to sunny Texas." He got real friendly and said, "We'll get you processed out, probably in the next twenty-four hours." Forty-eight hours later, in the middle of the night, I wound up in Fort Sam Houston, Texas, just outside San Antonio.

Basic was six-weeks long and essentially happened real fast. It kind of slipped by in a fog. The only thing that sticks out is making the drill sergeant puke on the morning runs. He was going to kill us and those of us who were athletes and runners ran him into the ground. That was one of the joys of our six weeks. Everybody that trained us was Regular Army. This was bad duty for them. They were really burned at having to train COs.

Now, the educational level of conscientious objectors in basic training was seven to twelve years above the normal basic trainee. There were some real sharp cookies—I mean I thought I was going to be hot shit because I had a BA degree—but, there were five or six Ph.Ds and a whole raft of Masters and LLDs running around there. Plus, the Uniform Code of Military Justice required that the Sabbath, from sunset to sunrise be respected. During this time COs were not required to perform any duty. We essentially had Saturday and Sunday off during basic training. Saturday for Jews and Adventists, and Sunday for Catholics and Protestants. So, we'd go to the Hilton Hotel, eat good Mexican food and drink some wine. There was a Penn State law student whose folks sent him $100 every week and we'd go eat a good dinner, go to the Quaker fellowship in San Antonio, and come back Sunday night. This really ticked the military off.

The COs were real varied. We had people having religious services at midnight, by candlelight. There were lots of "speaking in tongues" kinds of services and a lot of laying-on-of-hands for everything from inability to sleep to not being able to march right. There was some camaraderie. Not a lot, really. We interacted occasionally, with the most prominently exhibited behavior related to a Pentecostal perception, a Pentecostal reality. There was not a lot of political action either; not in basic. But we did bait a few NCOs who tried to intimidate us.

I got out of basic and went right into AIT in the same fort. Actually, I got misassigned initially. They started me in a clinical specialists school; and so, for about eight of the thirteen weeks, I'd get up every morning, get on a bus, and go to this clinical specialists school. After nine weeks they found out that I was misassigned. So, I had nine weeks of real advanced medics training. I mean, I could have been a surgical assistant. I could perform surgery out in the field if I wanted to. I got some real high-powered instruction. But, the last three or four weeks of the thirteen weeks training was conventional combat medics AIT.

In AIT, I still had no idea what duties I would be performing. I think I still believed that I wasn't going to go to Vietnam. I thought, "hey, they're not going to want somebody there who doesn't want to be there." I didn't think it could happen and I wasn't afraid. It was an exciting time. Classes were exciting. I enjoyed school and I liked the medical atmosphere. It was trippy and I was a real good student. I knew how to study and how to prepare. It was medicine that I was preparing for, not war that I was training for, and I found opportunities to talk about this.

I also participated in some antiwar activities while in AIT, distributing and writing some poetry for an underground paper called *Your Military Left*. I connected with and perhaps even converted some of the people there. I know of at least one person who instituted a CO appeal while I was there, maybe as many as five or six. I felt like I was working within the system, and was not violating the Uniform Code of Military Justice, or civilian law.

Your Military Left was published by some permanently assigned personnel with help from the local Quaker fellowship. I read this paper and the next weekend met some of the people who put it out. I found out from them that there was a CO discharge procedure. At first, I didn't understand this; I thought I'd exhausted all the appeals. So, they helped me institute the appeal process and I applied for a discharge as a 1–O conscientious objector.

Two chaplains counseled me. The first was a Catholic, an ex-Marine. He left the Corps, and joined the Army to be a chaplain. Now he was getting out of the Army and I got the impression he was also getting out of the Church. He wore a headband, and was almost radical in appearance. He was real supportive, but not real hopeful about my appeal.

The other guy was a Protestant chaplain, I had three or four visits with him. On one of the visits he left the office and I remember being skeptical about him because he wasn't being very supportive or helpful. I remember feeling a need to find out about him, so I opened a drawer and there was his service file. I found out that prior to becoming a chaplain, he had been an interrogator for military intelligence. I didn't panic, I had been counseled pretty well; so, I was feeling cool at that point. I just went ahead and filled out the CO forms, felt more militant about my position and decided not to talk to this guy anymore. He eventually gave me a letter, but it was a nonletter, not a real letter of support. It said, "I do not believe he's a 1–O, but I believe he's sincere."

I was given a pass the weekend after completing the CO forms. I went to San Antonio, and in civilian clothes, walked briefly in an antiwar march that ended at the Alamo. After that, I returned to the storefront Quaker Church with an elderly gentleman I met that weekend. He and I were chatting inside the building, getting ready for the church service when two men in civilian clothes entered the premises. They knocked the old gentleman to the floor and knocked over a stack of psalm books and pamphlets. They did not brandish weapons, but they let me know they were armed and said, "You're returning to the post with us." They took me out, put me in an unmarked vehicle and I was driven back to the post. They put me in a room with bars on the window. It wasn't a cell, it was a very bare, wooden room. It had a bed, a chair and a table, but no toilet.

I was there for several hours. I think I actually slept for a short time. I was given a military uniform to put on, one of *my* military uniforms, one with my name tags and stuff on it. Then, I reported to a major who I had talked to before about my CO appeal process. During that initial conversation he appeared very confused about me seeking a discharge, because he'd seen a very "strack" looking soldier standing in front of him. Now, this strack soldier had been arrested. So, in very abrupt, tough language, he said, "Okay, now you get your phone call." It was obvious that he and the captain behind him were waiting for me to whimper to my mother or somebody over the phone. The captain was actually chuckling smugly, hands behind his back, his

.45 on his hip. So, I called a Congressman I knew, a U.S. Senator from Ohio. Suddenly, the major's face went blank and the captain left the room.

I could not reach him directly, so I identified myself to his staff, told them my problem and asked for help. Well, about four hours later I got a change of uniform and was sitting down to a very nice meal in the transient barracks. No charges were ever filed, either verbally or in writing.

I lollygagged around the transient barracks for a couple of days. Finally, I was sent over to the Adjutant General's office. They notified me that my request for a 1–O discharge had been turned down. They also told me I had no other appeal options, and that I had orders for Vietnam.

I was given an eleven day leave and decided to go home. I did talk to a draft counselor at home who tried for days to reach somebody in San Francisco who could help. The final word was to report, as ordered, to the Overseas Replacement Center at Oakland, California and a lawyer would meet me there. Basically, they told me to refuse to board the plane.

So, I reported to Oakland, used the phone number I was given, and the lawyers told me they didn't know how to deal with the process given the time we had. Then, I asked the military people at the Overseas Replacement Center what would happen if I didn't get on the plane. They told me I could board the plane on my own or could board it in a bag, or something to that effect. I got on the plane and we split for Vietnam.

Dave Billingsley

Noncombatant service CO
U.S. Army 1970–1971
Vietnam veteran

I was a nineteen year old kid with a bag of medicine—and they called me "doc"—and it was real wild.

[AUTHOR'S NOTE]

Dave Billingsley grew up in a small college town of about 10,000 inhabitants. He considered his hometown to be "A little cultural womb where everyone was real philosophical." According to Dave, "Drugs, music and the counterculture were what was happening" in his hometown. Although he did not attend college, Dave did interact quite a bit with members of the college community. Dave remembered a lot of antiwar activity on the campus, especially a time when students surrounded the cars of military recruiters to prevent them from getting on campus.

Dave described his family as middle class, well-known and respected. His father was a "war hero" who served in the Philippines.

Dave found out about conscientious objection during a casual conversation with a Vietnam veteran who had served as a medic. The veteran assured Dave that by applying for 1–A–O status he was "guaranteed" to become a medic. The possibility of becoming a medic appealed to Dave, because he was opposed to the war and knew he was going to be drafted.

Dave then petitioned his draft board for 1–A–O, noncombatant status. He described the experience this way:

They sent the forms, I read them and decided I had

no objection to serving in the military. That was the background I came from, I grew up with it, "America, love it or leave it," and all that. I told them I just didn't want to kill anyone. They didn't give me any hassles, I didn't have a hearing or anything. Getting a 1–A–O was a piece of cake, because what you were saying to them was "I'll go, I'll serve, however, I would like to serve in this capacity." Well, that's no hassle for them, because they're still getting you in the service.

Unlike several of the other COs presented here, Dave was not harassed very much by the military brass. In his case, those types of occasions just did not happen. Nor did he actively oppose the war during his tour with the Army. Apparently, Dave did not affect the demeanor of many political or religious conscientious objectors and, therefore, was more easily accepted by his superiors.

His resistance to the war, and to things military, took the form of diligent care of the men in his company, escape through substances and by doing as little as possible when performing chores other than direct patient care.

Our interview was conducted while Dave went about the business of feeding and nurturing an infant and a toddler. During our interview he twice questioned whether or not he "was an appropriate candidate for this book, because although he considered himself a "nice guy" who could not kill, he also could not attest to a "bone-deep" commitment to conscientious objection. "Vietnam," he said, "taught me I have the capability to blow somebody away."

And yet, Dave expressed a strong opposition to taking life, and can be considered a selective objector to America's wars. Dave's honest and insightful narratives appear here and in Chapters 3 and 5.

Up to the point where you get inducted you're not dealing with real things; you're dealing with paper, concepts and ideas. Everything is talk; you're not dealing with anything real yet. All of a sudden, I go for my physical and go through all that shit. At the end of the physical I went to this room with all the guys and I took an oath. That's when it dawned on me, I thought, "I am in some real shit now." It was a little scary. There was one guy who wasn't going to step forward. They said, "Look, you step forward or we're gonna' throw you in jail." He finally did step forward, but I remember thinking, "Boy, he's a ballsy mother fucker."

I was shipped to Fort Campbell, Kentucky. We got there about two o'clock in the morning, and it was the usual routine. We got off the bus and these DIs got in our faces right away. They put us in this big room, probably about three or four hundred guys; and this guy's up there wearing a big smokey bear hat, hands on hips and he screamed, "If you got drugs, or if you got weapons, now's the time to turn them in and nothing will be said or done." After that he said, "Do we have any conscientious objectors in here?" I stood up; there were only two or three of us in the whole room. He hollered back to me "What religion are you?" I said, "Catholic." And he yelled, "Jesus Christ, boy they quit fighting those religious wars years ago."

That was pretty much the extent of my harassment; see, I went in under the system specifically set up to deal with the phenomenon of conscientious objection. They set up special basic training and a noncombatant MOS. Because I went in under that system it was kind of a cake walk for me. I was never put in situations where I had to say, "No, I won't do this."

The other two COs and I stayed at Fort Campbell for nine days. We were in a holding company doing shit work, mowing lawns, picking up cigarette butts and hanging out. One day they came down and told the three of us to pack our stuff. They took us to a bus station in some dumpy, little town outside the base. They stuck us on a Greyhound and we rode twenty-seven hours to San Antonio, Texas. I really believe they sent us by bus because we were COs. Anyone else would have flown.

Being at Fort Sam Houston was a whole lot different than being at a regular base. Fort Sam is a medical base, it's all doctors and nurses. They're all in uniforms, but it's different because they're professionals. Someone who's a lieutenant is not just a lieutenant, she's a registered nurse. There's a different mentality—I never saw a weapon the whole time I was there. We're talking about people who are educated, doctors, nurses and technicians. It was really different than being on a base with a bunch of drunken lifers who have been in the military for twenty-five years. Fort Sam was a whole different environment.

I went through six weeks of basic with about sixty COs. Most of these guys were really religious people. I mean, only about three or four of us were not deeply religious. So, the DIs made us the platoon leaders. The guys all got along, and we really worked well together. Most of the guys were very sensitive people who had this common bond, God.

The drill sergeants were all Vietnam veterans, most of them had been shot up pretty good, and some of them had had COs as medics. They respected us, because they saw our convictions were deep enough for us to say, "Fuck it, we'll play the game, but we are going to play it under our rules." The DIs were very aware of that. They ran our asses to death, but they weren't ball busters. Their theory was, "If you're not gonna' carry a gun, you better learn to fuckin' run."

In AIT I went to class eight hours a day, five days a week for ten weeks. The training was good, and I learned a lot. You come out of AIT feeling like you know a lot, but you really don't know anything.

Jim Kraus

Boot camp was day-to-day injustice. I can't imagine anyone looking back on boot camp and not being able to think that through. Intimidation is an art and certain people were intimidated. The funny thing is people really get scared away from even thinking certain things, but somehow I always felt I could think what I wanted. The military tried to get your thought pattern lined up, but they really didn't pull that off with me.

It was amazing to me that some of the recruits would do the hazing, or whatever, on behalf of the company commanders. If a guy wouldn't conform or was a little wimpy or something, some recruits would put him in a locker and beat on the locker. The NCOs wouldn't do this kind of stuff, because it was a little too dirty for them, but they could easily put the recruits up to doing it.

Once we had to jump off the high board into a swimming pool and swim to the side. Supposedly, if you're at sea and you have to jump off the ship, you have to know how to come up. It was also a test to see whether you could swim or not. It's pretty obvious there were other ways to find out who needed swimming lessons besides having people jump off the high board. Of course, it was also a way of terrorizing everyone.

There was a black recruit who couldn't swim. After a lot of argument, he jumped off, went right to the bottom, and didn't come up. They had this long pole and they put it out there. He grabbed the pole, and with every molecule in his body telling him what to do, started shimmying up the pole. As soon as he got near the surface, the guy who shoved the pole out to him let go of it. There was a moment of absolute terror for this guy. The pole hit the bottom and his head popped up. It was just a game they were playing with him. They picked on blacks especially, because they believed most of the blacks couldn't swim.

I don't recall any antiwar talk going on in boot camp. It was just people surviving, trying to cope. Meanwhile, I was trying to convince myself that I could still serve and still be human after boot camp. My original plan was to go through nuclear power training, apply to college again, go get a degree, and go to Officer Candidate School. After boot camp that was out. I'd seen enough disgusting stuff there to know that I didn't want any part of the Navy. I had already retrenched a bit.

My next duty station was Treasure Island in San Francisco. Now, that's where things began to change very dramatically for me. I took weekend forays into San Francisco that turned up some new books and magazines, especially the monthly *Ramparts*. I read *Ramparts* regularly in those days. Also, I started hanging out at the base library and reading whatever I could get my hands on, mostly Bertrand Russell. I read all of his letters and some of his books. I especially remember his letters, probably because they struck home. It was through his letters that I learned a bit of the history of the unilateral disarmament movement. This was the beginning of my awareness of the antiwar and the antimilitary movement that predated my lifetime.

For me, one of the most enlightening things that happened occurred during the summer of 1967 when the San Francisco newspapers went on strike. *Ramparts* turned into a daily, and I.F. Stone wrote a column for it. I remember his being the most exciting perspective that I had come across in my entire life. Things were starting to make sense. I was finally beginning to understand my life and my anxieties, not a lot, but at least there were now some things that looked like answers to questions that went all the way back to childhood.

My best friend in the Navy was from central Pennsylvania; so, he knew about the Mennonites. He wasn't a very religious guy himself, but because of his Pennsylvania Dutch background, he understood things like conscientious objection. He and I had to do a tour aboard a ship before going to Idaho to continue nuclear power training. We had been assigned to a ship going to the West Pacific, to Vietnam. I thought about refusing, about not going. There were all kinds of news reports about people who were resisting and going to jail. Neither of us, however, knew that it was possible to file as a conscientious objector while you were in the service. My friend and I went without a murmur; yet I, at least, felt more like a prisoner than a patriot.

David Brown

In-service, imprisoned CO
U.S. Army 1966–1968
Veteran U.S. Disciplinary Barracks,
Fort Leavenworth

I felt strong and very, very together.

[AUTHOR'S NOTE]

David Brown grew up in a family he described as "religious" and "middle class." Unlike most of the other COs none of his family, nor his immediate extended family, experienced military service. David attended Yale University studying nuclear physics, but left college with thoughts of going into the ministry. He saw himself as a person who was being called to be a "transmitter of life." Upon leaving school David was unable to get an occupational deferment for the work he was doing with the Salvation Army; he enlisted prior to being drafted. David informed the recruiter that he wanted to be a chaplain's assistant and entered the Army under the assumption that he would be allowed to do so.

Within one month of entering the military, David's general perceptions of basic training with its "emphasis on blood, carnage and 'kill, kill, kill' " led him to decide not to cooperate. He concluded that "The Army wanted to recreate me as 'the ultimate weapon,' but I could not let the government turn me into a killer." As he put it, he rejected "The spirit of the bayonet, which was to kill," in favor of "the spirit of God, which was to give life."

David filed two applications for discharge as a conscientious objector; both were denied. Imprisoned twice, he was the first CO to petition federal court for a habeas corpus, seeking release from the military. That petition was also denied. His story begins here and appears in Chapters 4 and 5.

* * * *

Once I decided I couldn't participate in the military anymore, I just told them, "I'm not going to fall out for basic training tomorrow." But, after a day of communication and confrontation, the drill sergeant convinced me that the first couple of weeks were just first aid and map reading; so, I gave it a chance.

Meanwhile, my wife discovered and contacted the Central Committee for Conscientious Objectors. They sent me a copy of the discharge regulations, the *Handbook for Conscientious Objectors* and their memo on CO discharges. I had been going through the training program and attending the lectures, and the obscenity of it all became clearer and clearer. So, I went to the orderly room and told them I wanted to apply for discharge as a CO. I'm not sure how I was able to do this, because I had no prior experience in confronting authority. It was a tense time. They tried to grab the paperwork out of my hands like it was classified information or something. But, I managed to convince them to allow me to apply for discharge.

I thought that while I filled out the CO forms I wouldn't have to continue with basic; but they decided I had to complete the paperwork first, then I would be removed from basic training. So, I was stuck with another couple of weeks of basic while trying to write the application in my spare time. I really wanted to complete the forms by the beginning of the fifth week, because that was when we were going to the rifle range.

I handed in a handwritten application, but they said it had to be typed! They consented to have it typed, but still wouldn't pull me out of training. So, I ended up having to go off to the rifle range. Finally, they brought my paperwork out to be signed. Well, the company clerk, damn his hide, had decided that I had given him more than he was willing to type; so, he reduced it to a very badly done outline. I was left with the choice of either signing this hash or continuing with the training. So, I just signed it, and the application I wrote was not officially presented to the Army.

I was removed from basic training and assigned to permanent KP. However, the first sergeant knew I was a good typist and pulled me into the orderly room. So, from the day after I was pulled out of basic training, until my first discharge request was denied, I functioned as a company clerk.

As graduation time approached I tracked down my application, and found that it had not left the post. They were trying to pretend that nothing had happened. They even gave me advanced training orders to report to Fort Benjamin Harrison to learn to be a stenographer. They just kept the application as a way to deal with me. But, I knew I was not going anywhere. I was determined to get out. In my mind I was giving the Army a chance to follow its own rules. I told them to cancel the orders and to process my CO application.

I came to realize that every job in the military was dictated by the needs of combat. Everything in the military is a combat support function. There isn't a job that is not combat support. Even a chaplain's assistant fires a weapon. It's part of the job; it's part of everybody's job. It's your first job. You're in the infantry first and then you do whatever else you're doing. It was absolutely clear that that's what the organization was about. Period.

My application came back denied. So, they put me back into basic at the approximate point where I was removed. I made it clear from the minute I hit the place that I was not going to train. I fell out with everybody, but I didn't even do the Physical Training. I was threatened by the squad leader, I got yelled at and called names, but I stayed cool and just stood there.

That evening they tried to get me to draw a rifle. The sergeant tried to hand it to me, but I did not put out my hands to catch it; I let it fall to the floor. At this point, I think he knew I was serious, because none of those guys wanted anything to happen to those weapons. Then, I refused a direct order to take the weapon. That was tense. I just screwed up the courage and faced it. I tried to be clear, said very little, just "No." I expected to get clobbered at any minute, but I wasn't. Being called names didn't bother me particularly; it was, like, part of the game. I just closed myself off to it.

They isolated me, like some kind of scum, moved me out of the squad bay to a room where nobody else was. In fact, they got me out of the company within thirty-six hours. I was sent to a holding company to await court-martial. That was tense, too; going to the stockade wasn't really high on my list. About a week later I got a special court-martial. There wasn't much to say, in fact, I was advised not to say anything at all—a "keep silent defense." At that point my position was to just get through it. I wasn't raising any issues; so, I didn't make a statement. They sentenced me to three months in the stockade.

Then, the brigade commander wanted to speak to me. He gave me the "fatherly talk." He said, "I'm going to assign you to a basic training company that has never heard of you. I'll suspend your sentence and give you another chance." I told him it was hopeless, but he reassigned me anyway.

As soon as I got to the new basic training unit I told them, "I'm not going to train, forget it, don't bother." The captain ordered me to go sign out a rifle, and gave me an hour to do it. So, I went back to the barracks, and an hour later I was called to the orderly room. He charged me with disobeying a direct order and sent me back to the holding company.

By this time I was getting some help; the American Civil Liberties Union had decided to take my case. The Army also gave me an excellent Judge Advocate attorney, he actually did the job I needed done—he got the charges dropped. It turns out the company commander didn't have any evidence. He just believed me when I told him I never checked out a weapon. They never called anyone in from the supply room to see if I had been there. Nobody even knew me, so they couldn't testify as to whether or not I had complied. So, there was no evidence and the charge was dropped. But, that led to my suspended sentence being lifted. And one day, after just giving blood at the bloodmobile, I came back to find out that I was on my way to the stockade. It was the week before Thanksgiving, that was a real kick in the pants.

CHAPTER 3

In-Country:
Conscientious Objectors in Vietnam.

Never think that war, no matter how necessary, nor how justified is not a crime. Ask the infantry and ask the dead.

Ernest Hemingway

John Lawrence

I arrived at the 90th Replacement Battalion at Bien Hoa in May 1969. They had our planeload trucked over to a building that had great big, wooden slats along the side, and a door in front. There was a guy standing on a table with a stack of blank yellow sheets and a stack of pink sheets. As each guy approached him, he would say, "Yellow or pink?" Of course, everyone said, "Yellow." When I got to him, I said, "Pink," so he gave me the pink sheet, you know, like, "Who is this guy, a fairy?" But, I liked pink. We all went inside this building, and the slats in the wood came down. The doors slammed shut and there were guards around us again. And I go, "Uh, oh, something big is coming." An NCO got up and he said, "All of you with yellow sheets are now members of the First Cavalry Airborne Division; those of you with pink sheets are going to go to specialized units." Most of the guys, eighty to ninety percent, were yellow sheets. You just heard this groan, like, "Oh gees" from the guys with the yellow sheets. I'm thinking, "Thank goodness for pink!"

I was sent to the 24th Evacuation Hospital. This was a mobile unit, like your MASH units, and I was in an emergency room. It was a direct casualty receiving center. We'd stabilize the guys and ship them out. We were a triage unit, where you categorized people when they came in. By Army doctrine, you're supposed to take the light-wounded first, treat them and then progress to the worst. We never went by that, we took them as they came in and tried to treat everyone the best we could. There were about five medics there, two general practitioners and a couple of nurses, one male, one female.

I noticed a trend with every campaign that came up. They would bring in a huge gob of medical supplies and we took in casualties. They'd have us primed and ready, because we were the direct receiving center; we had to have the supplies right there. We'd get hit with mass casualties; they arrived by helicopter, jeep or box ambulance.

My job was kind of gruesome, I did body identification.

When the casualties came in we would sort them. I would do minor, routine medical kinds of stuff, body stripping, you know, getting their identification.

In June 1969 the 82nd Airborne got chewed up royally. We got twenty-two casualties in our unit; but, I noticed they announced on the radio that there was only one. Because of my work, I got very familiar with the casualties; so when I compared their names to the ones listed in the *Stars and Stripes* I noticed discrepancies. I didn't notice the names of some of the guys that I tagged. So, I started asking questions. I said, "How can we have, say, only fifty casualties listed in the *Stars and Stripes* when we had so many more?" I was informed that, at the time, the Army had a system of dispersing casualties over several days so the impact would be less back home, folks back home wouldn't get the full count. Not only that, but they dispersed them over other geographical areas, you know, Vietnam, Korea, wherever they could sort through casualties. That way, it would diminish the number reported for Vietnam.

Also, if a casualty came into our unit and died before ten minutes were up, he was considered killed in action, a "KIA." So, at ten minutes the doctor would yell out, "Ten minutes!" At that point, anybody who died would be listed as having died of wounds, "DOW." So, the Army would take the KIAs and report them on the evening news. The DOWs would be sorted out, placed on a different casualty list and reported later on. Also, if you died "in-country," within the boundary of the land areas, that was one statistic; however, if you died offshore, on a Navy hospital ship, that was another statistic. You see, they took those statistics and really manipulated them.

The best way to know about war is to ask a medic. I've seen some of the most incredible things. I wish I could take everything I've seen and project it onto a celluloid tape, and let everyone see it first hand. There were mass casualties. Vietnamese civilians, Americans, Vietnamese soldiers, North Vietnamese soldiers. I saw just about everything there is to see and it has had an impact. I can't describe it; I've been in therapy for a long time trying to understand it.

We worked twelve hours on, twelve hours off and when mass casualties would come, they would just pile the bodies up on the ground and we'd pull them in and do whatever we could. We logged in 2,000 of all types in June alone, and you're talking about a handful of medics here. Other Vietnam veterans refer to me as a walking war memorial, because of the number of dead that I saw. It was just blood and guts of the worst kind.

Most of the ones that died were nineteen to twenty year olds. A lot of them were married; that made an impression that war is truly dark, the darker side of life. And only once do I remember a general coming through; never do I remember a priest or chaplain in our area. It was mass death, death on a grand scale, nothing like the movies.

When nineteen year olds are dying and the only person staring them in the face is a twenty-three year old medic, you become their father, priest and confessor. This whole dynamic relationship takes place in a matter of seconds. That's when you need your priest and your chaplain, your spiritual guide, but they weren't there, they were someplace else.

We had six little wooden stands that were built like boxes. The casualties would come pouring in on litters or wrapped in field gear. We'd just set them down on these boxes. Of course, we didn't have time to clean up, I mean, the casualties were just coming in one on top of another. If an arm fell off, you know, we'd just shove it aside. If it was an abdominal wound we just take and scoop it out. Brains, when they are damaged and come in contact with oxygen, gel up like cottage cheese, so there was gobs of that stuff laying all over the place. Blood congeals into massive globs, and it's really slippery when it's moist; we'd just take it and throw it, and there would be globs of blood and intestines and everything building up on the ground. It was like that all the time.

Children were brought in, blown to shreds, and I got really tired of that. I think I hurt the most with the nineteen year olds dying and the children, the kids, the little ones of Vietnam. There were four kids brought in from Ho Nai, two girls and two boys. All but one boy lived. The boy that lived had both of his arms and both of his legs blown off. He sort of became our company mascot; we kept him alive. I don't know what happened to him after the GIs left, but we sort of adopted him at that point.

We had an old wooden shed that we'd stack the bodies in. Things ferment pretty fast in 120 degree heat, and graves registration couldn't get out to us, because there were so many casualties and problems with transport. Heat built up in the shed and the bodies started exploding. A medic friend of mine had the grim task of cleaning that out. It's just that kind of world, over and over, day after day, hour after hour. You're just coated with blood, it dries and it becomes like rust. You feel like you've got rust all over your body. We'd eat our sandwiches and stuff while covered with blood and intestines.

I remember a captain came through, and there was a leg on the ground, almost a complete leg, thigh and everything, just laying on the ground. We had an incinerator out back where we threw body parts and they just burned up, stunk like everything, but we couldn't leave stuff laying around. We were too tired to move this leg out to the incinerator, and he walked in and he goes, "Who's leg is this?" and everyone looked at everyone else. We started going, "Is that your leg?" "No, it's not my leg, is it your leg?" He couldn't understand what was going on. So, finally he ordered someone to take the leg out and burn it up. That black humor is what kept us half-way sane.

Once Pat Nixon was supposed to visit our area so they sent in a whole battalion of MPs to secure the place. As I recall, it was an extremely hot day and she was supposed to come for a fifteen minute visit. The whole area was under Military Police Guard, 2,000 of these guys were around. Then the helicopters came and dropped different colored smoke grenades, yellow, purple, coded as to the degree of safety. The Vietnamese were kept out of the area. Just about the time her helicopter was to land, a box ambulance with two GIs pulled up. We're talking about 110 degrees outside so you can imagine what it was like inside that box ambulance, it became an oven. We couldn't get to them. The MPs wouldn't let us move from the emergency room area to the box ambulance, which was only about twenty feet away. They wouldn't let us move; I mean, we were frozen stiff, in place. She came, did her visit and pulled out. Well, we opened up the door to that ambulance—one guy did survive—the other guy fried. You know, she didn't know, but that's the kind of mentality that goes on in war; that's how valuable you are, and make no mistake about it. It's that callous, and you have the internalized realization that your life is also worth nothing. It's only as valuable as your friends make it.

Oftentimes, just to show the callousness of the situation, we'd be identifying bodies while they were still alive. Guys are dying and we want to rush through this thing, "What's your name?" You know, try to get them while they're still alive, it saved a lot of effort. But, on another level, I was becoming very sensitive. When you identify a body you have to take what's left of it and strip it down, take off all the rings and anything that's important to that body and give it an ID; it becomes an intimate, personal kind of experience.

There's an element about war that you just can't depict in movies, or books, or anything; there's something there. To me it was so dark, so evil. If there's truly a concept of evil, it was that immense waste of life. Life was zero, there was no value to life. If parents only knew how valueless their children's lives were; we really didn't care. You can't care, mass death is just that. It's naive for people to think that the military really does care about the individual. When you get into the military structure, the individual no longer matters. You're part of the whole, the group; and so, for me to sit down with these individual casualties and say, "Gee, I'm really sorry, I'll give you your last rites and really care for you," that's nonsense. The only people who care are the people back home who are going to have to accept the loss.

There were several people who became mental casualties in that unit. I met an E–7 sergeant that lost his mind. I didn't drink. I didn't take drugs. I was "Mr. Straight-arrow." I remember, when I'd be in the midst of all this slaughter, I would trip out in my mind. I would imagine this beautiful green field, tall green grass and a big oak tree in the center. I'd be laying down under this oak tree and I'd be looking up at this perfectly clear, blue sky. I'd concentrate on that, and I think that's what got me through. I remember that I was so tired most of the time, twelve hours on, twelve hours off and lots of activity; about the only thing you had time for is getting your gear ready for the next round. You'd just crash. You're just physically and mentally exhausted. It's like your body has deserted you. After about six months I told a friend of mine to get me out of there; he was in Personnel and he did.

A big chunk of us in the Medical Corps were conscientious objectors. I had one guy come and ask me, "Why do you believe the way you do?" But, he said it out of a real sincere desire to know. It wasn't hostile, he was really curious; you know, what's this dingdong doing, walking around here without a weapon? Also, I'll never forget a sergeant who came up to me, armed to the teeth, bulging with weapons and protective gear, looking at me in my fatigues, going, "You coward!" You get used to that after awhile. I think he was threatened. You know, you're around, rubbing elbows with these career Army types, they're going to be threatened by a weaponless creature in their midst. It doesn't fall into their masculine definition. But, there was a different mentality in a medical unit, a great deal more acceptance and tolerance. The purpose of the medical units was to preserve military strength and morale. I think the primary function of a medic is not casualty control, but morale. I wanted to think of myself as sort of a Florence Nightingale, that I was going to be constructive in such a colossal nightmare. And, our statistics were really impressive. If you got to our unit, so the Army said, your chances of survival were 97.6%, but that's if you made it beyond the first ten minutes.

Several times we had to treat the North Vietnamese and the Viet Cong; and once, I'll have to admit, I had to question my own integrity. We had gone through a whole gob of American casualties and they brought in a Viet Cong. He had an open chest wound, there were maggots crawling in and out of it. Of course, I know now that maggots are good things. They eat up the dying flesh and prevent gangrene. So, I was assigned to haul him down the road a quarter-of-a-mile to the POW hospital. These were just dirty, scrubby, filthy quonset huts, cleaned as much as we could, you know, washed down floors and cleaned-off blood and stuff. So, I was taking him down and I just stood there and stared at him. I had a great deal of resentment toward him because of my feelings about all these American casualties. Finally, another medic came out and said, "I'll take him down," and I said, "Okay." I was caught up in that whole mentality of "us versus them," and it reflected itself in that instance. War creates its own need and I did ego-identify with the American casualties. You want to believe that you can go beyond, you know, help your enemy. That's a hard concept. It's a big one.

I got reassigned to the 68th Medical Group. It was a communications bunker as well as the headquarters company for the 68th Med Group. This was a totally different world than the one at the 24th Evacuation Hospital. I was a courier and I went on "Med-Cap" missions. That's where we'd rendezvous at a village and give the Vietnamese people medical care. We were a force of good will. There was a lot of positive interaction there. The kids came running out to us and there was lots of good stuff.

I think the war ended not so much because of what was happening in the streets of America—although that was having a major impact—but more importantly, because over there morale was breaking. Whole units were refusing to fight; that was a greater threat to the military structure than any civilian protest. I know a lot of individual soldiers were refusing to go out on patrol, it was just growing dissent. One of the statistics I got, but I can't prove it, was that 70% of those in Vietnam were draftees. The regular

Army's morale was protected by being stationed in Germany or other noncombat areas; so you had a lot of people in Vietnam who really didn't want to be there. Vietnam was fought by the citizen-soldier.

The whole of Vietnam can be summarized in one event that happened to me. I was driving down a road in my jeep, approaching a beautiful green ravine. I mean, green over in Vietnam was really green. In the center of the bridge that crossed the ravine was this great big, fire engine red, tank-looking, thing. I came up behind it and stopped. Right behind me were these big five-ton trucks, a convoy. So, they wedged me in behind this big red thing. I couldn't go anywhere. There was nothing to do but look at the beautiful terrain, so I just sat there mesmerized by this beautiful, lush green. Then, all of a sudden this tank-thing turned its stubby little turret and shot out napalm. It was intensely hot, I felt like my skin was just melting off my body. In a matter of seconds, napalm completely coated the vegetation, and then it ignited all at once. The left side of the ravine turned into scorched black, with a few flickering flames on some limbs. There was no green left, it was all charred. Then I turned to my right and there was the lush green, and the turret swung around and fired out the napalm. The same thing happened, the green turned into this ashen, black, charred, wasted land. It was just that fast. It was just a wasteland.

That was the crime against the earth, defoliating the countryside, denuding it to where the Vietnamese were importing rice, instead of exporting it. The crime against the people was that everyone was a target. If you were right there in the middle of it, you knew you were up against the entire population. I think we came mighty close to being willing to kill them all. I realized I was in the midst of hell, the bottom rung of this reality. You see, the tragedy of the whole thing is the military took itself very seriously, to the point that it denied its own sense of value and ethic. And I remember watching the ravine burn, and the feeling I had was this *is* Vietnam.

David E. Wilson

Noncombatant service CO
U.S. Army 1968–1969
Vietnam veteran

We were put into situations that were like going to hell.

[AUTHOR'S NOTE]

David Wilson pointed to his parents' religious beliefs as critical in his decision to become a conscientious objector. The family belonged to a Christian sect, called the "Christian Conventions," that adhered to a literal interpretation of the New Testament. David described them as "Quaker-like" and "conservative"; they had no church, preferring to conduct services in the homes of their members.

Noncombatant military service was approved by the sect, and David's father and uncle had been conscientious objectors during World War II. His father performed the duties of an X-ray technician and his uncle was a medic in Europe. Neither relative talked about their military experiences. Another member of his congregation had been a CO in Vietnam. This man made it through the war without carrying a weapon; David found strength in that and decided he could probably do the same thing.

For David, applying for conscientious objector status was "learned behavior." it was based on the family model, and was not a product of soul searching or intellectualization on his part.

David received noncombatant conscientious objector status from his draft board, and shortly thereafter he volunteered for the draft. After a brief stop at Fort

Campbell, Kentucky David was shipped to Fort Sam Houston for medic's training. Upon completion of his training he received orders for Vietnam.

David Wilson's story is a shockingly frank and brutally human account of the impact of guerilla war on soldiers, civilians and noncombatants. It is presented below in detail, with concluding comments found in Chapter 5.

* * * *

I reported to the Overseas Replacement Center in Oakland, California. We were all locked up, nobody was allowed out of the compound. A couple of the guys literally tried to go over the wall. Apparently, these guys had a better idea than I did of what we were getting into. They were scared to death.

We left Travis Air Force Base in the middle of the night. From there we flew to a U.S. military terminal in Japan. We were allowed to get off and use the facilities, but nobody was allowed to go any further. There were armed guards, and they really kept an eye on us. There was no getting around them, they were there to keep us penned-up by the airplane, and they did. I felt like we were a bunch of cattle being herded into a slaughter pen.

Eventually, we landed in Bien Hoa. We no more than filed off the airplane when I saw all these guys standing by the side of the runway. They were going home. They were dirty and looked like they had been through hell backwards. They just kind of looked at us and shook their heads. I stood there and looked at these guys and I thought, "My God, these guys look like old men." And, they did. The oldest one in the group probably wasn't any older than twenty-five, but from the look on his face, I would have sworn that the guy was close to fifty.

We got on a bus that had all this wire mesh on the window. I'm thinking it's there because they don't want us to escape. So, I asked the driver what the hell was going on. He laughed; he said the mesh was there in case we got ambushed. It kept the grenades from coming into the bus. I thought, "Oh my God." That was my first realization that I was in some kind of danger. That feeling never left me; it started right on the first day and that underlying level of tension stayed there until the day I left. It got worse, but it started right there.

They took us into a supply room and starting issuing guns. I told the guy that I was a conscientious objector and didn't want one. He said, "What the hell are they doing sending somebody like you into a unit like this?" He said, "You're crazy, you ought to have your head examined." He started to laugh and told me, "You'll be back in a week."

Then, our sergeant came in and tried to talk me into taking a weapon. I refused. He got a little nasty, standing there yelling at me and calling me an idiot. He used every line imaginable to try to tell me that the lives of my buddies depended on me carrying a weapon. He said, "What if you are alone with a wounded guy, and here comes Charlie trying to kill you. What are you going to do?" I told him, "I'll just have to deal with that when it happens. If it ever came to that, my instincts for self-preservation would probably take over, and I'd probably use the weapon." So, he said, "Well, why don't you just take it now?"

But, I was stubborn. The Army had given me a bunch of crap about being a CO, I hadn't knuckled under and I wasn't going to. I got more stubborn as time went on. It pissed me off, and I just decided the hell with these people. They can't make me do this; and legally, there was nothing they could do to force me to carry a weapon.

I did meet up with one other CO while I was there. He started going out on patrols and the next time I saw him, he was carrying an M–16. When I saw this I began to wonder if things were going to get that rotten for me.

I wound up going to a big base camp in Dong Tam. For the first few weeks in-country I worked with a bunch of other medics in an aid station. People were nice to me, nobody was antagonistic about the fact that I was a CO. But, people knew about it the minute I hit the front door. It seemed like no matter where I went, somebody knew. It was almost like they couldn't trust me, like I was some kind of a weirdo.

After a few weeks I got assigned to a platoon that served as the front line of defense for the base at Dong Tam. My heart was in my mouth when they flew me out there. I was there for about five minutes when this lieutenant came out and asked me where my weapon was. I told him I didn't carry a weapon. He goes, "What!?" I said, "I'm a conscientious objector." He said, "Well, what the hell are you doing out here?" I said, "I was sent out here." At that point, he dragged me into his tent.

There first thing he did was bring out his M–16. He said, "Here, hold this." So, I took it, I just stood there holding the thing, and he said to me, "Do you know how to fire that?" I said, "No." He just kind of shook his head. Then he said to me, "I think you ought to at least let me show you how this thing works." I said, "I don't want to know." He said, "Well, what if you need it?" I answered, "Why will I need it? I'm a medic." And he said, "Goddamnit, we need all the firepower in this unit that we can get. If we get pinned down out there somewhere, that gun that you are carrying, or not carrying, might be the difference between us getting nailed." Well, I didn't believe him. I said, "That's a bunch of shit, you got thirty guys out there armed to the teeth, what the hell difference is one more gun going to make?"

Then, he demanded that I at least watch him run through the motions of slamming a clip into it, chambering a round and putting the safety on. I told him that I didn't want to know about it. He was pissed, just going out of his mind; he couldn't believe that he was seeing this.

After about fifteen or twenty minutes of this he finally figured out that he was fighting a losing battle. I was beginning to think, "Well, here goes my first assignment." I thought he would send me back to the rear. But, he didn't, I stayed with that unit until I left.

The lieutenant calmed down after awhile and sort of treated me with a certain amount of respect. The other guys were a little skeptical, but I became accepted as the medic. People started coming to me with their complaints about this and that. So, after about a week, I settled in.

Shortly after this our unit was assigned to do search and destroy missions. The first day out, we're walking down a trail, and all of a sudden I hear guys yelling and guns going. Everybody dropped. I looked up to see this Vietnamese guy running on a parallel trail, waving something. They shot him. It turns out he was waving his ID card.

Well, my first reaction was that the guy was hurt, it never occurred to me that the guy was Vietnamese; he was just somebody who was hurt. I started running over there and three guys jumped on me. It was like, "What the hell are you doing?" They thought he might have a grenade or something and he would take out some guys before he kicked the bucket.

Finally, a couple of guys went over there. He was bleeding all through the chest and abdomen; the guy's guts were damn near hangin' out. It was just a God-awful mess. I couldn't believe what I was looking at. The guys were pointing guns at him and made him keep his hands where they could see them. I thought, "Why are they doing this?" The guy was gesturing to them about his ID papers; they fucked up, they shot a civilian. They shot somebody that wasn't even carrying a gun.

They let me put dressings on him. My hands were shaking, this was my first time out in the field. It dawned on me that I didn't know what we were going to do with this guy. So, I looked up to the lieutenant and said, "We got to get a helicopter for this guy." He said, "You got to be kidding me, this is a dink." So, I stood and argued with the lieutenant until I could see that some of the guys were getting tensed up about it. They were really pissed at me for the stand I was taking.

Finally, the lieutenant said, "We don't have time to screw around with this, we're here to do an operation. We are not calling a helicopter for this gook." That was the end of that.

Well, I don't know if they did it to humor me or what, but me and a couple of the guys dragged this guy on a poncho to an abandoned hooch. We put him in there, on the dirt floor, and left him. We just walked away and left him. I'm sure he died.

We didn't get into all that many firefights; maybe two or three times a month we would be in situations where there was heavy, sustained fire. I only saw the people who were shooting at us a couple of times. We hardly ever had anything concrete to fight against; instead, we got a lot of booby traps, sniper fire and rockets. Two or three snipers would pin down our whole company for half an hour, every time somebody would move they'd start shooting.

As a medic, I was what they needed me to be at the time. If they needed a brain surgeon, that's what I was; if they needed a chest surgeon, that's what I was. I knew I wasn't those things and I was scared to death that I wouldn't be able to cope with serious wounds. So, a lot of what I did was automatic.

If somebody yelled for a medic, I went; and there were a couple of times when I came pretty close to buying the farm because I went. Guys would yell for a medic, I'd run and realize that I was the only idiot on my feet, everybody else was down.

Once we were ambushed by a suicide sniper. He was in a bunker covered up with brush. I heard all this firing and found out he shot the pointman. I heard them screaming for a medic, so I ran around the corner of this trail trying to get to where this guy was. I remember being in mid-air jumping to get there and my lieutenant reached up, grabbed me and pulled me down. I actually fought with him physically, got away from him and started crawling up to these guys. I got about five feet away from this bunker when one of the guys behind me shot a grenade into the bunker and blew this Vietnamese right out of there.

Well, our pointman was dead; I didn't even have the strength to help carry his body out to the rice paddy. I was totally in a state of shock; during the whole thing I hadn't been thinking, I had just reacted.

After the first couple of operations, the guys protected me. These were guys who were really skeptical about me at first, but I became something special to them, I became *their medic.* That kind of baffled me, because I felt like I was not actively involved in the war. I felt like it was their war, not mine.

Once our unit made a sweep of an island in the Mekong River. I was about ten guys back in the column when I saw the pointman step on a booby trap. Well, the guy behind him really got it. I watched his body fly up into the air, and was on my way before he hit the ground. When I got there, his flak vest was full of holes. The shrapnel had gone right through the damned flak vest. I cut the vest off and his whole chest was a mass of little holes. His eyes were glazed over, he couldn't talk. He was cut to shreds inside and was throwing up blood. I bound him up and we made a litter out of some fatigue tops and trees. Then, we carried him through about a half mile of mud that was up to our waists. The helicopter was waiting for us by the time we got to the landing zone. They took him to the hospital, but I found out later that he died.

This event was the beginning of the end for me. Once we got him on the helicopter, I sat down on a dike at the edge of the rice paddy and cried. I cried for about twenty minutes. I was so goddamned frustrated that this had to happen. This kid had only been in the unit for a week. I had only been there for a couple of months, but I guess I had been there long enough for things to affect my head. To me, he seemed like a child.

The guys didn't know what to do with me; my crying made everybody uncomfortable. I mean, guys just didn't act like that. Looking back on it, I realize that I did not have the kind of release that the others did. They could shoot their guns, shoot people, and all this other shit to get their hostilities and frustration out. I didn't have outlets like that.

Up to a point I was able to shut things out, I was able to do my job. I didn't think about it while it was happening, but when it was all over the dam broke. Perhaps crying was my body's own safety mechanism. I bawled like a baby after a couple of these incidents. When I finished crying I'd get up and go back to doing what I was supposed to do.

I guess I just wasn't emotionally prepared for that whole experience. I felt totally impotent. All I could do was patch guys up and hope to Christ that they got back to a hospital in time to be saved. I was mad and frustrated that there was nothing I could do to stop this idiocy—this lunacy. It wasn't a war, it was just goddamned stupid.

At one point we were down to about half strength. We only had about seventy-five guys in the field due to problems with immersion foot. Well, they sent us to sweep an area we had already been through at least four or five times. We were going down a trail when I heard an explosion up toward the front of the column. They called the medics and we found a guy in a ditch off the trail. He had stepped on a booby trap and was blown to shit. Two or three guys on the trail were also pretty badly wounded.

While we were trying to get things under control, the rest of the company had been sent down some other trails to provide security, and they hit another booby trap. I ran back down the trail and found this guy with both legs blown off above the knees. From mid-thigh down there was nothing but a mass of—I mean—it looked like somebody had taken his legs and shoved them into a meat grinder. I had to stick my hands into that to find the stumps of his legs. I put tourniquets on his legs and gave him a couple of hits of morphine. He was in shock and so was I. Other guys in the area had also taken some shrapnel, but they weren't hurt too badly.

Meanwhile, the NCOs were still sending guys down the trails to provide security. I couldn't believe those assholes. I got up and started screaming at them to get the hell off of the trails. I kind of lost it, I was just kind of nuts there for a couple of seconds. It turns out that out of seventy-five guys, twenty-five had to be taken out by medevac choppers. Two guys died there and a couple died later. I had been in Vietnam for five months and never saw anything like it. It was total carnage. And you know, there were no Vietnamese there, we didn't take a shot. It was incredible.

It took several days for me to get over this. I was angry. I had gone beyond being mad at the Army, I was pissed off at the U.S. government, and I am to this day. You see, we had been put into a situation where we had no control. We were being controlled by our superiors and by the U.S. government.

Meanwhile, even I got pissed at those bastards for setting booby traps on us, killing and maiming guys. I mean, I started looking at dead Vietnamese and feeling a sense of revenge. In my mind, I could see myself pulling the trigger on some of those people, even though I never had, and never did carry a weapon. But, seeing this stuff did strange things to people's heads.

Like, I saw three people executed while I was there. I mean literally shot in cold blood. This happened after we were hit with booby traps and the guys were frustrated and angry. Some VC who was in custody would look at a GI the wrong way and that was it, he died. Once, I heard this VC prisoner yellin' "Chieu boi!" meaning "I surrender." I looked up and saw a GI with an M–16 empty a whole goddamn clip into this prisoner's chest. The VC was down on his knees, yelling and the guy just kept firing, one burst at a time—it took an eternity for that guy to drop. I couldn't believe what I was seeing.

Another time, I saw five guys nearly kick an old man to death; he either couldn't or wouldn't tell them anything. Then, they blew the shit out of him, right in front of his family.

One day we had a suspected VC in custody; my lieutenant told one of the younger guys in the unit to take him out and kill him. He did it and came back all upset, just shaking. He came to me and said, "Doc, I don't think I'll be able to do that again." I said, "You don't have to do it again, that's ridiculous. If he tells you to do it again, tell him you're not going to do it."

I began to realize that these incidents happened during a day, or on a day after we had gotten a bunch of guys hurt or killed. It seemed like there was nobody else to take it out on, so they just killed people.

There were a lot of psychological pressures. We'd come back from operations covered with blood and mud, feeling like animals. We lived like animals; we ate in the mud, slept in the mud, fought in the mud, got hurt in the mud and died in the mud. It was like living in a slaughterhouse. We were put into situations that were like going to hell.

On a couple of occasions I got sent out on night ambushes with a handful of guys. I realized that if we ran into a squad of VC, we could easily be wiped out. I wondered why they sent me out there, because that was a situation where the absence of one gun could make a difference between guys coming back or not. But, the medics drew straws for stuff like that and I was the one who got nailed on both those occasions. So, I just did it.

The day I got hurt they dropped us off into one of two small rice paddies connected by a small break in the jungle. The one they set us down in had four-foot long punji sticks placed every three feet from one side of the rice paddy to the other. The choppers couldn't set down; so, we all jumped out from several feet in the air. It was a miracle that nobody got impaled on one of those things.

We got on the ground and started moving towards the second rice paddy. Well, the guy next to me stepped on a booby trap. He was walking about two feet away from me when he stepped on it. It blew his left leg off and knocked me unconscious. When I came to, I was lying flat on my back in the mud, with my right leg twisted underneath me. I felt like I was hit by a freight train. People were screaming for a medic, but at that point, I was the only medic on the ground.

I sat up and saw this gaping hole in my right leg, it covered about two-thirds of my thigh—just a puddle of blood. Then, I saw that my right hand was chewed to shit, blood running down my arm, and I was just baffled, because at that point I still couldn't feel anything. Finally, they realized that the medic was hit and they came up to help us.

I caught shrapnel behind my knee, on the front of my thigh, in my back and in my right hand. I told a guy how to put the dressing on my leg and asked for some morphine, but they wouldn't give it to me; they were afraid that I had a chest wound and they didn't want to screw up my respiratory system.

There was all this blood and I started feeling woozy. I thought I was going to die there. I thought about all the religion I had been taught as a child, that God was always there when you needed him, and how all that seemed to amount to nothing at this point. All I was aware of was an empty, vacant feeling; I felt like I had been totally let down.

They put us in a helicopter and flew us to a hospital ship on the Mekong River. There were no doors on the helicopter, so the air flew through it like a mini-hurricane. That revived me enough to make me realize that I wasn't going to kick the bucket. I thought maybe I'd lose my leg, but big fuckin' deal, I'd be alive. The air coming through also hit the exposed tissue on my body—all I could feel was pain. I thought I was going to go out of my mind. I remember screaming at the pilot to get that thing on the ground.

They got us to the hospital ship and sat our litters down on a couple of sawhorses. They immediately started cutting all my clothes and boots off and within a matter of seconds had units of blood going into each arm. I realized that if they were going to all that trouble I must be salvageable. I mean, I knew from experience that you didn't waste time on guys who were obviously gone, because if you did, somebody else's life would be put in jeopardy. It was a crude form of triage, I guess, but there wasn't really any choice.

I don't remember much about the time I spent in the hospital, because I was all doped up with Demerol. But, they took the shrapnel out of my body and saved my leg. I do remember a couple of nurses discussing whether or not I was well enough to be transported to the States. I recall waking up enough to yell that I wanted to get out of there. They did ship me out that day, back to Japan for surgery on my leg and hand. About a week later I was shipped back to the States for skin grafts and more surgery to restore function in the index finger of my right hand.

Harold O. (Pseudonym)

Noncombatant service CO
U.S. Army 1970–1972
Vietnam veteran

I saw doing this as my personal peace mission.

[AUTHOR'S NOTE]

For Harold, playing war and watching World War II movies were a big part of growing up in the 1950s. He recalled that he and his friends, "Played more war than stickball."

In his neighborhood, everyone registered for the draft when they were eighteen, "So they could drink alcohol." Raised a Roman Catholic, Harold grew to reject most of the church's liturgical dictates, but he adopted important moral and spiritual messages.

While taking courses at the New School for Social Research, Harold discovered the writings of Thoreau, Gandhi and Bertrand Russell. He came to the conclusion that the proliferation of nuclear weapons was "total madness." This led him to participate in a ban the bomb demonstration held in New York City in 1964. He recalled that the protest was not well received:

> I was among a handful of demonstrators marching down Fifth Avenue. People were screaming and throwing eggs at us; I thought we were going to be killed.

Soon, Harold began participating in demonstrations against the war in Vietnam. He also explored conscientious objection with a draft counselor from the Catholic Peace Fellowship. At that point, however, he found it difficult to relate his religious training as a Catholic to existing government requirements on conscientious objection.

When his draft notice arrived Harold tore it up and went underground, "Deep into the hippie movement." He spent time in Canada and Mexico before settling in San Francisco and "becoming completely swept up by the counterculture." He said:

> I was a pacifist, a strong warrior of truth and love and peace. San Francisco was a haven from the rest of middle-American madness that was going on at the time. There was freedom and openness in San Francisco. Everybody did drugs; drugs were our currency. I believe that what we were doing there changed the consciousness of this country, and maybe even of the world.

After more than a year on the run, Harold got tired of living with the constant fear of being caught. He decided to cooperate with Selective Service and turned himself in to the FBI. He was twenty-seven years old, one year older than the normal cutoff age for induction. Harold had also decided that he did not want to perform alternative civilian service; rather, he wanted to be drafted into the military as a noncombatant. He explained his position this way:

> At that stage of the game, I wanted to see Vietnam; I wanted to physically be in Vietnam. This was sort of a "Florence Nightingale" kind of thing, I wanted to do good. I saw doing this as my personal peace mission. So, all I had to do was sign the papers at the draft board and I was a 1–A–O.

After basic and medic's training, Harold decided to go into the Airborne Rangers and was sent to jump school at Fort Benning, Georgia. He said:

> I figured I was going to Vietnam anyway, and I was excited about the intense physical training and the prospect of parachuting. Also, I wanted to prove to

the other soldiers that I was not a conscientious objector because I had a fear of dying. That didn't faze me. Guys would say, "Oh, you're a CO, what the fuck's wrong with you." But, I shut a lot of people up with those silver wings on my chest.

In 1970, while on leave, Harold participated in a massive antiwar march in Washington, DC; a few days later he was in Vietnam. Harold's story appears here and concludes in Chapter 5.

* * * *

Vietnam was so fuckin' intense you would not believe it. You've never seen a combat movie done about the way it really was over there. Guys were armed to the teeth—it was John Wayne time—M-16s, C-4 explosive, everybody wore knives. You were put into an environment where people had a license to kill. A person could go up and down, as high or as low as they wanted to go, and some guys really got down to the depths.

I had that World War II image of GI Joe with the little kid in his hand, and the kid's got the helmet on, eating a Hersey bar, right? So, I'd give the kids all my food, sometimes I wouldn't have anything to eat. Well, all along the road there'd be kids yelling, "Fuck you, GI. Fuck you!" Then, I'd see guys ridin' on a truck take like, beans and motherfuckers—lima beans and ham, stuff that you wouldn't eat—and hit the kids in the head with the cans. Three to six months later, after all the shit came down, there'd be guys shootin' kids. Some kid would come up and say, "Fuck you, GI." Pow! They'd blow his shit away. Blowin' old ladies' shit away. Crazy sons-of-bitches.

A lot of these young guys thought all the Vietnamese people were the enemy. When I could, I did intervene to stop senseless violence against Vietnamese civilians and ARVN soldiers. Once, a guy I knew was roughin' up mama san, I said, "Fuck you, man. Back off. If you hit her again, I'm gonna' cut your fuckin' head off." And, I probably would have; that's how crazy you could get over there. He backed off. He said, "Okay, doc. Okay."

The violence among soldiers in Vietnam was unreal. In the beginning I had fights all the time. I saw fights between blacks and whites. Guys threw hand grenades at each other, knives at each other, shot at each other. I never saw an officer fragged, but I knew about a first sergeant that got blown away.

It was the pressure, exhaustion and disorientation that got to the guys. Mother nature humbled you over there. It was 140 degrees in the shade. The heat would fry your fuckin' brain like an egg. There were tigers and snakes; you had leeches all over your body. The mosquitoes would bite you until your eyelids closed and you couldn't see.

You'd hump eighty to ninety pound packs through dry elephant grass, eight feet tall, with booby traps all over the place. You'd hump until your throat was like sandpaper and your eyes were popping out of your head. You'd be so thirsty you'd kill for a can of Coke. You'd kill for a can of Coke.

We were in the boonies for the first nine-and-a-half months I was there. We'd hump until about nine o'clock. That's all we did. We'd lay low during the day and they'd lay low. This was during the height of Vietnamization; we were starting to pull out, so we were giving ARVN the job. We were not going out there searching and destroying at this stage of the game. The North Vietnamese and the VC had paid their price too; they realized things were going their way and they were content to lay low.

When the shit did hit the fan, you didn't know what was happening. Like suddenly, I get some guy's foot with half his boot in my face—and—and—some guy's leg is there, you know? He's all bloodied up and we patch him up and medevac him out. And, you patch up the other guys and medevac them out, and that's it. That's it. Just patch 'em up and get 'em out. I was trained that way, boom, it was automatic.

I was with a good bunch of guys. They just wanted you to

know your shit and to have your shit together, because their lives depended on it. The motto we had was, "we are going back to the world, no matter what it takes." And what it took was not taking any shortcuts, being able to cut the fuckin' mustard, and wanting to get back to the world.

We'd talk about the war lots of times. You know, what was our State Department's motive? What was our objective, and how the fuck were we going to accomplish it? These guys just couldn't picture themselves saying no to the war. It went against their whole concept of family and country. It was like, their uncles went to war and their fathers went, but nobody knew what Vietnam was all about. We'd sit and discuss it; yet, for them to stand up against the war, or for them to go to prison because they thought the war was wrong, was beyond them. We'd discuss and we'd argue, but we always had respect for each other.

I probably never convinced anyone about what I believed. And, no one knew I was a CO unless I told them or if a guard duty situation came up, because then I'd refuse to take a weapon. But, without an exception, when a soldier or an officer found out I was a fuckin' 1–A–O, I'd hear, "Hey, I thought you were squared away. What the fuck's the matter with you?" They never tried to trick me, but right up to the last day I was there they'd ask me if I wanted to sign out a weapon.

Being a medic came easy to me. The guys would say, "What a great guy doc is," that was important for me to hear. I knew I was a champion medic. I took the risks, and did everything military and to the max. I learned my trade and I learned it well. I was never afraid to use it; and because I was a good medic, the guys protected me to the max.

I spent my last few months in a Saigon hospital assisting doctors in the operating room. They let me learn as much as I possibly could. It was great, very exciting. The doctors were great guys, they'd often give up their days off to work on civilians. Captains and colonels, who could have been out playing tennis or at the officer's club drinking gin and tonics, stayed there to treat civilians.

Harold O. (Pseudonym)

I had a good time on my days off. I'd go to the orphanages and play with the children. I'd also bicycle through the streets of Saigon. There were beautiful, golden Buddhist temples, a great French Gothic cathedral and museums to visit. The restaurants were packed, the fuckin' bars were packed. It was a carnival atmosphere, a beautiful city.

There were a lot of different ways to get through Vietnam; the Rosary got me through. I said the Rosary all day long, from the moment I woke up in the morning, until the moment I went to bed; that's all I did. My uncle, who was a Trappist monk, kept me supplied with spiritual reading. In my spare time I read it; I read through the whole war. And, I came to realize that war was merely a continuation of the larger struggle of good over evil. So, being in Vietnam was a mystical period for me, like a religious experience.

Dave Billingsley

When I got orders for Vietnam, I went home and partied for two weeks. Then, I met my buddies in Oakland and we had another party the night before we were supposed to ship to Vietnam.

The next morning we all got up, put on our dress greens and flagged down a cabbie. He was a long-haired hippie who felt kind of bad taking us to the Overseas Replacement Center. When we got there, we gave him his money and then we reached in our pockets and pulled out some pot. We just gave it to him and said, "Here man, we're not going to be needing this." He really freaked out, because it was like we were saying to him, "Hey, we're not really much different than you." And, he knew that.

We stopped in Japan for refueling; so, they let us off the plane to go into the snack bar. We walked in, and there sat a bunch of guys who just came in from Vietnam. These dudes must have been in the clothes they had on for more than a month. They were dirty, I mean funky; the boots were red, just red—there was no black left on them. Their skin was red from the red clay. Their clothes were faded out. These dudes looked like death warmed over—the thousand yard stare—they looked hard, they looked like some bad mother fuckers. And, I remember thinking, "Holy shit, what am I getting into here."

When I got to Vietnam I was like a sponge. I was in awe of what I was seeing; it was so foreign, I just took it all in. The Vietnamese people were dirt poor, living in grass huts beside the roads. There was barbed wire everywhere I looked. Everywhere. You never saw so much barbed wire in your life. I mean, Christ, there was enough barbed wire in Vietnam to go around the globe twenty times. And weapons, everybody had a weapon.

They took us to Long Binh to wait for assignments. I saw this little club there called "Alice's Restaurant." Then, a helicopter flew over and it had a peace sign painted on it. It also had a speaker hanging out of it, and they were playing

132

Sgt. Pepper's Lonely Hearts Club Band. So, I went into Alice's Restaurant to get something to eat, and everywhere I looked there were dudes with peace signs around their necks, beads, headbands. And, I'm thinking to myself, "Where the fuck am I?"

I'm in-country about ten days and they sent me to the 15th Medical Battalion, a MASH unit. I walked into this place just as a couple of medevacs came in. I'm standing there looking at this wounded North Vietnamese soldier. This guy wasn't Viet Cong, he was NVA, with the uniform and everything. He's got IVs in him and he's bleeding to death. They were trying to save him. He looked back at me, just cold—cold as fuckin' ice. I stood there and watched him die. Then I watched them zip two young Americans up in body bags. I'm standing there thinking, "This sucks, these two dudes are dead and I don't even know who they are." And I'm thinking, "The people who are most important to them, brothers and sisters, wives and children, mothers and fathers aren't going to know anything for a couple of days." I thought of the grief they would feel—the pain—and I knew about it already. Then I thought about the NVA guy and I realized his family might never know what happened to him. That was a real bizarre concept to think about.

Eventually, they gave me a bag full of medicine. Any drug you wanted, you name it, I had it. Everything. I had uppers, downers, syrups, stomach and muscle relaxers, everything. But, I didn't know anything about drugs. We didn't do pharmaceuticals in AIT. They never told us about anything. The only thing we ever covered was morphine. I was a nineteen year old kid with a bag of medicine—and they called me "doc"—and it was real wild. But after awhile I got very confident about what I was doing; once that happened the guys became very confident in me.

I got assigned to a firebase to replace a guy who was rotating out. This firebase was a little carved out area about the size of a football field. We had about a hundred to a hundred fifty guys there. We were as close as we could get to being out in the boonies without being grunts. It was like the last bastion to the frontier. It was as close as you could get to seeing the war first hand without actually being there.

We were out in the middle of nowhere, there were no lights; so, when it was dark, it was black. I mean, you'd put your hand in front of your face and you couldn't even see it.

I was there about four days and this real rancid smell came through. They sent out a squad of guys and found three dinks out there, dead and rotting. They got caught where they shouldn't have been and got hit by some rounds from our firebase. They really stunk. So, some guys took them over to the trash dump and burned them up.

Nobody ever gave me any hassles about being a CO, because I was a medic and I was in Vietnam. The basic attitude was, "I don't give a damn what you are, you're here now, and we're all in the same pot of shit." Maybe I wasn't hassled because it was during the latter part of the war, it might have been different earlier. By the Seventies, attitudes toward the war had changed. By then, everybody knew we weren't going to win. The idea was to do what you could to keep your ass alive, and to do anything you could to keep out of the field. I spent ten months in the field.

Everyone was aware that if you got fucked-up in Vietnam there was no one back home who would pat you on the back. This was not an honorable thing we were doing over there. No one at home was going to say, "You were fighting for freedom, we're proud of you." Everybody knew this; I was there three weeks and I knew it. It was very clear cut.

They issued me a .45 and I kept it. I never used it. I only had six rounds for it, not even enough to fill a clip. I used to lug it around, you know, John Wayne style; but, I didn't like it. I couldn't hit the broad side of a barn with it and couldn't get the ammo for it. So, I got rid of it. It wasn't a big deal. I took the gun after I saw death. I thought, "Bullshit, if some mother fucker is going to shoot at me, I'll be damned if I'm not going to shoot back." I mean, the bottom line was that fucker on the other side could give a shit about what my convictions were. He didn't care and he wouldn't want to know. It was immaterial. My whole thing was I had this weapon, but I would never really have to use it. My job was to take care of guys, my job wasn't to shoot people.

All the guys in the artillery battery knew I was a CO, but that didn't matter to them. I was "doc," what my convictions were didn't mean shit to them as long as I was there when they needed me. To be a medic in Vietnam and to have said, "Okay, I'm going to be your medic, take care of you, and I'm not gonna' carry a gun" was a very personal thing that the guys accepted, if you proved your worth in the field. It was like, "Either this mother fucker is crazy or he's into some deep, heavy, personal shit," and the guys accepted that. Medics were highly respected in the field. If you were a good medic, guys would die for you. Because, you could be the difference between them living and dying, and they knew that. So, they took real good care of you.

My job was to ease pain and to deal with field sanitation. I burned shit, I mean I burned tons of shit in Vietnam. But basically, I was a pain easer. Whatever that pain might have been, a sliver a guy couldn't get out, jungle rot on his feet, stomach cramps, fevers, pink eye. I gave out a lot of malaria pills, I gave a lot of shots for venereal disease, and took care of problems like heat prostration. I was always taking care of people, and it was always, "thanks, doc." I took good care of my people, I took my time and evaluated their situation. If there was something I couldn't deal with, I'd send people to the rear. I was the medic, when it came to shit like that, nobody argued with me.

I had a lot of guys who'd be down and needed to talk. They missed their old ladies, they got "Dear John" letters and stuff like that. You just had to be realistic with them and hear them out. Once, this supply guy was going to blow the first sergeant away. I mean, he locked and loaded on the first sergeant. So, the guys came and got me to go talk to this dude. I go down, and this kid's sittin' there with an M–16 pointed at his forehead with his thumb rested on the trigger. I talked with him for quite awhile and got him to put the gun down. He was just flippin' out; he just couldn't deal with it anymore. So, he and I flew back to the base on a chopper, and I unloaded him on a chaplain. That's the whole thing about being a field medic, you stabilize and unload. That's your function; you are the front line, you stabilize and get them back to the professionals.

The bottom line about being a medic is that you react, you perform. You're the only one who's been trained to do these things and you are expected to do them. You cannot walk away from the situation, it's not even something you can really think about. There's not time. The name of the game is to just react.

Tom Fischer

In-service, discharged CO
U.S. Air Force 1970–1972
Vietnam veteran

We can't put Vietnam behind us, we have to put it in front of us.

[AUTHOR'S NOTE]

Tom Fischer considered himself to be "a pretty patriotic person" in 1969. He actually felt guilty about being in school while his peers were involved in the war. Tom described himself as, "A pretty young and unaware eighteen year old" who was "out of touch with the anti-war movement."

Tom's desire to serve in the military was tempered by his inclination to help others. Therefore, he met with a recruiter to discuss the possibility of serving in a medical unit. He said:

> I wanted to be a medic. I wanted to ease the suffering and the pain. The recruiter assured me that my background as a hospital orderly would enable me to go in as a medic. So, I joined the Air Force.

Tom recalled that, "I pretty much operated on fear in basic training; when the Training Instructors (TIs) shouted, I jumped." He worked hard to do everything right and actually won an award for being the best trainee in the basic training squadron.

After basic training Tom discovered the recruiter's assurance about medic's training had little to do with the Air Force's plans for him. His request for medical training was ignored and he was sent to Security Police school to be a dog handler.

Tom Fischer

Tom became disenchanted with military violence while attending Security Police training. The TIs expected trainees to hurt the dogs to get them to obey, something he could not do. He said:

> I hated what we had to do to those dogs. It soon became clear to me that I wasn't suited to do this. It was a signal that I wasn't up to the violence.

Upon completing training Tom Fischer was sent to Vietnam. His story begins here and continues in Chapter 5.

* * * *

I was assigned to Phu Cat Airbase in Vietnam. It was like a small American city; they had clubs, a swimming pool and it was pretty secure. Guys coming in from the field thought this place was heaven. The perimeter had lots of firepower that was set up so no one could come across the wire. But, we were surrounded by mountains, so it was hard for the Air Force to make the entire area secure.

We got rocketed once or twice a week, but there was very little damage since the place was so big. When there were a lot of rockets we always expected sappers to come across the wire. They never came across while I was at Phu Cat, but you were always ready for that to happen.

When I first got there they didn't have a dog for me; so, I had to take an M–60 out to a bunker every night. They were long, scary and lonely nights; usually, seven nights a week.

When I finally got my dog, my job got even scarier, because in a bunker you were well-protected. With a dog, you went all the way out to the limits of the perimeter, so the dog could catch whiffs of people trying to come in at night. Mostly, we patrolled inside the perimeter, but you were out there by yourself. Dog handlers were the first line of defense. So, if anyone at the base was going to come face-to-face with someone, it was going to be a dog handler. I was always aware of that possibility, but I just went ahead and did my job.

I wasn't there too long when I experienced death for the first time; a jeep got blown up with some people in it. I had to go outside the perimeter with my dog to secure the area. I circled around while they got the jeep out and cleaned up the guys. I was real scared and sad. It was then that war became real to me; I knew right then that all the illusions about what war was, and what war wasn't, simply came down to people dying.

A real vengeance was felt on the base after those guys got blown away. The goddamned jeep was put down by the post office so everybody could look at it. It was meant to get the guys to rally around what had happened. Like, "Now we'll get 'em." It was real sick.

The mine that blew up the jeep had been set pretty close to a tower; so, the guys figured that whoever set it probably looked like they were going about their daily business. All of a sudden everyone was a threat, and guys on the towers started shooting at mama sans and papa sans who were tending their crops. I'm sure some people who were just trying to feed their families were shot and killed. The people just became objects in this game.

About a month after I got my dog, three guys decided they were not going to go out on patrol. They talked among themselves, came to the conclusion that what they were doing was wrong, and decided they weren't going to do it anymore. So, they handed in their guns. They offered to go out with their dogs, but they refused to take the guns out there.

This was the first time I was exposed to guys in the service who were discontent with what was going on. I started hanging out with them and got to know them. For several months, while they waited for their court-martial, we'd sit around the hooch and talk and get high. They were the ones who got me to reflect on who I was and what I was doing in Vietnam.

They were a real varied group. Little John was a short, slightly older guy. He was real sincere and pretty quiet, but there was a lot of stuff going on inside him. When he did talk, it was clear that he was not going to be able to kill somebody. Charlie was a real Abbie Hoffman prototype. He had lots of energy and was into freaking people out, being absurd and flamboyant. Then, there was Crawford. He was not as articulate as Charlie nor did he appear as serious as Little John. Crawford was just this gentle kind of guy who was sick of going out at night with a gun and a sentry dog, and sick of being in a position where he might have to kill someone.

These guys tried to find out what they could do legally, but nobody really steered them towards conscientious objection as an option. Eventually, they were charged with "desertion in the face of the enemy." They got six months in Long Binh Jail, did time in the States and were dishonorably discharged. I went to their court-martial and was amazed at how military justice was such a world unto itself. Basically, the military could do anything they wanted to do with you. The trial was real expedient, and they threw the book at them.

At this point, there were two forces operating inside of me. I was gradually coming to a position of opposing the war. I still thought we were doing the right thing, that our country wouldn't do anything that was wrong. But, other things kept grating at me like, "Fuck man, why shoot at people out planting their fields?" It bothered me that guys were doing this, but I still went out and did my job.

Another event that influenced me happened on a night when we were under a high threat of assault. A large NVA unit was in the area and it looked like they were moving toward our base. So, everybody was on edge. That night, my dog picked up a scent. I knew from his movements that he just didn't detect an animal; he had something. I knelt down and radioed in to pinpoint the location where the dog was pulling me. Then, I pulled back.

The guys moved in with armored personnel carriers. They started throwing everything out there, M–50 and M–60 machine guns, everything. It was a real show of might and strength and violence. I stood there and watched it happen. And, it just occurred to me that if there were people out there, that was it, they were dead. Afterwards, I spoke with the guy in charge of the personnel carriers. He was really gung-ho, and talked about needing a good body count for the base. He thought it would be good for morale.

This event helped me to realize that I was part of this thing. I had carried a gun for seven months and had been pretty straight and narrow—a good troop—but I realized then that I was contributing to what was happening.

A few days later I called in from patrol and asked to speak with the captain. He came out to the perimeter and I said, "I don't think I can do this any longer. I'm pretty sure that if someone comes across the wire I won't be able to shoot. I don't want to be in this position any more." He talked to me about the consequences and then sent me back to kennel my dog.

Before I decided to do this I contacted a group of civilian lawyers called the "Lawyers Military Defense Committee." They were based in Saigon and both counseled and defended GIs. I found out about them from my friends who were court-martialed. So, I wrote to them, and they got back to me. They informed me of my rights and gave me advice about applying for a CO discharge.

So, I walked over to the JAG office and asked for a CO application. They just kind of looked at me, because no one in the history of the base had ever done that before. They gave me the application, but I had to tell them the correct procedures, because they didn't know.

I requested a discharge rather than noncombatant status for a couple of reasons, some noble, some not so noble. First, although I had never pulled the trigger, I felt like I was part of the chain. If I stayed in the military, no matter what job I did, I was still supporting and affirming what we were doing there. Just by being there I was contributing to an organization that believed in solving problems by going in, and with force, trying to subdue an entire population.

The not-so-noble reason was it had become clear to me that the military was bullshit. Any dreams I had about that were gone. The jobs were terrible and tedious. There was no creativity, you followed orders and nobody wanted to hear your opinion. You weren't a person, and you didn't have a mind. I couldn't imagine doing this for two more years.

I was threatened by my squadron commander after I applied for CO status. He said, "You can't do this. You can't put your weapon down and you *are* going out on your post tonight." I said, "No, I'm not going out on post tonight. I applied for a CO and you have to put me on another detail, because if you put me on post tonight, you are going to be in a lot of trouble." Once he found out that I was right he put me on details. I started doing real shitwork like filling sandbags and cleaning toilets. But, it was better than carrying a gun.

Other things changed. I started to be on the outs with the guys I shipped over with. I think I became sort of a threat to them. One guy called what I was doing "bullshit" and said all I really wanted to do was to get out of the service. I got lots of questions about my views on nonviolence and what I would do if somebody tried to rape my grandmother—things like that. So, I pretty much got cut off from the people that I cared about.

They kind of ignored me or tried to make me feel guilty. Even though I worked hard on the details I got, guys would say, "We're out there protecting your ass. Our asses are going to get killed while you're doing this bullshit CO thing." If they wanted to hurt me or make me feel guilty, that did it, because I really cared about those guys. That part was hard, but no one ever threatened me.

I got a three-day pass to go to Saigon to meet with the lawyers. I had three days to sit down and write a document that would either get me out of the military, or get me sent to jail. The lawyers told me they were there to help me, but they weren't going to tell me what to write. They just gave me things to think about and told me what to include. That was a hard three days for me. I was under the gun; I had to search my soul and to discover what was important to me. You know, what about violence? What about religion? What about God? It was both defending yourself as a person and looking inside to see what was there. It was real intense.

On top of that, this was the first time I was really exposed to Vietnamese life. I had spent seven months on an American base; all of a sudden I was in Saigon, in the middle of all the hustling. You know, "Do you want a woman? Do you want to change your money? What kind of drugs do you want?" It was a bit overwhelming. Then, I got caught in the middle of a firefight. I came out of my hotel and there was shooting right outside the hotel. I hit the ground and saw the hotel guy run out to roll this tin guard down over the front of the hotel. Just before he rolled it down, I half-crawled and half-ran back inside the hotel.

Most of the time I spent writing, alone in the lawyer's office. One night, about three or four in the morning while I was still working on my CO application, this real gentle Vietnamese music came floating in from across the street. It was beautiful, a real moment of peace during a time of internal and external anguish.

I got the application together and brought it back to the base. I felt really cut off, like every move I made was under scrutiny. Even people who were not really gung-ho saw me as a threat, even the guys who did drugs. None of these guys were into bucking the system very much; certainly, none of them wanted to get a bad discharge. So, they didn't want to talk much about what I was doing.

On the other hand, I did help three other guys to go CO. I told them how to do it and helped them with their paperwork. I also helped by communicating between the base and the lawyers. Eventually, the lawyers in Saigon referred to me as their "northern referral agent." They would send me down to the stockade to visit prisoners, and I'd relay messages on what they could or could not do. So, I was getting to be a real pain in the side of the military authorities.

I felt real good about doing this. I felt powerful. I started to feel like the military didn't have me anymore. I started to rebel and felt good about myself. I felt like I could take some risks, that I didn't have to be so full of fear. I realized I did have some rights in the military, it was just that nobody told me about them.

I was sent to the chaplain for an interview. He recommended that I be put into another career field. He called
the American troops there, "his boys." He said, "If my boys
were in danger I wouldn't hesitate to pick up a machine
gun, go out to the wire and start mowing the enemy down."
So, that's where he was coming from, I guess "his boys"
were on the right side of God.

The officer that interviewed me was a major, an F–4
fighter pilot. He was a hard-liner who really gave me a
hard time. He just couldn't relate to what I was saying. He
considered nonviolence to be unrealistic, saying it didn't
have any place in the world. He concluded that I wasn't a
CO, just a real mixed-up young man; so, he disapproved my
claim.

I wrote the base commander about this. I told him that
the major who interviewed me was not objective, that he
was caught up in defending his position and he couldn't
listen to what I was saying. I told him I didn't get a fair
shake and requested another interview. Well, he granted
me another hearing and the new guy recommended that I
be discharged as soon as possible. He thought I was sincere, that I had thought about what I was doing for a long
time, and that the influences in my life confirmed what I
was saying.

Meanwhile, while I was waiting for a decision on my application, my buddies and I fell into a pattern. Those of us
on details would get up real early and hook-up with the
guys coming in from night patrol. We'd get together and
get high; then, those of us with details would leave, and the
others would go to bed. There were a lot of drugs on base,
and I got into it; I never used drugs before I got to Vietnam.
But, drugs were becoming a big problem in all the services,
and the Air Force was not excluded from the problem.

Anyway, we smoked up some heroin one morning and the
SPs came, guns drawn, and took us for a urine test. We
flunked the test, and in an hour we were gone. I was medevaced to a detoxification center in Cam Ranh Bay. I
didn't do drugs that much, so I didn't go through real
heavy withdrawal, I felt pretty good. After two weeks we

were flown back to a hospital in Texas. I spent a month there, just kind of in a holding status. There really wasn't any rehabilitation going on, and people still did drugs; the patients just paid the guards to bring the stuff in.

I'm pretty convinced that I was set-up. The military wanted to get rid of me; they were tired of putting up with my bullshit, and tired of me and the other COs being protected by civilian lawyers. So, I think I was probably railroaded.

I had lost track of my CO application, so I went to the JAG lawyer and asked him to track it down. Actually, just to get guys out, the Air Force was offering discharges under general, or even honorable conditions to people with drug histories. So, if I wanted to get out I probably could have, but I really wanted the CO.

The JAG officer found out that a favorable decision had been made cn my application. It was just sitting on a desk somewhere. The Air Force then offered me the choice of being discharged as a CO or taking the drug discharge. I told them I wanted to be discharged as a CO, I had worked real hard for it. The principle of the thing was important to me; so, I was discharged as a conscientious objector.

Steve Akers

Noncombatant service CO
U.S. Army 1971–1972
Vietnam veteran.

My own form of patriotism is working with kids.

[AUTHOR'S NOTE]

Steve Akers described his upbringing as "typically middle class." As a boy he participated in church youth groups and became an Eagle Scout. He wanted to be a veterinarian, but considering his "average grades" and interest in other cultures, eventually moved toward the social sciences.

In college he started to think about war "in human terms," and to question how he would fit in. He was not brought up to believe in pacifism, that became, "Something that was generated along the way." For example, Steve once did a major paper on Mohandas Gandhi, and by doing so, discovered the works of other pacifists like A.J. Muste and Martin Luther King.

Steve reportedly "agonized" over the decision to apply as a conscientious objector. But after concluding that medicine was a "caring branch" of the service, he announced his willingness to serve as a noncombatant.

Steve was trained as a psychiatric technician and was stationed in Vietnam between January and November 1972.

Steve's narrative is unique in that it documents an unusual attempt to transcend the military role and to connect with the people of Vietnam. Additional comments appear in Chapter 5.

* * * *

By the time I got orders for Vietnam I had pretty much rationalized the fact that I would be helping people either as a medic or a psychiatric technician. I really didn't know what was going on there, but I knew that I had reached a point of no return. I considered my options, Canada and so forth, but since I was interested in different cultures I rationalized going. I thought it might be an interesting experience.

I was sent to Da Nang with about ten other guys from my AIT class. We were to focus on problems related to drug abuse among the troops. We insulated ourselves in our work, trying to do the best we could to heal minds and bodies. To me, that was valid, because it had nothing to do with war per se; you could do the same things in the United States. So, being in a medical unit was a blessing. There was a real feeling of creating an alternative to being in a war situation.

By the time I got to Vietnam, American involvement was winding down. Officially, our guys were not out in the field; but, we were receiving casualties and we were sensitive to sapper attacks. The sappers would try to get into the bases, they'd cut the wire, throw hand grenades and do different things. Sometimes we'd have to put flak jackets over those guys in hospital beds who couldn't move, and then we'd jump into sandbagged bunkers.

So, guys were still getting injured. We also had a number of guys who were shot-up with heroin by the girls they were with. Sometimes it was a lover's quarrel, other times it happened randomly. By 1972, this was a common casualty experience for us.

The heroin was so pure, the guys used to smoke it. It was also fairly easy to get. I had an apartment about a block from Tan Son Nhut Airbase. I'd look over the railing and watch a lady who sold fruit exchange packs of heroin. She'd give it to a guy on a motor scooter, about twenty exchanges an hour. I called the MPs who got in touch with the municipal police. The next night there was a guy with a rifle standing on that corner. Eventually, several streets in the area became off-limits to our personnel.

The Army was interested in the process of getting guys off drugs and they sent a team of specialists from Walter Reed Army Hospital. We'd collect data for them from our heroin users. We gave users the Minnesota Multiphasic Personality Inventory, we'd take pictures of their pupils as they were getting off heroin, we'd measure reaction time and take blood samples. I'd say these guys were definitely guinea pigs.

One reason I think guys got involved with drugs was the boredom and senselessness of being there. In 'Nam, those of us in the rear were called "rear echelon mother fuckers" (REMFs). We had it relatively easy. We were able to employ people to shine our boots, press our uniforms and everything. So, some guys just didn't seem to find outlets for their feelings of boredom. There was nothing really around for these guys to relate to. A lot of guys felt out of place, away from family and everything that made sense to them. Being in Vietnam was like being on the moon.

It seemed like these guys didn't make the mental connection between smoking heroin and addiction. To them, getting strung out was okay, somehow it helped deaden the psychic pain from the boredom and alienation they felt.

My outlet, and my way of finding out about what was going on there, was through the people of Vietnam themselves. The first three months I was there I made an active effort to learn the language. I tried to get to know the people at the PX and stuff like that. I enjoyed meeting them. The Vietnamese seemed to be flattered, because the majority of GIs didn't show an interest, except other than getting to know some "chick" or something like that. Eventually, some of the people I got to know took me to weddings and birthday parties. By doing these things I got a more realistic picture of the Vietnamese people.

I even taught English in Da Nang for three months. We would teach high school kids for a couple of hours and then go out to eat in an open cafe. One day we were sitting in the cafe and a guy comes up and drops a note on the table addressed to me. Real cloak and dagger stuff! It said, "Please come with papa-san to the river and meet me." It was from one of my students. She wanted to meet so I could help her send a letter to her lover in the States. She had a three year old daughter and was trying to get the family together, nothing more sinister than that!

A lot of people I met in South Vietnam revered Ho Chi Minh, but disagreed with his economics. He was seen as the savior of his country who freed them from the Japanese and the French. People in the South felt an affinity for the people in the North, but they wanted their own chosen options. My thinking was that we should have sat down with Ho Chi Minh years before and worked something out.

Jeff Engel

I landed in Bien Hoa on December 13, 1969. I was separated out with eight or nine others and given the third degree. People in fatigues without either name or rank insignia interrogated me for about forty-eight hours. It was actually one of the more frightening things that happened during my whole time there. These people knew things about me that I didn't know. They knew that my sister had a silver tooth. They knew my mother had a stillborn child. They knew that in 1962, I had gone to Canada to a church convention. They knew the people who rode with me and the places we stopped along the way. I was scared shitless and in awe of their command of these facts. They had a variety of profiles and perceptions of why I was behaving the way I was. No threats were ever made against me though, essentially they just had questions about my intentions and designs.

I wasn't locked up. I was in a barracks; but for twelve to twenty hour stretches they would walk up and down the room talking to me. I ate three meals, they talked to me while I was eating. For two days I was not released from them, except to go to bed. I was with them from sunrise to pulling the covers up around me at night. None of their questions were about my religious motivation. There were questions about my participation in communist or political organizations. Things like, "Why do you do this? Why do you do that?" Lots of theoretical situations, you know, "What would you do in this or that situation?" They would set up real involved scenarios and paint me in the pictures. Then they'd ask, "What do you do now?"

Well, I said to myself, "They've got to do this. I was involved in antiwar activity and this is a combat situation. There are different rules here. They want to make sure that I'm not going to be an armed adversary behind the lines or something." So, I answered the questions.

Finally, they just stopped. An officer, a major, came in with a stack of orders for me. First he grabbed me by the arm and said, "Come on, let's go. We're through here." He ushers me outside and gives me a shove. I turned back and he tosses the orders at me. Some of them fell to the ground, and while I'm picking them up he pointed at me and said, "You know something, you're a troublemaker. We're going to kill you in Vietnam."

At that moment there was a click in my brain. Everything became clear, all of it. From my high school speeches, the believing, to just who and what was the adversary? It hit me, "Hey, wait a minute, they don't give a rip about my religious beliefs. Some nebulous soldier, a Viet Cong, a North Vietnamese, is not the adversary. My own government and the military, is the adversary." And to this day that wounds me, just not as badly.

I remember going and sitting on a bench for a long time. Just sitting and thinking, smelling the diesel and feces being burned in the back of an outdoor toilet, watching the bare hills and barbed wire around the base, feeling the heat, like being on another planet. I had no romanticized vision that this was Dante's inferno or some dream state that I was in. Reality is what came back to me. I watched the childlike faces, childlike faces with hollow eyes and I said to myself, "It's survival, my job is to get out of here, in one piece, as quickly as possible, and to get as many of them out as I can." I spent fourteen months doing that.

Eventually, I was assigned to the headquarters company for the 1st of the 27th Wolfhounds, a unit within the 25th Division. We were in a fire support base about forty-five minutes outside of Cu Chi. This was a transient site for units going out on missions. We had a battalion level aide station with a physician and a group of medics working there. Plus, each company had two to four medics that worked with the platoons in the company.

My orders read "1–A–O, Medic, Conscientious Objector." I remember being asked, "Are you going to carry a weapon?" And I said, "I'm not planning on it." My dad had given me a buck knife with my name engraved on it; that's what I planned to carry. I excised boils with it. I shaved with it, carved melons with it. It was a tool I had with me.

I suspected I was the first conscientious objector that any

of these people had experienced. Well, it turned out there were other COs, and a number of them carried weapons. It wasn't an issue with the regular Army people or any of us who were COs. They just did it. I needed to perform as a medic. So, I carried fourteen extra pounds of medical equipment instead of a weapon.

Eventually, I was assigned to a platoon and from there went out on field missions, unarmed, except for my buck knife. On one occasion I remember going out the gate, single file. I had this carefree attitude, talking with all the guys in the platoon to establish why I wasn't carrying a weapon. They all felt comfortable about it. The essential theory was, I'm carrying all these medical supplies, there's thirteen to twenty guys with weapons, if it gets to the point where I need to carry a weapon, there's going to be one available. So anyway, I was going out the gate and the gate guard said, "Hey doc, where's your weapon?" And I said, "Oh, gees, I must have forgotten it!" Then, I reached down and I said, "It's okay, I've got my buck knife." I walked out the gate leaving this guard staring, with mouth agape. Of course, all the guys in the platoon thought this was funny as hell.

I spent ten months in the field running around with these guys. On a typical day, I'd get up in the morning and see how everybody was, I'd check rashes, boils, coughs and whatever. Then we'd get orders for the day and we'd walk somewhere.

In the field I had to help people a lot of times, thirty times, fifty times, I don't know. Hell, I don't know if I received enough training or not, but I was a hell of a good medic. I was better than a lot of others. I saw my job in terms of being able to do what was necessary out there. I think it had something to do with my age. I was twenty-five by the time I got to Vietnam. I had my head screwed on a lot better than a lot of the eighteen and nineteen year olds who were medics with me.

I got some people out of the field. If anybody used drugs of any kind, I recommended a psychological or medical profile and said, "out!" Not all of them left the country, but I know two or three did. At least one or two got out of the military due to emotional or substance related problems. I got very good at this during the last couple of months in the field, because I had made some contacts in Saigon and knew the forms to use.

We went to Cambodia in 1970, probably before the actual May Cambodian invasion. We made some forays across the border in a place called Parrot's Beak. A lot of "search and destroy" missions, twelve days in the field returning for a couple of days of standdown. We were there for thirty days. That was my highest sustained level of combat. Everyday for thirty days there were shots fired, shots returned, somebody wounded, somebody medevaced. I put twenty-eight people either directly into body bags or loaded them into helicopters. I probably loaded the same number of wounded. The majority of them happened in Cambodia.

Once we had contact, and a young American Indian boy was killed. I was in the process of preparing him for medical dust-off. The rest of the platoons were out, away from me. I was by myself, in Cambodia, with this body. About fifty yards away I saw three dark clad individuals running across an open area. I didn't know my platoon's distance or their angle from me in relationship to these fellows. I didn't know whether these men in dark pajamas were "bad guys" or just villagers who were trying to get out of the way; or even if they'd seen me. The dead fellow's weapon was laying there and I picked it up, checked it out and chambered a round. I remember feeling uneasy about that, but that's all I had to do; nothing happened. They left. That was the only incident where I actually picked up a weapon and felt the need to have one.

While I was in Cambodia my church held an international convention. The week prior to the convention the high muckety mucks convened to deal with the agenda. Well, one of the issues the board had to confront was whether rock and roll music should be played on the church's college campus. Also, that year the President of the college invited a Catholic, the "anti-Christ" to some, to be the guest speaker at graduation. So, they had to confront this issue. The third issue was a rewriting of the church's position on war and peace.

Well, they spent the entire week dealing with numbers one and two and never even got to the last question. They didn't even talk about the issue. I got a letter about this two weeks after I got out of Cambodia. I read this knowing where they'd been that week and where I'd been. I'd been body-bagging people, and I was pissed. I mean, I ranted and raved; I was really mad—and powerless. I wanted to go rip throats.

Jim Kraus

We were on the *USS Princeton*, a helicopter aircraft carrier, on a nine-month tour to the West Pacific. It carried a battalion of Marines and a squadron of helicopters. It was the summer of 1968 and we were floating a mile off Vietnam, by the DMZ. We were in a situation where we were close enough to the fighting and the suffering of the Marines that we could think about it, and we had the time to think about it. We would talk to them about what was going on, but it was like they spoke another language. They thought differently; it was hard to talk to them at all. They'd go off for a week and they'd come back and be all bandaged up, and even more reticent than ever. We'd eat with them, but talk very little. Mostly, we just observed them.

I was in a division of maybe eight enlisted men. By this time, all of us in that division knew the war was wrong, that it was unjust, and as far as we could tell, most of the Marines knew it too. One of the most vivid memories I have of that time is sitting on the catwalk, a metal grating that went around the perimeter of the flight deck. You could walk on it and sit all the way forward on the ship. It was kind of a place to get away, to stare down at the water and sing or talk. The Marines would go up there sometimes, too. They'd go out there and sing a song by Country Joe and the Fish called, *I Feel Like I'm Fixin' To Die Rag.* They sang that song all of the time.

Not just the songs we sang, but the music we listened to had an impact on the antiwar feelings more and more people had. In 1968, there wasn't much going on in music that was not antiwar. We all brought tape recorders or record players on the ship, although the record players didn't work too well at sea. We all listened to the Doors, the Fish, Jimmy Hendrix. These were long, long hours and nights waiting for some officer to call for us to repair a broken radar. Meanwhile, we just sat there with our headsets on listening to music.

But sometimes we went up on deck for grimmer duty than radar repair. The crew of the ship had to lift the body bags out of the helicopters. This was a rotating assignment. We'd go up on deck and take the bags down to the ship's morgue. I had to it just once. I think at the time I was pretty numbed by it. Yet it's the kind of thing you do—and it keeps coming back—and I suppose it's the most vivid memory I have. Actually—it was a kind of an epiphany—I mean, it really made me see through a lot of stuff.

Another one of the rotating duties that came around every so often was machine gun watch. Now, we were a mile offshore, and everyone was concerned that we would be mortared or something. So, the ship's company was supposed to stand machine gun watch. I refused to do it and got away with it. I think they realized they were better off just keeping this quiet than to make an issue or an example of it—because too many people were on the verge of doing things like this. I knew at that point I wasn't going to shoot at anyone, so I thought they might as well know it. However spontaneous my refusal was, just knowing I had the power to refuse gave me a funny kind of reinforcement, a sense that the individual had power to alter things.

One other guy, an American Indian, also refused to do the machine gun watch. But that was something between our chief and us. The chief and the warrant officer he worked for were pragmatists; I mean, they said, "Here we've got a bunch of guys who are intellectuals, and yet they're the same guys who have to fix the radar. We'll just have to put up with some of their idiosyncrasies." Basically, that was their attitude. They were willing to let us get away with it. They probably also realized that if they started to make martyrs out of us, they'd have big trouble.

All through this time, I'd been making plans to marry my high school girlfriend, and as soon as the ship returned to California, I took a two-week leave to get married in Hawaii. When my wife and I got back to California I began the first of two six-month nuclear power school assignments. The first was at Mare Island, near San Francisco, where I was mostly concerned with theory and had little time to think about anything else. However, when I began working on prototype reactors in Idaho, it was an entirely different story.

Stephan Gubar

I landed in Long Binh, Saigon—scared shit. The plane was air conditioned, but the ground wasn't. It was like walking into a sauna or a steam bath; I just couldn't breathe. All of a sudden there were incoming rounds—rockets or mortars—close enough to feel the explosions. I don't know how I saw myself at that point. I'm on an airstrip, with no place to hide! The first thing that struck me was that everything I had heard about Vietnam was probably true.

I got assigned to the 199th Light Infantry Brigade, a mechanized unit. The commanding officer of that unit used to pick all the conscientious objectors, because he thought they were better medics; and so, after about a week, I joined the 199th. As duty went, I guess it was better than being a grunt; it was a lot easier traveling in a mechanized unit than to grunt around. One of the other nice things about a mechanized unit is you could sleep under the tracks, you didn't have to dig in. We would circle around, like a wagon train. All the tracks and guns were facing outwards, it was an artificial perimeter made up of armored personnel carriers, two Sheridan tanks, light and mobile assault vehicles. You felt like you had protection, but it was all an illusion. We probably wound up being in more firefights, because as a mechanized unit we were mobile. We could obviously move much faster than a foot unit; but, as a tour, it was less physically demanding and therefore, easier. I think it was just as emotionally demanding, if not more.

The usual rotation for a medic was six months in the field and six months in a firebase, although that wasn't always so for COs. In my experience, COs frequently did less time in firebases, they were reassigned out to field units. As I said before, I always had the sense that the Army continually challenged convictions. I always had the sense that I was being challenged to pick up a weapon and to participate in the shit. I felt like the Army was saying, "What would you do if you found yourself being shot at and you had the availability of a weapon?" My answer was "I don't know, but I don't want to find myself in that situation." But, I did. So, I think it was a constant test—"Are you still a conscientious objector?"

The second track commander we had was almost fragged. He was a gung-ho son-of-a-bitch, but nobody else in the unit was. Once, up toward the base of the Central Highlands, we came upon some wagon tracks. It was late afternoon and this guy wanted to follow the wagon tracks. Everybody said, "If you want to follow these wagon tracks, you go ahead and follow them." Wagon tracks frequently led to bunkers. He couldn't believe that no one was going to follow his command. He took off with a sergeant and they came back really fast. Later that night he called in covering fire from artillery and had the wrong coordinates, so we spent a lot of time underneath the tracks. He wasn't too well-liked, and it became obvious he wasn't going to live too long. So, he left the field really early.

Our next track commander was a guy who had been a teacher. He was a physical education major in college, a good looking, well-built man. The first night he was there, he called me to his track and he said, "I understand you are a conscientious objector." I told him that was true. He said, "Well, I really don't care, as long as you do your job. If you don't do your job, you're in trouble." So, I said to him, "I understand you're not a CO." He said, "That's obvious." I said, "I don't care, as long as *you* do your job." Medics had that kind of latitude because we were needed.

The next day we had a firefight along Highway 1. North Vietnamese regulars had put a land mine in the road and continually engaged our unit for about four hours. We were left with virtually nothing. The medic from the other platoon was wounded, so I was running around. A medevac came in early, took hostile fire, and then we couldn't get a medevac in after that. Typically firefights were really short, but this was sporadic fire, enough so we couldn't move too well and we couldn't get another medevac helicopter down.

The NVA was using B–40 rockets. Going in, the B–40

rocket put a hole in a track the size of a silver dollar and it puts a tremendous hole in the other side. It bounces around inside, and doesn't come out clean. The drivers were the most vulnerable persons on the tracks, because they sat on an elevated seat and worked the levers by reaching down inside. They rode pretty high and were obviously susceptible to land mines and B–40 rockets.

That day, during the quiet periods, I spent a lot of time holding a man who had been virtually cut in half. I knew he was going to die—and he knew that he was going to die—and the only thing I could do was hold him. The hardest thing was dealing with someone you knew wasn't going to make it.

After that contact I drove an APC, because we didn't have enough men left to get the vehicles that could move away from the site. We left and circled-up for the night. The only officer there was the physical education teacher, the guy who came into the unit the day before. Most of us had tiny bits of shrapnel all over our bodies, and we were picking that stuff out. I was going around with tweezers, checking people and trying to clean up the surface, minor kind of things. I stopped at his track and he said, "I've got to tell you something. I want you to know I'm resigning my commission." He went on to explain that he understood where I was coming from, that it wasn't a game anymore. This was a young captain, a really bright man. He had passed through the ranks quickly, but it was all a game until he found out what it was really about.

I kept winding up in combat situations. That's why I sort of felt that as a CO, I was being tested. The Army reacted real strangely, they just kept giving me medals. They couldn't believe anyone would do their job without a gun. They just didn't know how to take it. So, they gave you a medal. I wound up with four Bronze Stars, two Oak Leaf Clusters, and a recommendation for the Silver Star. I got these just for doing my job, but the Army looked at it as being special because I didn't carry a weapon. And that's funny, because even if I did carry a weapon, I wouldn't have had time to use it. When the shit hit, you had to go! It wasn't so much the Army saying, "Thank you," it was just them being amazed that someone did their job. They didn't expect it.

Another interesting thing is the language they used in the commendations. This one says, "Award, the Bronze Star Medal for Heroism." And it reads:

> immediately, and without regard for his personal safety, a medical aide maneuvered one hundred meters across hostile terrain and through intense hostile fire, in order to aid and evacuate wounded personnel. He then took an exposed position and engaged the enemy throughout the remainder of the battle.

Well, that's utterly absurd, because I didn't even have a weapon with which to engage the enemy. This is a standard form and they didn't know how to change it.

It was kind of funny, I was always given a medal in a room somewhere. Normally, medals were awarded in formation. The unit commander would come down and do all that shit. But I remember the track commander saying to me, "I knew you wouldn't want to go through the formation shit," and he was right. I didn't think, and I still don't think, that I did anything spectacular or heroic. Getting medals didn't make me feel anything, really; it was just amusing, amusing.

Being a medic is a strange thing, because you've got to be everything to a unit. Like, when guys got "Dear John" letters, I was the guy that sat and talked to them. I was older than a lot of the guys, I was all of twenty-two. Most of the guys were nineteen or so, so it was like being a father, confessor, psychologist, everything. Sometimes it was really easy, like putting a pressure bandage on. Sometimes, it was really hard, like deciding when somebody was dead, and just moving on. The first time I saw somebody get killed—I didn't want to believe he was dead. That was a tough decision, because I never wanted to think a man died because I decided he was dead already. Sometimes, people died from shock and from fright. You had to make a conscious effort to calm them down, right in the middle of everything that was going on. Sometimes they'd figure they were dead and they'd just give up.

I was treated very well, for a CO. The guys couldn't believe I wouldn't use or carry a weapon. It's not that they cared about it, because my job didn't deal with weapons. And they knew it. They didn't even play with me; but once, they thought they could offer me a vicarious kind of understanding of what they were doing. One time the guys were exercising the rubber gaskets on the guns of the tanks by firing blank rounds. This guy said to me, "There's no round, you're not firing at anything, would you like to see what it's like?" So, I climbed down inside, fired this big cannon and got a black eye! Things like that happened once in awhile, good natured kinds of stuff.

When I first got into the country, I had a lot of friends. I knew everybody in the unit really well. When I left, I didn't know anybody. I didn't want to, because—the hardest thing—is to lose friends. The last guy in Vietnam I called a friend was a guy by the name of "Shorty." They used to take people out of the field when they were about sixty days short. But, we were having some problems so then it became thirty days short—and you get really scared, really scared. I didn't want to see anything happen to Shorty, so, if he had a boil, I'd medevac him out. He would come back after literally having a boil lanced and I'd find some other reason to send him back out. He spent the end of his time flying back and forth to Bien Hoa. That's part of the power a medic had. I felt good about doing that. But, after him, I had—no friends.

Getting through the day involved trying to find a way to cook C-rations to make them edible. After about six months, you knew that was impossible. So, getting through the day became hoarding and trading. Hoarding the peanut butter until you got the jelly, so you could put the two of them together and put them on a cracker, if you could get hold of a cracker. Or, trading off the franks and beans to some FNG for anything you could eat. Waiting until you circled-up at night, so that you could get high—we got high a lot. That was getting through the day.

They used to drop sorties in, there was a case of beer and a case of soda included in each sortie. You could tell the people who drank from the people who smoked dope, because everybody who drank, took beer and everybody who smoked, took soda. Everybody, *everybody* I knew did something to make it through Vietnam.

Once we got a new top-sergeant. He had us line up in formation at five o'clock in the morning, which we never did in Vietnam; he paraded up and down telling us if we had to use drugs to get through this experience we weren't men. He berated us for a good fifteen minutes, with a beer in his hand. So everybody used something. It was a situation you couldn't escape, it was horrendous, you couldn't get away from it. I was always trying to get out of the field—never managed to. That may have been related to the fact that I was a CO, but I don't know, I can't be sure.

The guys I knew in-country didn't want to be there. There were very few gung-ho people. If they were gung-ho when they got there, after awhile they weren't gung-ho anymore, at least in that unit. And it wasn't that they were sloppy, it was just that they didn't want to kill anybody; they didn't want to be killed either. We were just happy to kind of move around. Even the lifers just wanted to get through. It was a bunch of guys that just wanted to get through.

Part of the American war machine propaganda, from induction on, was to dehumanize the Vietnamese people, to portray them as less than human. Shit, they weren't even called people; they were called "gooks." And so, Vietnamese people were mistreated all the time. It was not an unusual thing to see the mistreatment of the Vietnamese people, whether they were ARVNs or suspected Viet Cong. Mistreatment was part of the corruption that existed in the South. The Vietnamese were people whose industry was prostitution, drugs and black marketeering. These aren't things people choose to do, these are things people are forced to do. They were forced into it by circumstance, they were forced into it because they had to have food, because there was no gainful employment other than the war. So, this is what they did. And, it's only a simple step from thinking it's okay to force a population of women into prostitution to killing a person because they're a suspected member of the Viet Cong. That's not a giant step. It's a very small step.

My anger wasn't directed toward the Vietnamese people. The Vietnamese people were neat in the sense that they were fighting for their country, they were fighting for their lives. Those people who were conscripted into the South Vietnamese Army were just like me, they didn't want to be fighting this war, killing their brothers. My anger was directed at the Army, and the government. I never wanted to retaliate against the Vietnamese, but I sure as shit would have liked to punch out the President.

I got in trouble in Vietnam. I was arrested, detained and interrogated for fraternizing with civilians. I was squatting, talking through a fence with mama-san and a couple of other people. Now, it was very strange to see an American squatting. Suddenly, the Vietnamese took off, and this MP jeep came and arrested me. They said those people were running drugs and prostitutes in the area. I didn't have any drugs on me, but the MPs produced about ten caps of heroin.

They put me in a connex container which served as a holding pen. It was made of corrugated metal, maybe six feet by six feet, and maybe seven or eight feet high. It was attached to the side of a building—in the sun. I sat there for a couple of hours, baking. And then I was interrogated by a Civilian Interrogation Detail; I had nothing to tell them. Finally, they released me and told me I was going to be court-martialed.

I was really worried, because again, I had this fear of prison, I didn't want to be in Long Binh Jail. So, I did a lot of things. I went before a promotion board and got promoted. Also, the Freedom Foundation of Valley Forge had an essay contest, and one of the categories was "The Military." So, I wrote an essay for the Freedom Foundation and was awarded the prize. And in Vietnam, the Army had this thing called the "Soldier of the Month." Every month they would pick somebody. So, I became "Soldier of the Month." I figured if I was court-martialed they had to look at my record, and it would help if I had all this stuff in it.

While I was waiting to be court-martialed, there was a fight in one of the bars just outside Saigon. We wound up with the American military remnants of the fight. Who did I see come in, but the CID person who kept me in that connex container for two hours. He had a very large cut across the top of his head. I asked one of the doctors for permission to do the suturing. So, there's a CID person, who's now probably in the CIA, with a tremendous scar on his head. To this day, I don't feel badly about that. Plus, I was never court-martialed.

CHAPTER 4

From Thought to Action:
Resistance, Prison, Discharge.

. . . I am doing my share to perpetuate the principles
of freedom for which my country stands.

–The Soldier's Creed–

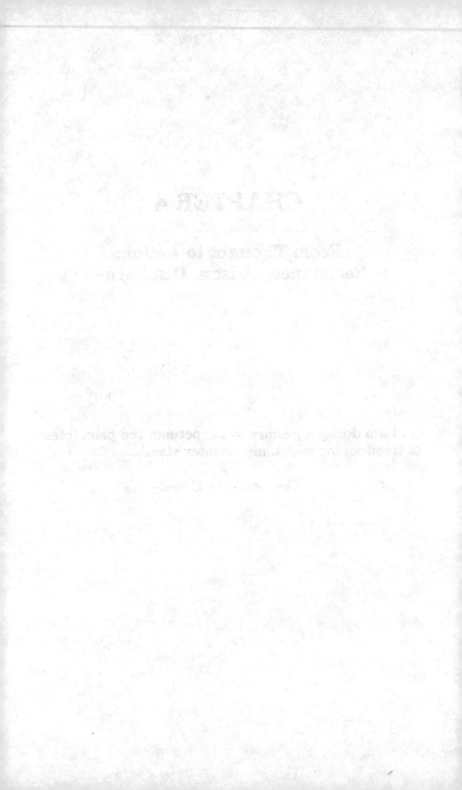

Jeffrey Porteous

I handed in my application for discharge when I got to the Overseas Replacement Center at Fort Lewis, Washington. I was then taken to a holding company. Everyone in a holding company is waiting in place, waiting for something to happen; a transfer, a discharge, further orders. In the meantime we cleaned latrines, did dull, meaningless jobs. While there I began to meet guys just back from combat in Vietnam. They would have a bit more time to do, so until they were discharged, the Army would assign them as clerks, or training officers. These guys reeked of Vietnam, they couldn't help it, it just poured off them. One time, doing KP, I remember overhearing a young captain explaining to one of the cooks how he'd blown a Viet Cong's head off with his service pistol. He held his arm out in front of him, his hand cocked, his forefinger pointing at the cook as he explained. He was still mad about it, and excited.

Our company clerk, a gentle kid, beset with facial tics and tremors, told about coming face-to-face with a Viet Cong in a forest clearing. Both men had stepped into it at the same moment, the clerk raising his rifle first. It happened to have been an M–60 machine gun, and he described the sight of his rounds ricocheting off the other man's backbone, then coming out the top of his head, a shower of bullets and bone fragments and the man's brains spewing out the topless top of his skull. When they told these stories, their fear always came through, but also a kind of inarticulate pride. With the officers it seemed closer to aggressiveness. Perhaps it was simply enormous gratitude at the fact that they were still alive.

At some point during my stay at the holding company I did something I shouldn't have done, or didn't do something I was supposed to do, whatever, the result was a revocation of my suspended sentence for AWOL. I had to do my ninety days. I felt angry and hurt about going to the stockade; but I also felt proud and self-righteous. I was convinced I was doing the right thing.

When escorted into the Fort Lewis stockade you are locked in, then unhandcuffed, then issued a mattress and led back into the body of the prison, into "C" block, which is a caged bay of two-tiered bunkbeds. When I first arrived, there was a group of young blacks standing in their skivvies, in heated discussion around one of the bunks. I heard the names Stokley Carmichael and Rap Brown. I laid out my mattress, just listening and thinking that this is where my education would begin.

My days in the stockade were filled with routine. One of the tricks of prison is that you begin to understand and appreciate the value of routine. Routine is the agent that makes your days endurable, because it hides time, makes it invisible, each day running into the next, each week indistinguishable from the last; until it all becomes a kind of dream.

There were no trades in the stockade, it being a holding pen. There was just a lot of laying around in that compound. I was very fortunate, though, to have my wife nearby, I could see her for a few hours on Sunday. We would talk until the last moment, and then she would leave me with books. I read Kierkegaard there, and Blake, and Norman O. Brown. And I met many fine, fine men.

I was also thrown into the hole for being a smart-ass, for lipping off to one of the guard officers, a lieutenant from the margins of Texas someplace. To look at his face was to know that no member of his family had ever been made an officer and a gentleman before, and he'd had to bust his hump to get there. The problem being that "there" was behind barbed wire in the stockade with the rest of us. But he was going to make it. You could just tell that.

There was another officer whose job it was to inspect us first thing each morning. He'd step from prisoner to prisoner, regarding the shine on the toes of our shoes. One morning I asked why he always looked at our shoes, why he didn't look in our eyes? There was no guile in the question, rather it was an attempt to cut through. I mean, look at it, if recruits were almost invisible to the caste system of the service, you can imagine how prisoners in the stockade were viewed, something on the order of inventory, something to be kicked, counted and fed.

When I got out of the stockade I was assigned to another holding company, where I met several other COs. There were Buddhists, Jehovah's Witnesses, Seventh Day Adventists, radical Catholics, politicos. Most were very fine young men, some were extraordinary. Amongst them all I found a circle of friends, friends I grew very close to. Included among them were Rudy Byrd, Tom Cox, Jerry Gioglio, Howard Koby and Richard Lovett. There was an acute intelligence in this group, a certain kind of energy I could identify with. We were all fighting the same thing, in twenty different ways, all saying, "This is wrong. This I will not do."

We would go to a GI coffeehouse in Tacoma and talk to other soldiers about our experiences and about the alternatives to war. There was some antiwar activity on the base, too, but I didn't get involved; I wasn't a joiner, I was a pretty shy kid. But I did join some of these guys for a trip to Seattle for an antiwar demonstration.

During this time, my application came back disapproved. I sent it in again, again it came back to me disapproved. The night of its final disapproval I was given an order by my company commander to report to the Overseas Replacement Center. I knew this was coming and had talked to my lawyer about it. So, I saluted the company commander and said, "Sir, for reasons of conscience, I respectfully decline to obey your order." I was then taken to an office, kept under guard and sent back to the stockade the next morning. I was there three months awaiting my general court-martial.

I felt a bit like a spectator during the court-martial. But, it wasn't my trial, what was on trial was the Vietnam war, and the officers of the court knew it. And they weren't about to let the war be on trial. The whole trial had a kind of queer, dreamy atmosphere to it. I couldn't see any of it for one thing. My military lawyer had advised me to take off my glasses, they were wire framed eyeglasses—hippie glasses at the time—he thought they might get me another year. So, I didn't wear them, I couldn't even see the faces of the men who sent me to prison.

The courtroom seemed to consist of three tables shoved together in front of an ordinary classroom. The presiding officers sat behind them. There were no NCOs, no enlisted men. The issue was decided on the narrow grounds of whether or not I'd disobeyed an order of a superior officer. Several COs from the holding company were there and a few of my friends from the stockade managed to get there. I don't know how they did it, but they were there. I had four people testify as character witnesses, my parents, a mother of a friend of mine and my wife.

My civilian lawyer managed to get in a long and eloquent brief about the war. Then, I was called to the stand. The prosecutor asked if I had disobeyed my company commander's orders, I told him I had. He had no other questions. Then my civilian defense lawyer asked of my opposition to the war. My heart was a knot, my tongue tied even tighter, though I finally managed to say what I could, simply that the war in Vietnam was wrong and I didn't want to be part of that wrongness. I wanted to separate myself from them and it, and I felt morally impelled to do so.

We were then excused while the officers conferred. When called back a few moments later, I was ordered to stand in front of the room, where I saluted the front table and was sentenced to three years hard labor and a dishonorable discharge. The last thing the presiding officer said, before I was led back to the stockade, was that the trousers of my uniform were too short. For the next trial, the colonel advised, the guards should get the prisoner a pair of pants that fit. This seemed to have upset him a good deal. A real martinet, I guessed. Though I could never tell. I only got my glasses back after I'd been taken out the door.

I went back to my friends in the stockade, happy to be back among the living. There were eight or nine COs in the stockade at the time; we supported each other a lot, before and after our trials. Some guys got short sentences and did their time in the stockade; but the majority went to Fort Leavenworth.

As COs, we were constantly telling our stories to people, doing good organizing work. Some guys were thinking of getting out of the stockade and going to Vietnam; we were doing our best to convince them not to do it. I was proselytizing, I told people what I thought. Some guys would say, "What are you going to tell your son when he asks you what you did during the war?" As if I would be so shrivelled from trying to answer that question. But that wasn't acute enough to touch me. And no one ever called me a traitor or a coward—it never happened in those words or any other words approximating that.

The Army's stockade at Fort Lewis was a relatively new building, less than twenty years old. But it had been filled for so long, by emotions so intense, that the place seemed gutted, ugly, filled with ghosts. I saw men being harassed, fucked with, driven to suicide attempts, insanity, and to odd acts of beauty and kindness. I heard men being beaten, heard them screaming through the walls of "B" block at night.

B block was maximum security, the stockade's "hole." The whole inside was painted gloss black. It had a steel pallet, no mattress, a sink, a lidless commode, and an overhead light that never went off. The cell was fronted by a row of black bars and beyond that by an iron door with a peep hole in it. You could reach out and touch both walls. I was thrown into the hole twice, spent a couple of weeks in there. Once I was put on "rabbit food," which was dried bread and dried corn flakes, three meals a day, with water, because you had your sink. I had a buddy who was down there too, and we'd meditate—we'd do these long chants until we got pretty high. I took mescaline there once, a friend who brought my food smuggled it in to me. He also brought some funny papers. I remember thinking they were the saddest damn funnies I'd ever seen.

Late that summer they formed a line of us inside the stockade compound, handcuffed us, and took us all to the Seattle-Tacoma airport. We flew out that morning, arriving in Kansas City in the afternoon. We then took a prison bus the twenty or thirty miles to the base.

If you get into trouble in the Army or Air Force, bad enough trouble that you're given a general court, then Leavenworth is your eventual destination. The penitentiary is old, built early in the last century. High sandstone walls and red-roofed guard towers surround the main cell blocks, which are housed in a massive central building dubbed "the castle." Entrance to the castle is through a steel door set in a windowless, red brick wall rising ten or more stories above your head. Here we were ushered in, then herded through a central rotunda, vacant except for a single guard shack, then more steel doors, and the first sight of cell blocks rising eight stories above us. We were lined up, stripped, searched, photographed and fingerprinted. It was all relatively benign, but I didn't know that then. It was reels of "B" movies unwinding in my brain. All of a sudden I was there, *in prison.* I remember standing real quiet, waiting, keeping a real steady eye on everything.

Each day we would be let out of our cells to go to breakfast, then back to be counted, to work, back for count, lunch, then count, work, dinner and evening recreation, and about four more counts. It took a couple of weeks for the routine to assert itself, before time began to pass unnoticed.

During recreation time we would carry on long group conversations, comparing notes, a kind of on-going critique of the system that put us there. There were robbers and murderers and thieves—I knew a fellow who had shot his entire chain of command. Several had real strong feelings about the correctness of the U.S. being in Vietnam, so we'd engage with them. Of course, much of the population at Leavenworth had already been converted—they'd seen it, they'd been there. Like, I was very tight with a Special Forces guy named Harris. He did two tours in Vietnam and just quit. They tried to send him back for another tour and he said, "No, I'm not going back there."

The population shook itself out into three broad categories, "the brothers," "the heads" and "the cowboys." But within these categories were represented every kind of story. For awhile, I worked next to a country kid, a cowboy, who happened to be a small-time thief. He was also quite harmless.

But the other end of the scale was represented too. In my wing there was a big, bug-eyed dude named "Frog." Frog was in for murder, and in Leavenworth for life. For entertainment in the evening, he liked to check out the white boys in the showers. One night, after dinner, he had a buddy filch my towel from outside the showers. So I borrowed someone else's, to wear up to my cell, until I could get one back to him. Then, later that evening I ran into Frog up on the catwalks—and I said something to him. Frog looked down at the kid standing before him, and asked what in the world I was talking about, a smile all over his bug-eyed face. He was huge, and we were above tree-line in the tiers; he could have made a human airplane out of me. One toss. But he never bothered me after that.

In the evenings, we would all listen to music on the radio. Each one-man cell had a headset and three jacks, and each jack played a different kind of music; rhythm and blues, country and rock'n'roll. And since we had all segregated ourselves according to our respective inclinations, there being just three of them, this worked out fine.

But one group out of the three was inclined to sing along with their music. All you had to do was take your headphones off and quit listening to rock'n'roll. Inside all that concrete, the acoustics were something else. After twenty years, I can still remember words to the Motown hits.

And, of course, there were friends. All the general court-martialed COs from around the country were there, maybe 25–30 of us. We hung out talking, reading, arguing, proselytizing, celebrating birthdays and Christmases, making plans for when we'd all get out. It was a time in my life, perhaps the only one, in which I knew exactly what I was doing—and why.

Jeffrey Porteous

On Sunday, a protestant clergyman would come to the prison to minister to the COs. We'd sit in a circle and talk about our feelings and our different beliefs. It was wonderful, it helped you remember you had a positive emotional muscle in your body and that you could use it. Also, come Christmas 1969, the COs got cards from people all over the country. Somehow, our names had been put on lists and we got cards wishing us Christmas cheer and telling us to persevere, that there was a commonality of concern with us and with what we were doing. We posted them on the walls where we worked and the guards would rip them down; we'd put them back up and the guards would rip them down again.

After some months had passed my wife moved to Kansas City. There was a guard named Golden who patrolled the visitor's room when she'd come out on the weekends. He looked like he'd been a surfer before the Army—he had California written all over him—and my wife, who was blonde, and young, and pretty, didn't escape his attention. Nor, as it turned out, did I.

One night I was summoned to the rotunda, to the main guard shack. This was never good news, but I hadn't done anything, so I went out, more curious than anything else. It was Golden, and he was by himself. I walked up to the shack, reported to him, and was handed a pink DR slip, a disciplinary report. He had written me up for being slow in getting back from work that day. It was a lie. Three DRs and they carted you off to the hole. I was so fucked, standing there, I started stuttering, trying to tell Golden he was full of shit. He just laughed, and told me to get my ass back to the cell block.

That weekend, during visiting hours, as I was with my wife, young sergeant Golden walked by and gave us both a big smile—and that night, after dinner, he repeated the DR process. Once again, I could not speak.

I went to see the executive officer the next day. But he was a young second lieutenant, more uptight about being in the joint than I was. He told me, "Leavenworth is a big place, you don't want to make waves." Which meant he didn't want to make waves, which meant I was back to square one. Then, a few days later, a tier-guard told me someone wanted me out in the rotunda.

Golden was standing, waiting for me. I saw he'd brought a friend. I didn't know if that was good or bad. I had tried to think about what to do, but I'd been unable to think, and hadn't come to any conclusions. What could I do? But as I received the slip from his outstretched hand, I found myself shaking my head, and laughing. I do not know where this laughter came from, surely not me, but I'm thankful, because Golden's face fell like a buckshot duck, and then I really laughed. Really. And his friend blurted out something like, "C'mon, man, just leave him alone." And that's exactly what he did, his face so red it was black, ripping the DR out of my hand and telling me to get the fuck back to the wing. So I went, though I was no longer laughing, and never saw him again.

One day, after I had been there fifteen months, I was sent to the Administration Building, then ushered into an office. There were shades on the lights, and I was told to sit on a chair with a cushion. A corpulent young captain who sat behind a big wooden desk said, "How'd you like to get out of jail today?" The prick. "It seems like your orders came through about five days ago, I don't know what the fuck-up is, but we can let you out right now—today," he said, smoothing out a piece of paper on his desk, "if you'll just sign this waiver." It was a form saying I'd drop all rights to sue the Army for any damages, past or future. I had never even thought of that before, though once he'd brought it up, I didn't want to do it. I told him I'd think it over. But I wanted out. I walked around, saying goodbye to the guys still in medium security with me, then I went back to my cell and wrote a poem in pencil on the concrete wall. It read something like, "I've been here before you, and I've done this, and I've kept faith. I keep faith with you who are to follow." Then I went back and signed their piece of paper.

They cut me loose and I walked the whole twenty miles right on into Kansas City. It was summer, and it was sunny. I walked in one perfect, uninterrupted direction for hour after hour, caressing the warm bricks on the building-sides as I passed through their towns. I stood still to watch the manifold miracle of women simply walking by, of children playing in the parks, of dogs running free, quietly letting all the good, gainful shit fill back in. In prison we were all guards, no matter what we thought. But once out, you could let it all down, and the whole warm world rushed in at you at once.

I had gotten out of the penitentiary five days before my twenty-second birthday. The whole decade had changed, it was 1970 and I was out. I was free.

Mike Ferner

The military housing my wife and I occupied was right along the perimeter of the base, right on the fence. On Armed Forces Day, the "Movement for a Democratic Military," a GI-civilian organization in the area, decided to hold a demonstration they called "Armed *Farces* Day." They marched around the perimeter of the base going right past my house. I ripped off a sheet from the surgery ward, spray painted a peace sign on it, and stuck it on the fence. Then, I sat down on my back stoop, waiting for the march. Well, the Shore Patrol was hiding in the bushes; they saw this sheet and went out of their minds. They came roaring up to my house and were jumping up and down, livid, turnin' purple mad! They hauled me away in a pick up truck and kept me locked up until the demonstration was over.

They released me, but they had arrested me. I could have taken nonjudicial punishment, but I requested a court-martial instead. Base policy was to post court-martial charges on the bulletin board. Somebody, God bless his soul whoever he was, saw this charge sheet and sent it to a reporter, figuring it was worth a story. The reporter contacted me and did a story about my situation.

Coincidentally, right around that time, an Air Force colonel ordered an illegal bombing in Indochina. All they did to him was bring him back, slap him on the wrist and reassign him. That was the analogy the reporter used, a comparison of what the military was doing to me and what they did to this colonel. Well, the day after this article came out, they dropped the charges against me. This was the first time I tried something and won, and it gave me encouragement. I saw that you could beat the system, even if it was by a lucky accident.

I also wrote a couple of letters to President Nixon, telling him what an asshole he was. I put down my name, rank, serial number, address, the whole shot. I called him every name in the book; I mean, I was pissed. I figured they could hang me for this, but man, that son-of-a-bitch was blowing up all these people, so the least I could do was write him a nasty letter. I never got a response; but later, when I shipped out to California, I walked in and handed the guy my orders and he said, "Oh yeah, we've been waiting for you, Washington called." I thought, "Well, somebody's been listening."

I worked at the Great Lakes Hospital for a year-and-a-half. During that time I began to question the militaristic part of me that had been real strong when I was younger. Bits and pieces of that remained. It took a long time to work through this, and to finally decide that war was wrong—that it was not the thing to do. In the meantime, I continued to have other, contradictory thoughts, like, the war represented a historical period and I should experience it to the max.

Now, I worked on a psychiatric ward and a neurosurgery ward, and I saw a lot of brain and nerve damage caused by battle wounds. In the surgery ward we pieced guys back together who were only a couple of years older than I was. Those guys had pieces of their heads missing, and stuff like that—I worked on those kinds of cases for a year-and-a-half—and, as I talked to more and more Vietnam vets, it really began to sink in. I slowly began to challenge a lot of the views I had about duty, God, and country; that is, what duty was and how we should carry it out.

Another image affected me, and has stayed with me vividly. My duties included meeting medevac planes, loaded with the wounded, that were coming back from Vietnam. We'd go to the Naval Air Station on a bus fitted out for stretchers that were stacked four-high. The inside of the plane was altered in the same way.

One day, after the stretchers were loaded up and the bus started back to the hospital, a seventeen year old Marine laying on a stretcher turned to me and said, "Doc, do you think you could help me, my hand's stuck in the side of the stretcher between the window." I pulled the sheet back, and saw his forearm wedged in a very uncomfortable position. When I went to free it, I saw that it was only his forearm. He'd lost his entire hand in Vietnam. Here was a kid, even younger than me, who would go back to his hometown, and make his way for the rest of his life, with a hook instead of a hand.

The real turning point was running into some older guys who had graduated from college before they came into the military. They did drugs and listened to music that I thought was odd. They also talked about things I thought were odd at first. But they struck me as being very good people. I was taken by them, and they befriended me. They were very different from the other guys I had been hanging around. I remember getting off-base, as much as possible, with a couple of these guys. We talked about a lot of things; so, I was finally able to bounce some ideas off people who were receptive. Up to that point, those thoughts had just been running around in my head. Now, I could bounce them off these guys to get feedback and reinforcement. I also began to read antiwar literature. This helped me to solidify those ideas that were leading me against war.

After a year-and-a-half of duty at Great Lakes Naval Hospital, I got sea duty, on an aircraft carrier off the coast of Vietnam. As soon as I realized what my orders were I put in a request for a transfer. My reason for doing this was not, as the Navy later claimed during my CO process, because of fear of combat duty off Vietnam. Chances of personal danger on a carrier were slim, at any rate. I requested a transfer because I saw carrier duty as being more directly involved with the war than I could justify. That fine line of what I could or could not allow myself to do was beginning to be defined. But I was still feeling my way along.

The request for a transfer was turned down. So, my only options were to take my month's leave, and then report to the ship, or to desert. I went on leave and decided to look into finding a counselor. I ran into a guy who was counseling out of a run-down church in Toledo. He told me what I could do legally, and encouraged me to develop my own thoughts, ideas and judgments. He also gave me the name and phone number of a counseling service in Oakland, California.

When I got to Oakland, I located the Pacific Counseling

Service and asked them for help. The counselor there showed me how to prepare an application for discharge as a conscientious objector. So, I started writing this thing, re-drafting it three or four times.

At the time, I was on the Naval Base in San Francisco Bay. The ship I was supposed to be on was at sea, off of Vietnam. I assumed they were going to fly me out to the ship, but I told them, "I'm not going out to that ship, I'm not going to cooperate with this." Finally, I had decided to make my stand, and to take the consequences.

They decided not to fly me out, that I should wait for the boat to come back from Vietnam. So, there I was, I waited for three weeks, did some serious partying in my off-duty hours, hung around, fine-tuned my application for discharge, and talked to the counselors some more.

Finally, the boat got back. It was a World War II aircraft carrier, the kind you'd see on *Victory at Sea*. An old boat, but it was a workhorse that didn't break down like the newer boats. That thing had the record at the time for on-line flight operations, twenty-four hours-a-day for fifty-four days, this rusting, aging hulk, the *USS Hancock*.

The first day it arrived I walked in there and handed them a twenty-page application for discharge. The guy I handed it to didn't quite know what to do, and I was surprised at the lack of static I got for submitting it. I guess it was because everyone on that boat just wanted to get off of it, and go back home.

It took a couple of weeks until they finally realized what I'd been up to. Then I started getting negative feedback from some of the officers. They tried to talk me out of it, using the patronizing, fatherly approach. One lieutenant commander, the head of the medical department on the carrier, called me in. He went on about, "I looked at your records and you're a very intelligent guy" and blah, blah, blah. It was bullshit. He asked me, "What do you think is going to happen if people start thinking about the fact that they can file for discharge as conscientious objectors?" He said, "What do you think that's going to do to the morale of these people? Don't you think it's going to make them feel like their time in the service and the work they are doing is worthless?" I remember, very specifically, looking at the guy and saying, "Maybe they *should* start thinking about this." He just kind of looked at me, like, "hmm, this line of talk isn't going to get very far."

In my CO application, I basically talked about the experiences I had patching guys up, thinking that something was wrong there, and how I wasn't going to be part of it. When you file for CO status, they send you to a line officer, a chaplain and a psychiatrist. While I was waiting for the boat to come back I did my psychiatrist interview. My first reaction was to question the whole process. I thought, "These guys think I'm nuts, because I don't want to participate in this crazy, fuckin' war; but obviously, they're the crazy ones."

When the boat came back I saw the chaplain and the line officer. The interviews went really well. The psychiatrist and the chaplain recommended that I get out. But the officer listened to my story, read my application and wrote a report that said, "Mike is sincere, but he should not be discharged, he should get noncombatant status and finish his tour." I had ten months left in my four-year tour when my claim was rejected.

Meanwhile, I was getting help from the Bay Area Military Project which was hooked-up with the Pacific Counseling Service. The attorney there thought I had grounds for an appeal. At that time, the criteria for CO status centered on whether or not the applicant was sincere. So, he wrote the appeal.

My stand was if they didn't discharge me by the time the boat was to go back to Vietnam, I would cease participating in anything the Navy wanted me to do. If that meant the brig, so be it. I told all the lifers this and they thought I was nuts, but the word got around that I was serious.

After the *Hancock* got out of drydock, we'd go down to San Diego for flight operations. They were getting the ship ready to go back to Vietnam. While we were on flight operations I tried to get the Navy for everything I possibly could. If we dumped garbage, I'd check the charts to see if we were beyond the limit for legally dumping the trash. I'd mark down the times we were within that limit and write to Congressman Dellums and others. I'd say, "Look at what's going on, isn't this illegal?" I did anything I could to get them.

Since I was not cooperating very much they took me off my job in the sick bay. They gave me the job of inspecting the bathrooms. The enlisted men's quarters were just abominable, especially those that were six or eight decks down. Some of these bathrooms were awash with four or five inches of raw sewerage. Men had to walk in there to take showers and to try to clean up. I started writing these things up and sending them to the officer responsible for sanitation. I'd report problems like inadequate urinals, the need for soap and towel dispensers, and so forth. I read the rule books, and used the regulations. I wrote up everything that wasn't up to snuff. They got three warnings; the fourth time, you had to write them up. I used a section in the Uniform Code of Military Justice that said even an enlisted man could write-up an officer if they were breaking the regulations. So, I started writing-up officers, and that really got to them. Like, "This guy can't even inspect bathrooms without screwin' up."

I also figured I'd do what some of my friends called "copping an attitude." For most, this meant breaking regulations and getting busted all the time. But my "attitude" was to abide by the regulations one-hundred percent. I started cutting my hair more often and shining my belt buckle. I was trying to drive them nuts with their own regulations, that was my "attitude."

Now, I had already requested a couple of, so-called "Captain's Masts." This was a attempt within the Navy to try to be more progressive. Basically, it was a request to see the commander of the ship, base, or whatever. It was like a grievance procedure; if you went up the chain of command and your request wasn't dealt with, you met with the commander. The "Captain's Mast" was like going to binding arbitration.

Well, I read these regulations as soon as they were issued. The officers on the ship weren't really aware of them; so, I just ran my requests up through the chain of command. One of my requests was to be able to circulate pamphlets on how to apply for conscientious objector status. Of course, none of the officers would okay this, they thought it was crazy. They just kept passing it up the ladder until I got to see the captain of the ship. Of course, he thought I was some kind of basketcase up there asking to pass out this type of information.

Another time, I drafted a petition with a group of counselors and antiwar activists; we were attempting to stop our ship from going back to Vietnam. It basically said that since this was an old World War II aircraft carrier, and the peace treaty had already been signed, it had no business going back over there. We were requesting a Congressional investigation regarding the need for it to go back again.

We pulled into San Diego one weekend, I got off the boat, and on city property, I collected signatures as the guys came off the boat. I got a good response. I went back on the boat and decided to do the petition on the ship. One guy helped me do this on shore, but he wasn't about to do it on the boat. So, I did it before my work shift. I got up early and started circulating the petition in the cafeteria. Well, one of the lifers saw the petition and ratted on me.

The next day I got busted and hauled up to the captain. This was the second or third time I'd gone to see him. Well, he just lost it, he was screaming at me. I didn't say anything. He screamed at me for about five minutes, reduced me in rank, fined me two hundred bucks and confined me to the ship.

So, I called my lawyer and we got the American Civil Liberties Union involved. Ultimately, they took a deposition on my charges that the Navy violated the First Amendment by not allowing me to petition or distribute literature on the boat. Our case was simply that we had the right to do a petition. The Navy's position was that when you're in the military, your First Amendment rights are suspended. I was discharged before the case was settled, it actually took about eight years to adjudicate.

I heard stories of guys doing even more serious stuff. There was a guy on the *USS Ranger,* the sister ship to the one I was on, who was charged with dropping two six-inch bolts into the main reduction gears that transferred power to the shaft powering the boat. These gears were located right along the bottom of the boat, probably twelve decks down. A guy dropped this shit in there and wrecked those gears forever. To get to the problem, they had to cut out a section of twelve steel decks to lift the damaged parts out and replace them. It took them six months and millions of dollars; it was a celebrated case in the Bay area. They found some guy they accused of doing it and brought him to trial. Sabotage in time of war meant the death penalty, which had never been meted out to anyone during the Vietnam era, but it was a very serious offense. This was a major case, and after a political fight to keep his trial from being transferred to the Philippines, the guy was acquitted.

The Navy actually had Marine guards on many of the larger boats. Any ship above a destroyer had a Marine detachment on it. They put Marines on these ships, in part, to prevent acts of sabotage; plus, they had Marine guards around the fighter planes. I'm sure the Navy's original intent wasn't to prevent sabotage, but eventually, that's what their jobs came to include. Guys used to throw handfuls of nuts or bolts into the engines of these planes; pilots would start 'em up the next morning and blow the engines. Marines, with M–1s, would guard these things so *their own people* wouldn't sabotage things!

There was a lot of sabotage on my ship; a lot of frustration was being vented. Not big time stuff, like on the *Ranger,* but a lot of low-level sabotage went on—salt poured into this, turpentine dumped into that, things thrown overboard. It was basically antimilitary as opposed to antiwar stuff. I didn't know very many people who were doing it, but it happened everyday.

I strongly suspect there were no other conscientious objectors on board, people just hated being on that boat, they were just pissed-off and frustrated; you know, "Show me something to break and I'll break it," that sort of thing.

Actually, it was a little disappointing that the destruction going on was not directed in any particular political manner. I tried to get the word through the grapevine that if people were interested in conscientious objection they should come see me. One or two guys came by, but that was it.

There was a time when I seriously doubted my sanity. I was bothered by the fact that nobody there seemed to consider what I was doing as sane. Nobody I knew, except for my one friend who helped me to petition, felt what the military was doing was wrong. There were thirty-five hundred guys on that boat, I probably knew a hundred or a hundred and fifty, and nobody thought what I was doing was sane, let alone agreed with me.

Most people had absolutely no idea that conscientious objection existed within the Navy regulations. They never understood that what I was doing was a Navy procedure. They just thought it was crazy. So, I was really isolated. I'm on the boat, out on the ocean playing war games for two or three weeks at a time, having only one person I could really confide in. I began walking around the ship wondering "Am I crazy? What's going on here? Why am I the only person out of thirty-five hundred guys feeling this way? Am I nuts, or what?"

I worked this through and finally reached a point where I felt inner peace. I no longer thought I was crazy, and even if I was, I didn't really care. I knew what I was doing; I had gone through enough experiences, had written enough about it, and had seen and heard enough about Vietnam to know I was no longer going to participate. If they wanted to call that crazy, so be it.

This was one of the few things in my life that I have been absolutely sure about. I decided they could do whatever they wanted to do with me, but I was not going to cooperate. They could put me in the brig for the rest of my natural life and I didn't care.

Being on that carrier helped me to see my role in the Navy very clearly. It became evident that everyone's job was directed to one end—catapulting those fighter bombers off the end of the flight deck and into combat. Whether it was loading bombs into planes or working in the sick bay, our work, every day, was directed to the same purpose. No matter how detached or uninvolved a corpsman's job could be considered, it was directly supporting something I could no longer be part of.

I waited for five months for a decision on my CO claim, it must have gotten lost on somebody's desk or something. But, the day I got busted for doing the petition on the boat, it was miraculously found. Later that same day I was told I was going to be gone within two days. A happy day in my life!

This is what happened. My lawyer contacted the Bay area Congressmen; they, in turn, wrote telegrams to the Secretary of the Navy, the Commander of the Pacific Fleet and to the captain of my boat. Boy, you talk about the shit hitting the fan. It hit the fan royally! The next morning I was called down to Personnel and processed out of the Navy. The Personnel clerk told me, "The captain said to get the fuck off the ship." I was escorted, with a military guard, out the gates of the Naval Base. I was so elated, you couldn't have brought me down to the ground if you had skyhooks to pull me down.

Richard Lovett

In-service, discharged CO
U.S. Army 1967–1969

We were on the outside, inside.

[AUTHOR'S NOTE]

Richard Lovett came from a family background sensitive to violence as an acceptable expression for settling disputes. There was no history of war resistance in the family; however, Richard did report that "cultivating an independent frame of mind" characterized his father's side of the family.

Early on, Richard came to the conclusion that "Other people were a reflection of myself. I found that I had difficulty crossing the boundary of deliberately doing physical harm to another. I believed that violence was not an acceptable mode of life."

In college, Richard found himself becoming more and more concerned with issues surrounding human dignity and the importance of life. Attracted to the civil rights movement, he took a job in Washington, DC with the Office of Equal Health Opportunity. He also enrolled in Catholic University as a graduate student majoring in philosophy. He focused his study on ethics and metaphysics developing a "Deep, intense, intellectual preoccupation with the connection between values and civil rights." He read Satre, Camus, Kierkegaard and Thomas Aquinas, masterworks that advocated, "Total respect for coming to the independence of one's own conclusions."

While these studies kindled a keen interest in concerns like civil rights, they also turned Richard within. He became preoccupied intellectually, and that, he re-

ported, "Created an inhibition to be an activist, per se."
He became sort of an "intellectual activist," who saw
himself as "Not very pragmatically connected to the
workings of the world." He said, "My training was bi-
ased intellectually and involved very abstract systems
of thought."

When draft deferments were eliminated for graduate
students in the mid-sixties, Richard found himself in-
capable of dealing with the Selective Service bureauc-
racy. As he described it:

> receiving my draft notice sort of overtook my frame
> of reference. It was hard for me to catch on that
> there was this mechanism set in motion by Selec-
> tive Service that I had to deal with. At that point I
> hadn't learned to put ideas into action. The draft
> and the war were shadowy worlds to me. I saw them
> there, but I was incapable of seeing how they fit in
> for me, or how it would affect my destiny.
>
> Conscientious objection never occurred to me. I was
> so overwhelmed with what was about to happen
> that I didn't have the conscious room to deal with it.
> Conscientious objection seemed esoteric, a category
> that, I assumed, automatically excluded me. I saw it
> as connected solely to the Quakers or to similar reli-
> gious persuasions. I was not able to connect the ten-
> ets of conscientious objection to me, I just couldn't
> project and define myself that way. I guess I was
> totally hooked up into the bureaucracy's way of
> looking at me, rather than in me taking control of
> my destiny.
>
> The draft situation made me feel like I had no con-
> trol, I felt victimized. I took the physical examina-
> tion, realized I was on an assembly line, and started
> looking for ways to modify the outcome. I saw a re-
> cruiter who talked me into Officer Candidate
> School, and I went through with that idea.

Richard Lovett

Richard Lovett's story continues below and concludes in Chapter 5.

＊ ＊ ＊ ＊

I did basic and advanced Infantry training at Fort Dix, New Jersey. It was hard for me to relate to what they were training us to do. Part of me could not readily accept that they were preparing us to do something as awesome as killing people. Mentally, I resisted the magnitude of this reality. I guess this was a way of protecting myself, of not letting that reality take total control of me. I was distancing myself, giving myself space, so that I didn't totally hook into their system.

The routinization of the training was very numbing. There was a lot of depression, for everybody, during basic. People fell asleep all the time, not just from fatigue, but from depression. It was a mass stupor.

The whole effort was geared to pulverize your mind, an attempt to obliterate your prior life so you had nothing. Realizing this, and hearing the rationale the officers gave for being in Vietnam is where my resistance started. I concluded that I was either responsible for believing what they were saying, or responsible for not going along with their thinking. I tried to identify with the so-called "cogent" reasons they gave for our involvement in Vietnam, and I found they weren't very cogent. That was the dividing line for me. I decided I could not let these people lead me into a conviction, and then into their plan of action. I couldn't do that.

After AIT, I went to Officer Candidate School in Fort Benning, Georgia. I was there for fourteen weeks. I still had not totally given myself over to the military experience; part of me was still removed. Even though the trainees were older and college educated, I was unable to become "one of the guys" or to get into the esprit de corps.

The Army wondered if I had the right dedication, the right mettle to be an officer. They tried to break my will, to humiliate me, and I thought, to get me to either resign, or to resolve my will for leadership. For example, once, for no apparent reason, the company commander called me into his office to berate me, and to make me do an hour's worth of push-ups in my sleeping bag. I guess I just did not have the charismatic energy that the Army thought an officer should have.

While in OCS I met some people who were looking for options to deal with this situation. These were the sort of rebels who didn't actually pick up the cause. But, they were dissidents in terms of not believing in, or respecting the Army's authority. One, in particular, knew of conscientious objection; the rest were cultivating other options to change their situations. For me, this was the beginning of a passageway that helped me see a whole other world.

Eventually, the Army told me I was not up to snuff and transferred me back a couple of weeks into another OCS company. But, I had had it with OCS. I realized I was not willing to give orders to other people that I, myself, didn't believe. I told them I wanted to resign. They gave me a hard time about it, but I insisted that they execute my request. This is where my consciousness started to be liberated, this is where I finally became resolved to a course of action.

Eventually, they dropped me from OCS and put me in the holding company. During training they'd march us past this place, point to the guys who were there and say, "Look at those derelicts, look at those bums." They'd say, "You guys end up falling out of OCS and you'll become bums like those people." Obviously, I was becoming one of the "bums." It was there, at the holding company, that my liberation really started.

While there I met a fellow who mentioned he was a conscientious objector. He told me what it was about and how to apply for CO status. Nebulous though it was at the time, I decided this was a realistic option, and that I was going to file an application for discharge.

I went down to the orderly room and asked for the paperwork. They were very hostile and tried to talk me out of it. But strangely enough, because I had such resolve, it didn't really bother me. I just wasn't intimidated. I had been triggered into a compulsive, active state of mind. My decision was made, and it was irrevocable. They could shoot me or put me in jail, whatever, but I was not going to do what they wanted.

In the interim, orders came down for me to go to Vietnam. Now, my obsession was to get the CO application going and to have the issue clarified, right then and there. But, the chaplain I was sent to told me to accept the orders, and to take my leave. He suggested this would give me more time to prepare a quality application. I accepted this as good counsel, and that was what I did.

I went home for three weeks, but I didn't use the time to fortify my case, and somewhat foolishly, I didn't seek any assistance. I sort of sequestered myself and got caught up with two ideas. Number one, I saw applying for CO status as a very private, subjective experience, something that was only happening to me. It was hard for me to see this as a more universal problem that other people were actually involved in. And secondly, I was feeling a sense of guilt. On the one hand, I had come to realize that being involved in the military was something I could not do, but then again, I felt guilt because other people were not able to do what I was doing. I had the luxury of being able to do this, and I felt bad for those kids who did not have the freedom to do this.

The day I reported to Fort Lewis was one of the most tremulous days of my life. I had this overwhelming image that I was going to show up there, tell them I wasn't going to Vietnam, and with no buffer in between, end up disappearing. The day before I got to Fort Lewis I visited an American Civil Liberties Union attorney in Seattle. Doing this made me feel much more secure. I felt like nothing untoward was going to happen to me, that I wouldn't disappear without it being a reportable event.

I handed in the paperwork, and of course, the military people became very abrasive. But it was like a kinetic activity. Once the adrenaline started flowing, everything seemed to fall into place. So, once they became outrageous, I became more calm. I came prepared for the worst.

Eventually, I got thrown into the holding company barracks at Fort Lewis. That was the best thing that ever happened to me! I ended up in a barracks which housed an undefined coterie of people with different problems—medical problems, emergency discharge problems, conscientious objectors, people up on criminal charges—a whole medley of different personalities that you'd find in the normal range of events in the Army. It was a real counterculture, full of misfits, people that just didn't belong. Everyone there knew they didn't belong, so there was an internal support system that everyone respected. There was this whole other perspective on the Army, it was like being on the outside. We were on the outside, inside.

There were a lot of COs there, and that sort of cemented this whole reality for me, it was just wonderful. The COs became a coherent group. Of course, the politics of the country that opposed the war was very powerfully in front of us. So, we not only felt an obligation to each other, but we also felt a need to take part in that larger reality. And we did, very blatantly. We made trips to the GI coffeehouse in Tacoma, went to antiwar seminars, and listened to antiwar lectures in people's homes. By doing this we became more coherent to people outside of the Army. This was very important to me, because I was coming from such an introspective angle, and it was opening me up.

My application for discharge was basically a narration of the untenableness of war and violence. I saw no compensating rationale for the violence that goes on in war. I felt no conviction to justify undertaking a war on the pretense of achieving certain ends. I also cited the importance and sovereignty of conscience, and how my background made it impossible to justify participation in the war in Vietnam.

When the company commander read it he asked me the meaning of one of words. I realized he was checking to see if I had, in fact, written the document. His fixation was that I had a support system out there making me do this, that I was being corrupted and undermined by dissidents.

I applied for discharge because I didn't believe in violence or in supporting the implementation of violence; I could not accept a noncombatant position. They tried to make me feel guilty by saying, "Well look, you can't shoot people, but maybe you can help bandage them up, be a medic or something." But doing this was still participating in the horror of war. I felt it gave credence and rationale to the war; it was defending and making war more viable. I just could not accept it; the integrity of what I was doing would have been violated.

My first application for discharge was turned down. I felt bad, obviously, because I felt pride in what I was doing. Of course, jail was a very imminent kind of thing that loomed over all of us. People were going to jail, and one guy, given rush orders, was abducted to Vietnam.

I applied a second time and it was also summarily rejected. I was not given any reason why the applications were disapproved, but the usual connotation was that my claim didn't fit my background. At the time there was still some ambiguity over whether or not a Catholic could fit the definition of a conscientious objector.

At this point I had about nine months left on my enlistment. I was told orders were coming down to transfer me from the holding company to an armory company on the base. I told them if the orders were cut I wouldn't go, I'd go to jail. Well, for some totally fortuitous reason, the orders never came down.

Then, when I had about four months left on my term of service, I applied for CO status a third time. The first sergeant was all upset that I did this, he thought there was no point in doing it. But I believed in the integrity of following through; I told him, "This is what I set out to do and this is what I am." I was persistent about it and wanted to pursue it. So, I did another application; it was still being processed when I was discharged. It turns out the Army approved it ex post facto. I received a letter at my home telling me I had been discharged as a conscientious objector.

This made me feel very good. I finally felt legitimacy for everything I did, and pride for what I had accomplished.

James Willingham

In-service, discharged CO
U.S. Air Force 1969–1972
Vietnam veteran

I wanted to be part of something better.

[AUTHOR'S NOTE]

Jim Willingham described his upbringing as "traditional." As a young man he had a "fairly conservative personality," but was "not into shooting guns or other aggressive types of behavior." Both his father, who was a pilot, and his stepfather were in World War II.

Jim joined the Air Force ROTC while in college, but differed from most trainees in that he was a more "quiet and sensitive type." By his senior year he had become known as "the class pinko" because, he said, "I didn't want to fly fighters, drop bombs or kill anyone."

In flight school he chose to learn to fly cargo planes, a type of training usually given to "lower ranked people in pilot training." He continued to distance himself from the "macho and aggressiveness" of the other trainees, and began to have serious doubts about serving in Southeast Asia. At age twenty-three he achieved the rank of second lieutenant and earned his wings.

Upon receiving orders for Vietnam, Jim said, "I decided to put all my conflicts and doubts behind me, to go over there and try to do a good job." But, by the time he took his R&R he began "feeling alienated about the war." The amount of destruction he saw began to play on him, and as he put it, "All these Vietnamese people were poor and struggling, and there I was tripping around with all this money. It seemed a little absurd."

After returning from Vietnam he was stationed in California, and then in New Hampshire, for additional training. Shortly thereafter, faced with possible temporary duty in Vietnam, he applied for discharge as a conscientious objector.

* * * *

I came back from Vietnam with a feeling of personal accomplishment. I actually became a flight instructor over there; so, I felt that I had achieved something tangible. I was progressing in my career, I was making good money, and I had a recommendation for a regular commission.

I also came back feeling bitter about the destruction I'd seen. I saw a lot of defoliation, bomb craters and wreckage. I saw a lot of bomb damage in eastern Cambodia. You could actually tell where Vietnam ended and Cambodia started, Vietnam was defoliated and plowed flat, Cambodia was pretty much bombed out.

I wasn't stressed out or agitated, I was sad. I was kind of broken hearted, it was sort of a shattering of dreams. I was brought up to believe in the fight for freedom and democracy; I guess I had a naive and simplistic idea about what America was supposed to be. But, I saw Americans behaving in degrading and irresponsible ways in Vietnam. It made me sad and angry.

One day, I saw a sign that advertised a meeting of the Vietnam Veterans Against the War (VVAW). They were a group of Vietnam vets who were strongly opposed to the war. I had evolved to the point where I was thinking about getting out of the Air Force; so, I went to the meeting.

These were earthy people with long hair and a natural spirit of rebelliousness that I was attracted to. One guy who impressed me had been a Navy officer, rather conservative looking, middle of the road. Another vet said that he would not stop until America got out of Vietnam. I asked them about getting discharged as a conscientious objector, but nobody knew how.

I was in California, in KC–135 tanker training, really apathetic and unhappy. I kept seeing the bomb craters and bomb damage, and I decided I didn't want to be a part of it anymore. I wanted to be part of something better. On the other hand, I realized I was about to give up a dream that I pursued for about six years. I was totally disillusioned and alone. I wanted somebody to pat me on the back, but there wasn't anyone.

While I was on leave during Christmas 1971, I decided to file for a CO discharge. When I told my parents about what I was doing my stepfather said he'd never forgive me and my mother said, "James, you'll never be able to get a job." I must admit that I was really afraid of being labeled a conscientious objector for the rest of my life. I thought it would be just like having a bad discharge. I came from a real conservative background; my parents thought it was important to do everything right and to get an honorable discharge.

When I went back to KC–135 school I didn't have any connections and wasn't sure what to do. Then, one weekend I went up to Sausalito and found a book called *The Handbook for Conscientious Objectors*. That referred me to the Central Committee for Conscientious Objectors in San Francisco. I talked to them just once. They gave me some basic information, patted me on the back and put me in contact with other guys in the military who could help. I was scared shitless, but at the same time, there wasn't any possibility of turning back. That was it, I was going to go for it. In January 1972, the Air Force gave me orders to ship to Pease Air Force Base in New Hampshire. From there I probably would have been shipped TDY to Vietnam. So, one morning I told the student commander I wanted to file for discharge as a conscientious objector.

When I got to New Hampshire I had to write up a formal application for discharge as a CO. I based my claim on the fact that a lot of people were making money off of the war. I also didn't think the destruction was justified; and I didn't like the way we treated the Vietnamese people. I got letters of reference from two guys I had known in Vietnam and from a couple of guys in training school. They all said that they couldn't agree with me, but they believed I was sincere.

There was constant pressure, but I wasn't really harassed that much. I guess it was easier for me since I was an officer. Mostly, they wanted to keep me apart from other people. They thought that I'd be bad for morale.

I didn't want to fly and managed to get myself grounded. I was given alternative duty, a variety of tasks. By that point I was feeling so antagonistic that I said, "The heck with it." Once they asked me to lead a group of Airmen who were doing an inventory. I never showed up for it. I started staying off the base a lot, as much as two weeks at a time; I just had to be available if they called me.

I became pretty active while I was waiting for a decision on my CO claim. I was in three or four demonstrations; one was held right outside the base. By that time I was expanding into a more loving kind of awareness. It felt good being there.

Off-base, I had a lot of friends who were pretty angry about the war. I hooked up with a woman from the Quakers who gave me a lot of support, and I met a lot of Vietnam vets who belonged to VVAW. There was also an underground newspaper around called *Off The Brass*.

I talked to two other guys who were applying for CO status, both were officers. One told me, "All I want to do is build houses." Essentially, he wanted to do something constructive, rather than destructive. But, these guys were uptight about getting involved in antiwar actions. They didn't want to be controversial and risk getting hassled; so, they sort of low-keyed it.

It was a psychologically and emotionally difficult time. I was sad, angry and scared. I had fierce headaches I'd never had before or since. I was kind of anxious and uptight, just waiting and waiting for a decision.

Finally, one day I got really uptight and decided that it didn't make any sense for me to give up my career and all the goals I had been working for. I came to the conclusion that I wasn't against all wars, but I was definitely against the war in Vietnam. So, I went and told the squadron leader that I wanted to withdraw my CO claim. But, that feeling only lasted for one day. I went to the chapel to meditate and to think things over. In the Book of Psalms I read something like, "You have traveled a long and rocky road, slippery in many places. You almost fell, but you will have the courage to continue." I realized then that I was going to go ahead and get out of the Air Force.

I went back to my squad and told them I wanted to resign my commission. By this time, there were enough antiwar officers around that the Air Force came up with a deal allowing you to resign your commission and be given an administrative discharge under honorable conditions. So, that's what I did, and I was out in a week or two after that. I was discharged in June 1972.

Going through the CO experience made me respect myself; I felt good about following my conscience. Sometimes I think that if I had more resilience and strength of character I could have followed through on the CO discharge. If I feel guilty it's because I didn't follow through. But, at the time, it didn't seem particularly important how I got out. I did not want to participate in the war anymore and I was sick of the military. I didn't have to go to jail, although I was willing to go. I could have done a little better, but I did participate in antiwar activity and I know I influenced a lot of people.

Robert D.

I drove an ambulance in Germany, spending a lot of time in the field. I was a very liberal sort of a guy, my hair was so long I stuffed it up underneath my helmet. I also had sort of a Fu Manchu moustache. I got away with a lot; but once I did get an Article 15 for having my hair too long. As punishment, I got dropped back in rank to private.

Most of my GI friends were antiwar and antimilitary, some handed out newspapers opposing the war. I knew one guy who applied for a 1–O discharge. Other COs would meet with him to give him help and advice. He was real sincere, but the Army wouldn't let him out.

I did my job, but I didn't take anything from anybody. Like, my ambulance was my territory. I was responsible for it, I took care of it, and nobody came in there without my permission; under no circumstances were weapons allowed in my vehicle. Only once did somebody take a weapon into my ambulance. On that occasion I walked over, grabbed the weapon, opened up the back door and pitched it out. The next thing I knew, I was flat on my back with this guy's fist in my face. Two guys pulled him off me, then this sergeant asked me why I wouldn't allow weapons in the ambulance. I said, "Because I don't believe in killing anybody and I don't want to be involved in killing anybody." I told them, "The last thing you're going to do is to put a weapon in my vehicle, because that is a piece of machinery that kills people." All he could say was, "Oh, one of those guys, huh?" Luckily, it ended right there; I had no further problems.

If I were to sum-up my experience and advise the young, I'd say I put in my time, and feel I served my country. I didn't hurt anybody; I didn't have to hurt anybody. I'm proud of what I did, and I'm not ashamed of anything that happened.

People who don't believe in taking life, and suspect they might be drawn into the military and forced to do things they don't believe, should act—right from the start. Not acting on beliefs was a mistake guys made during Vietnam, and a lot of them have to live with that now.

Tom Cox

At Fort Monmouth I was assigned to a six-sided building called the "Hexagon." It was the headquarters for the Third Army or something. The chief of staff and the commanding general of the post were right down the hall from where I worked.

One of my duties was to set up and clean an interview room for the general. When GIs from the area were killed their families would come in—wives, mothers, children—for a posthumous ceremony. When the families came in, I would kind of be there in the background. The commanding general would make a little speech, give them medals, and they'd break up and cry.

What got to me was how phony the general acted when he did these ceremonies. I mean, I saw him in his more candid moments, so I knew what he was like. Finally he'd leave, and little by little the family would leave too. I'd change the room around and get it ready for the next family. I probably witnessed about a dozen of those—they were real emotional, real hard to take. It made me think, "God, you are just so expendable, you're just a number, they could care less. If you go to Vietnam, you die, they have your position filled the next day and nobody but your family cares about it."

Those experiences influenced me a lot. Also, during this time I attended an antiwar rally in New York City and read some books by Dick Gregory and Joan Baez. The combination of these things helped me decide that I wasn't going to go to Vietnam.

One day my commanding officer called me in and said, "Orders have been cut to send you to Vietnam." I said, "No, I can't do that, sir. I can't accept them." He asked me if I had applied for conscientious objector status. That was the first time I ever heard the term. I said, "No." Then he started screaming at me at the top of his lungs. I didn't have a chance to say a word. The last thing he said was, "I hope the next time I see you you're in the stockade."

He sent me to a JAG officer who told me that if I didn't

accept the orders I'd be court-martialed and would get from one to five years in prison. He said I didn't have a legal defense for my actions; so, I changed my mind and decided to desert.

I accepted the orders which meant I got about $400 and a thirty day leave. But most of all, I was free and had time to think. Some friends, who knew a little about resistance, took me to Philadelphia, to the Central Committee for Conscientious Objectors. Here, for the first time, I got an explanation of what conscientious objection really meant. I talked with these people for about three hours. They thought I fit into the classification and said I should apply for discharge.

When I reported to the Overseas Replacement Center at Fort Lewis, I handed them a letter saying I was applying for conscientious objector status. They singled me out from the rest of the men, brought me into a room and tried to talk me out of it—a "father-to-son" routine. But, when they saw I was sticking to my beliefs they got a little more pushy and tried to pressure me into giving up my stand. There were a few threats made about how I was going to do a lot of time, how people in prison were going to beat me up, stuff like that. Finally they said, "Okay, okay," and put me in a barracks pending some kind of action.

Eventually, I got sent to a holding company with other people who were seeking discharge or reassignment. This was a major turning point in my career as a resister, because I hooked up with other COs. Rather than spread us out in different companies the Army kept everybody in the same place. I guess they did this so we wouldn't share our ideas with the other men.

There was a real supportive atmosphere at this holding company; we had about twenty-five people who, in one way or another, were taking the same stand. People of different ages and religions, from every kind of background. It was just marvelous for me, exactly what I needed at the time. I had all this input from these people, a real learning experience.

The commanding officer of the holding company wasn't

particularly fond of the COs, so we got some pretty crummy details—cleaning the latrine, shoveling manure for the colonel's stable, and cutting firewood for the officers. The details were pretty menial and rather boring. We'd fall out in the morning and be assigned this kind of stuff. But, since we were COs we didn't have to carry weapons or participate in any war training.

Well, we fell out one morning and were told we had to go to Chemical-Biological Warfare Training—you know, put on a gas mask, go through a gas chamber, that kind of thing. There were three COs in formation that morning and we refused to attend the training. We told them we didn't have to participate because we were COs. Eventually, we were charged with refusing an order and faced a special court-martial. Two of us remained free pending our court-martial. The other guy, who was considered more of a threat, was taken immediately to the stockade. He had no lawyer, had his court-martial in a matter of days and got sentenced to the maximum, six months in the stockade. I got a suspended sentence of sixty days, one reduction in rank and forfeiture of all but ten dollars of my pay for four months.

Preparing an application for discharge as a conscientious objector is like writing a term paper for college, like a thesis. The Army had it set up as if it was a game, and the people who were less educated, or who didn't have a good way with words, were at a disadvantage. Actually, I submitted two applications, my first one was really poor and was rejected. I didn't know how to put a strong statement together, so I just told my story, straight from my heart. That was really naive, because the military was looking for reasons to discredit what was written. Basically, I told them that I should not be part of the military. I didn't even feel that I should be a noncombatant. At this point, I was feeling that even in a support role I was contributing to something that I didn't think was right. I would still be serving, I'd still be in Vietnam. I considered what the United States government and its Army was doing in Vietnam as morally wrong, and I didn't want to be part of it. As a noncombatant I would still be a representative of the U.S. government, a paid representative at that. We didn't belong in Vietnam, and short of the ultimate goal of getting everybody out of there and stopping the war, my next goal was not personally participating in it. So, my position was I should be discharged.

By this time I had decided to go to jail if my CO application was not approved. I decided to do the time rather than desert. My philosophy was that I wanted to get it over with, to do two or three years in prison, or whatever they wanted, as punishment for not being in their war.

One weekend I got arrested for hitchhiking back to the base. I stayed in jail for five days and when I returned was considered AWOL. So, they revoked my suspended sentence and put me in the stockade. Some people from the holding company were already in the stockade, so when I got there people knew me and welcomed me. The stockade's conscientious objector contingent was pretty strong and supportive. Plus, everybody there, AWOLs, COs or those who wouldn't wear the uniform had refused to cooperate at some point along the line. They just didn't fit into the military structure.

I didn't face any violence in the stockade; and, other than the obvious discomforts of being behind bars, it wasn't too bad. The racial situation wasn't too bad either. The black people definitely hung out together and stayed in a certain group and the white people were separate, but there wasn't unbearable tension. However, it was hard to get information in or out of the stockade. The Army was pretty strict about visitors being blood relatives, wives or fiancees; so, I couldn't see my friends from the base. That was a little alienating.

After fifty-odd days I was released. Then, with the advice of a chaplain, I put in a second application for discharge. By this point, I had become pretty active, and the fact that I had already been in the stockade gave credence to my new claim for a CO discharge. A lot of Army people knew that I had been involved in counseling other GIs, demonstrating in Seattle, passing out literature and that spoke well for my sincerity.

While I was waiting to hear about my CO application I was picked up for handing out literature on the base. The MPs turned me over to the Criminal Investigation Division (CID) who questioned me. I didn't want to give the CID guy too much information, because I didn't know what they were after. I told them about my philosophy as a conscientious objector and about my moral objections to the war. They really didn't want to hear that. They wanted to talk about politics. They wanted to know about the type of organized opposition there was on the base, people who were left, politically. They wanted to know names which I wouldn't give them. They wanted to know how many people were talking about the Chicago 8 trial. They wanted to know who talked about socialism. They wanted to know who was buying and selling drugs. I told them I really didn't know any and kept turning the conversation back to conscientious objection.

Shortly after that incident I was told that my second CO discharge had been approved. I felt so good, I can't describe it. They sent a guy with me to speed up my processing out of the service. He had special instructions to march me to the front of these long lines of guys who were also getting out. The clerks would stop what they were doing and take care of me first, move me right through. Then, they escorted me to the bus station and gave me a letter saying I could never come on a military installation again, for the rest of my life. The first sergeant's parting words to me were, "If I ever see you on *my* base again, I'm going to kill you."

They dropped me off, I waited until they left and hitch-hiked back to the holding company to say goodbye to my friends. Then, I lined up a ride to Seattle. That was it. I was free.

Howard Koby

In-service, discharged CO
U.S. Army 1968–1969.

I wanted to be fully recognized for what I believed.

[AUTHOR'S NOTE]

Howard Koby was raised in a Jewish, working-class neighborhood in Brooklyn, New York. "There," he said, "you did what you were supposed to do, if you got drafted, you picked up and went."

Howard described his mother as warm and compassionate, and his father as a person who often expressed hatred for the violence that occurred in World War II. Howard's father had been in Civil Defense during the war; however, he told his son he would have proclaimed himself a conscientious objector if he had been drafted. Howard's father also recounted personal horror stories from his youth in Poland. He told his son about the brutality of the Cossacks, and how family members survived by hiding in holes dug in the ground. These stories greatly impressed Howard who told me, "A lot of what my father said about war stayed with me all these years."

In college Howard took a low-key approach to campus politics. He did not consider himself to be as militant as a lot of other students were at the time. While in school, he also discovered and came to adopt Buddhism as his religious persuasion.

Howard was twenty-four years old when he graduated from college. He knew very little about conscientious objection at that point. Nevertheless, he experimented with resistance by deciding not to notify Selective Service of his graduation. They found out anyway, and he was drafted just a few months after leaving school.

Howard considered basic and Advanced Infantry Training to be "instruction in premeditated murder." He said:

> I was very much against what was going on. The whole idea of the Army repulsed me; I hated every minute of the training. About half way through AIT I thought about not handling weapons, but I didn't do anything, I just held it all in. I knew I didn't want to kill, I didn't want to be killed, and I didn't want to be forced into situations where I might kill or be killed. These thoughts started to surface in basic, and really built up during AIT.

After AIT, Howard got orders to Vietnam. He said:

> I didn't know how I was going to do it, but I knew I was not going to Vietnam. I was brought up a free man and suddenly, there was no freedom. I found myself in a position where I would have to fight for my beliefs.

Howard Koby decided to reclaim his freedom. His story continues below.

* * * *

After AIT, I got a two-week leave and orders to report to Fort Lewis, Washington for the flight to Vietnam. During those two weeks, things started to happen. I was on the outside; so, I was able to contact people and to make inquiries.

I went back to New York and immediately visited the American Civil Liberties Union (ACLU). They turned me on to counselors who knew about conscientious objection. The counselors told me how to initiate an application for discharge; they also put me in touch with an ACLU lawyer in Seattle.

After that, I talked with my father. I told him I had orders for Vietnam and I was going to put in an application for discharge as a conscientious objector. I told him if I didn't get the discharge the only other alternative was prison. He looked at me and he said, "I believe in it and I'll stand behind you. I would do the same thing." Looking back, I'd say the reassurance and support I got from my father was *the* thing that helped me decide to go through with this.

By the time I got to Fort Lewis I was totally prepared; I knew exactly what I had to do to put in an application for CO discharge. I was also totally alone. I didn't have the names of anyone to contact on the base, so I asked some guys if they knew anyone around who was a CO. Someone told me about a guy named Tom Cox, and I looked him up.

I met Tom in the coffee shop at the Overseas Replacement Center. I told him I was putting in for a CO discharge and asked for his help. Tom had already filed for a CO discharge, and when he heard what I was doing he simply said, "Far out." Then, we went off into a corner of the coffee shop and rapped all night.

Tom gave me some important bits of advice. He told me what would happen when I first handed in my application. He informed me that this would be my first experience of harassment. He warned me that they would call me a lot of names, and in order to continue, I had to be strong enough to come through this.

So, the next morning I walked into the sergeant's office. I stood right in front of him, feeling all the strength in the world, knowing that what I was doing was right. I said, "I want to put in an application for conscientious objection." He looked up at me like he was going to throw me out of his office and said, "Oh no, not another fuckin' one." So, I repeated myself and cited the Army regulations that gave me the right to do this.

That did it, he reached into his desk and gave me the papers. Then he said to me, "Under what religion are you basing your claim?" I said, "Buddhism." He looked at me and said, "Who the fuck are you kidding." But, I just stood there. He looked me in the eyes and something happened— I think he saw the sincerity and the truth of what I was telling him—and he kind of melted. He saw that I wasn't bullshiting him. So, he gave me the papers, told me to read them and pulled my orders for Vietnam. Then, he advised me that I was going to be sent to a holding company while they processed the application.

When I walked out of there I had renewed strength. All during basic and AIT things had been brewing, but I never took any action. Now, finally, for the first time, I stood up. I knew then I had the strength to follow this through.

There were two or three pages of questions on the CO form, I spent a whole day just reading and studying them. One asked something like, "Do you believe in the use of force?" Of course, they were referring to physical force, but I didn't write about that at all. I wrote about life-force. I talked about the universe, the life-force that keeps the universe together. I went on for about a page talking about the universal force. They gave me ten days to complete the application, so I spent the next ten days doing a lot of soul-searching and writing.

Then, I joined a Buddhist community in Seattle and mailed copies of my application to noted Buddhists and professors of religion. Two people from the University of Oregon and someone from Lewis and Clark College read my stuff, and they sent letters of support to attach to my application. I also attached letters from friends and people who knew me well.

I never had any thoughts about trying to get noncombatant status; I applied for a discharge. It was either out or jail. I had already decided I would go to prison for my beliefs, and there were times that I really thought I was going to go to jail. Now, Canada was only about 100 miles away from Fort Lewis. However, I never went to visit Canada, because I thought that if I did, I might not come back. I didn't want to handle it that way; I wanted to be recognized for who I was. I wanted to be fully recognized for what I believed, even if it meant going to prison.

When I got to the holding company I met a lot of other COs. I learned a lot from each of these guys; and because we were all together, we supported one another and gained strength from each other. When new COs came in we would all try to help them. We became counselors, we became experts. Often, the new guys would be scared and very unsure of themselves. We'd tell them to find strength in their convictions, and to ask themselves if they would go to jail for their beliefs. We told them that to be a CO they needed clarity about themselves. See, you had to ask yourself if you truly held all your convictions. Then, you had to be able to write them down. You needed information, but you also needed strength. We'd talk and talk, and you could sense the new people getting stronger.

While I was there, one of the other COs, Jeffrey Porteous, had his application turned down. He was eventually court-martialed for disobeying orders. That was a sad day. When they loaded Jeff on a truck to take him to the stockade, I told him how badly I felt that he had to go to jail. He looked back at me and said, "Don't worry about it Koby, I'm free now." I'll never forget that.

At one point, I had to go for an interview with the company commander. This captain, who was supposed to be interviewing me, kept telling me about his experiences in Vietnam. He said he had three tours there and told me about the Viet Cong he killed. I found myself asking him, "How do you feel about killing all these men?" And, he came out with a classic statement that truly sums up the Vietnamese war; he said, "I don't kill men, I only kill ideas." I'll never forget that either; it made me sick. So, I said to him, "Look, we're talking on two totally different planes of thought, I really don't have anything else to say to you." I left, and of course, he recommended that my application for discharge be disapproved.

This same guy gave me a list of chaplains to choose from, because a chaplain had to attest to the sincerity of your claim. Well, there were no Buddhist chaplains on the base, so I told him I'd go see a Jewish chaplain. The guy he sent me to seemed anxious to talk to me—until I told him I was a Buddhist. Then, at first, he was sort of against me. I tried to show him beliefs that were consistent in Judaism and Buddhism. For example, they both advocate compassion for other people. So, I tried hard to explain this to him. We had a long interview; eventually, I convinced him of my sincerity and he recommended that I be discharged. It was funny, as I was leaving his office he said to me, "You know something Howard, once a Jew, always a Jew"—and then he nicknamed me "Moishe Buddha."

My application was shipped to Washington, DC and several months later it came back disapproved. I was very disappointed, but I wasn't crushed. The Army disapproved me on the grounds that, quote, "The claim was not based on a recognized religion." Now, Buddhism is probably quite a few thousand years older than Christianity, and maybe 60% of Asia is Buddhist. But, the Army did not consider Buddhism a recognized religion!

I decided to reapply, which you could do as long as the new application was substantially different from the first. I believed the first one was disapproved because the military didn't understand what I was talking about. So, in the second application I explained Buddhist doctrines more completely.

I also went to see an ACLU attorney, and we decided to file a writ of habeas corpus. We did this to force the Army to prove that Buddhism was not a recognized religion and to justify their decision to keep me in the military. We went into the District Court in Seattle, and of course, the Judge threw it out. But it did make the Tacoma newspapers which, I feel, generated more support for what conscientious objectors were trying to do.

Shortly after that I submitted my second application for CO discharge. Unlike the first one, which took months to process, this one came back approved in three or four weeks.

You know, to this day, I really don't think they understood what I was talking about. I've come to the conclusion that the Army let me out because they didn't want me to cause any more trouble. They didn't like going into civilian court, and I was getting too strong and too opinionated. Sometimes I think they let me out because they just didn't want to deal with me anymore.

Bill Burke

After AIT I was assigned to be a supply clerk. But, I began to feel guilty about helping the Army supply materials needed to carry on the war. I didn't want to hand out weapons and ammunition or to be in a position that was combat related in any way. So, I applied for noncombatant status as a conscientious objector. I didn't ask to be discharged; I just wanted to help people by being a medic or a chaplain's assistant.

After I applied for CO status they sent me to see a chaplain. He was a nice guy, military for twenty-some years. He had run into other COs in the past and was supportive. He interviewed me for a very long time and approved my application for noncombatant status. Actually, I had an effect on him. The Sunday after we spoke he conducted services at the chapel I attended. In the sermon he mentioned that someone had come to him to tell him of his beliefs. He said, "I've been in the military for a long time and I've been thinking one way for a long time and now I met somebody who has helped me to see another way." Then, he went on to say how easy it is to shut out ideas and never give things any thought. I was encouraged and impressed, because he didn't know I was sitting there.

After that I had to see a psychiatrist, a very degrading experience. Now, I was in a company with some certified nuts. I mean, these guys Article 15'd left and right, did drugs, hallucinated half the time—I mean psychos. They weren't going to see a psychiatrist, they sent me to see a psychiatrist!

The psychiatrist was an arrogant, uppity major. He picked up that I resented being there and asked why. I said, "I think it's a shame that I'm applying for CO status and I'm sent here to see if my head's on straight and yet I've got a first sergeant who's gone to 'Nam five times, trying for a sixth, and nobody's sending him over to see you!" I thought I floored him with that, but it never even registered. It was comical in a sense; but, he was so military that he didn't even pick up on it. He just went on with his questions, spending a full hour with me.

In his report he wrote that I was psychologically sound and clear for administrative or disciplinary action. In other words, he didn't give a damn if they hung me in the square. Frankly, it pissed me off, the low point in my quest for noncombatant status.

Finally, I was interviewed by an administrative hearings officer. We locked horns right off the bat; we just slugged it out. At one point he asked, "What if you were walking down the street with your wife and a guy jumped you with a knife?" I answered saying I'd try to disarm the guy rather than trying to kill him. And he said, "I wouldn't want to be your wife." I told him that was fine, because I wouldn't want him to be my wife either. The interview was one big confrontation, but he recommended that my application be approved.

It took eight months before my application came back approved. Basic training was the pits but waiting for the decision, in a combat unit, was ten times worse. I always refused to handle weapons and I never went into the field on maneuvers. They went into the field every month for a couple of days and I'd say, "I'm not going, period. This is a military operation, I'm pending CO status and you can not force me to go out there." They'd get pissed-off, but never physical.

My platoon captain hated me. I was a pain in the ass to him. He hoped that my application came back disapproved, because the first thing he was going to do was order me to carry a weapon. Then when I refused, he was going to march me over to the stockade. There was nickle-and-dime stuff like that every day. But, I wasn't worried; it was always just verbal.

A lot of guys were fascinated by what I was doing. They had no idea what was going on, but they respected me, because the captain couldn't do anything to me. They liked that. They couldn't buy into my beliefs, but they respected them, although most of them thought I was from Mars.

Bill Burke

Eventually, my CO application was approved and I spent the rest of my military time as a chaplain's assistant. Technically, I could not be a chaplain's assistant because the assistant is required to carry a weapon to protect the chaplain. So, my first sergeant, this tough talking, foul-mouthed, heavy drinking, woman chaser who'd been to Vietnam five times said to me, "You tell the chaplain you are going to be his assistant, and I'll protect the chaplain." He said, "Just do a good job, I don't want to hear from you." I told him, "Don't worry about me, I'll do a damned good job; I'm where I should be now." He said, "I know you will." So, this hard-assed guy took my side and that was it, I became the chaplain's assistant.

Michael Rosenfield

After basic training I got assigned to a missile site just outside of Pittsburgh, Pennsylvania. Our main job was to protect Pittsburgh from air attack. My MOS ended up being "Law Clerk, Clerk Typist," but my main job was to line the softball field and to pass out tickets for the Pittsburgh Penguins hockey games and the Pirate games. A fairly easy job; all you had to do was keep your mouth shut, but I wouldn't do it. I called myself "the model antisoldier." I did everything the wrong way.

At the time I was reading *The Autobiography of Malcolm X,* a very powerful book that had quite an influence on me. One of the passages in the book read, "Once the slave realizes that the slaveowner is no better than himself, he rebels." I typed this passage up on a piece of paper and put it on the board behind my desk. The lieutenant I worked for told me to take it down. I refused telling him it was a quotation from Abraham Lincoln. He said, "Take it down, you're not allowed to have it up." Meanwhile, there were all these gung-ho, promilitary slogans on the wall, "A good citizen is a good soldier," "Kill the enemy." All these insane slogans covering the walls. I said, "Wait a minute, look at all these asshole slogans on the walls. If you can keep that trash on the walls, then I can keep this here." He said, "I sympathize with your feelings, but it's against regulations, you have to take it down." So, I refused to take it down and they gave me an Article 15 for insubordination. I got fined $30 a month for two months.

Some of the other guys appreciated the fact that I was standing up to this stuff. They'd say, "We support you, but you're nuts for doing this." I said, "You're nuts for not doing it. You guys pretend you're good soldiers when you're not. I'm not a good soldier and I tell them." I wanted everybody to do what I was doing, but nobody else would. Anyhow, since the guys supported me, when the orders were cut for my Article 15 they distributed them through me. So, copies never made their way to my personnel file or to the finance office. I was never fined.

This event was a turning point for me. I came to realize that either the Army intimidates you, or you intimidate the Army. I decided I would intimidate them; they were not going to intimidate me—even if they gave me orders for 'Nam.

One day the general who ran the missile site walked in. I'd never seen him before. I didn't know him from a cake of soap. The guy was an alleged alcoholic who didn't know what was going on at the site. So, he walks in and everybody jumps up to show respect. I just sat there until he walked through. After everybody sat down this sergeant came over and said, "What the fuck were you doing? Why the fuck didn't you stand up when the general walked in?" I looked him in the eye and said, "Do you think the general stands up when I walk in?" He screamed, "AAAHHH!" I asked, "Is it in the regulations?" He said, "No, you do it out of respect for the general." I said, "Well, I don't have any respect for him. If he stands up when I walk in, I'll stand up when he walks in."

I got so rebellious I joined an underground newspaper in Pittsburgh. I was a reporter for them and wrote a column under the pseudonym "GI Joe." I wrote about how fucked up the military was and how fucked up it was to be in the military. I also covered demonstrations, draft resistance and stuff like that. I was very bitter about being in the military and wrote a lot about how we should stand up and do everything we could to stop the war. By that point I had totally lost my sense of respect for the military. It was totally alien to me, I knew I had no business being in the military. I knew I was in the wrong place, like being a stranger in a strange land.

Because I wasn't cooperating the Army gave me a lot of terrible jobs to do. Fortunately, they also made me the "gofor." I was sent all over the place and picked up the mail everyday. Well, I would read everything that came through and one day I came across a regulation regarding discharge as a conscientious objector. I did a double take, I couldn't believe it. I didn't know you could get out as a CO once you were in. I just couldn't believe it.

I read the CO regulations over three or four times and realized that while I didn't have religious grounds to apply, I did have the moral grounds that might qualify me as a conscientious objector. So, I asked for the application form and they said, "You don't want to do this, they'll never grant it." I told them this was exactly what I wanted to do, I filled out the forms and submitted them.

There was no question in my mind that I was a CO. I couldn't kill anybody, and even though I had a noncombatant MOS I didn't want to be part of a killing force. One of the things I did as a clerk typist was to type orders of people who were being sent to Vietnam. I realized I was typing orders to send soldiers to go kill people in Vietnam. So, I couldn't let the military do this to me, I couldn't let them control my life anymore.

After I submitted the CO papers I figured the Army would try to screw me. So, I got some help from a counseling service in Pittsburgh run by the American Friends Service Committee. There was a lawyer there who told me about the whole procedure, what to do, what to say, things like that.

Eventually, I had an hour-long interview with a major. He talked about fifty of the sixty minutes; I only got a few words in edgewise. All he talked about was why we should be in Vietnam, how important it was to stop communism, and how important the military was for the survival of democracy. He did say he had no reason to believe that I was insincere; and that was important, because if they found you to be sincere they would grant the discharge.

I also saw a chaplain. He tried to convince me to change my mind. He was military first and a member of the clergy second. He wasn't a CO and therefore he wasn't somebody I really could talk to. He wrote a three sentence report that basically said inconsequential things. It was very neutral; so, he wasn't going to help me and he wasn't going to hurt me.

One day I was notified that my CO discharge had been granted. I was so happy. It was like being let out of prison. I was screaming. I was running and hugging all the officers and everybody. I was just ecstatic!

Over the years I've wondered if I just wanted to get out of the military because I hated it so much, or if I really was strongly opposed to killing, violence and being part of a military force. But, I realized that those things are inseparable. I *was* pissed off at what the military was doing. I *saw* it in basic training, I didn't need to see it firsthand in Vietnam. I knew what was going on there. I've come to realize that I felt so strongly about being in the military because it was the antithesis of what I am all about.

Lou Judson

In-service, discharged CO
U.S. Army, 1971–1972

I saw military and nationalistic warmaking as ritualized bullying.

[AUTHOR'S NOTE]

Lou Judson lived on Army bases for the first eight years of his life. His father retired as a colonel in 1959. As a child Lou was quiet, describing himself as adept in avoiding confrontations. Lou's involvement with music and study of broadcasting led him to associate with members of the counterculture; people he considered to be "more radical than most kids."

For Lou, "The draft was unreal, something I couldn't imagine dealing with." Thus, when Lou quit college he never notified his local board of this change, nor did he ever apply for CO status. Lou received a total of seven induction notices, but refused to report the first six times. In March 1971, faced with accepting induction or going to prison, Lou reported to Fort Ord, California for basic training. He summarized his experience of basic training this way:

> I became incredibly aware of the inhumanity with which the Army treated people. The training was designed and calculated to humiliate and beat the humanity out of you. They tried to make you into an efficient machine. You had no free will; I felt like a slave.

Once, on the rifle range, he put down his weapon and refused to continue target practice. However, he agreed to continue after a thirty minute tongue lashing at the hands of his company commander. From that point on, he attempted to meet only minimum standards. Paradoxically, the very next day, Lou's company commander informed him that he considered Lou to be OCS material. Not interested in becoming an officer, Lou was eventually assigned to be a radio specialist at a nonfunctional radio station in Fort Benning, Georgia.

Unlike several of the other COs presented in this book, Lou had a relatively easy time of it. He experienced very little harassment after he filed for discharge. Indeed, an officer was actually helping him and others to get out of the service. Then again, in 1972, the Army was cleaning house; 80 percent of those who applied for CO discharge were approved, up from 55 percent the year before. Lou's narrative appears here and in Chapter 5.

* * * *

Shortly after I got to Fort Benning, I found out about the local GI coffeehouse and about the Central Committee for Conscientious Objectors. They put me in touch with a counselor and some other people on base who shared my views. The counselor they referred me to was actually an Army captain, who later became a major. He was expecting to get out of the military in a couple of years and was helping guys get out of the service. He counseled people off-base, in his home. He was open about it, he wasn't sneaking around; but, he didn't do it on Army time either. He gave me some pamphlets and talked to me a lot. So, I discovered what the requirements were for discharge as a CO and started working on it. I guess I had been in the military for about four or five months.

In a sense this was the first concrete spiritual experience I ever had. I had to document my beliefs and how those beliefs prevented me from participating in war. I had to think about things I never really thought about. Before this, I never had a concrete picture of what God was to me.

I didn't have a strong religious background in my home. I started going to church when I was a teenager because my parents thought I should have some religious training. But, I wasn't sent early enough for it to form the core of my beliefs. I didn't personify my beliefs like others did. For me, God was not a person directing things with His will; rather, I saw the energy of the universe, and everything that is part of it as divine. So, coming to a position of conscientious objection was not a spiritual or intellectual process; it was a very concrete sensation in my body. I just knew there was nothing violent that I wanted to participate in.

In my application for discharge I told them I didn't want to be in the Army and that I had a righteous, moral reason for not wanting to be there. When I was young I realized that bullies and people who wanted to hurt others were not intelligent and did not contribute to human well-being. As an adult I saw military and nationalistic warmaking as ritualized bullying. I was baffled by the thought that somehow the world would be a better place by killing people, or by one country being better than the next country. I found it hard to verbalize this; so, the challenge for me was to satisfy what the Army wanted to hear while being true to myself.

While waiting for a decision on my application I hung out with other people who were working on CO discharges or were sympathetic to the idea of conscientious objection. There were maybe ten or twelve people on the base who I called friends. I even stayed away from the coffeehouse in town. It was full of GIs and I didn't want to be around GIs.

The COs I knew were pretty independent people. We would hang out at the home of the captain who was counseling us, we'd watch television and get together for picnics and things like that. I hated being in a military environment; so, I separated myself as much as possible, only being on-post when required. I even bought a Volkswagen bus and lived in it. I parked it at the homes of my friends who lived off-post.

Once, I was driving it on-post and was pulled over and searched for marijuana. I didn't have any, but they spent two hours, with dogs, searching the drawers and the cabinets. They were overwhelmed with the amount of stuff I had in the camper, but after all, I lived in it, so I had a lot of stuff. They were real gung-ho about it, but they were totally inefficient; they didn't even look under the back seat.

I was in the Army exactly a year—had no rank at all—when I heard I was being discharged. One day, the entire base was called out to the parade field to honor some visiting dignitary. I was out there in formation marching around when this private comes running across the field yelling out my name. People pointed me out to him and he said, "The commander wants to see you in his office *now*." I thought I was in big trouble, but I hadn't done anything.

We were right out front of headquarters, so I just walked in. I was immediately led into the commander's office, stood at attention in front of his desk, and he said, "You're a free man, your papers came through, get out of here." I did exactly that. I left headquarters yelling happily. I told everybody I knew, packed my stuff and I was gone. It was great.

John Vail

By late 1968, a number of organizations and newspapers had been started by GIs at various military bases. The Army's response to this problem was to break up the groups by shipping everybody somewhere else. They finally realized that what they were doing was facilitating the proselytizing, because guys would go somewhere new and start another group.

I heard that an organization called "GIs United" was having a meeting at the University of North Carolina. So, I went to the meeting and got involved. At first, there was a core group of about seven guys. But, it grew to about fifteen or twenty. There were a few COs, some Vietnam vets and other antiwar GIs involved. Most of the guys were white, but there were three or four black guys who were active.

One guy, from the 36th Medical Company, was the first GI to get a CO discharge from Fort Bragg. After he got out he joined the staff of the Quaker House in Fayetteville, North Carolina. The Quaker House, and later a GI coffeehouse called "Haymarket Square," were our meeting places. We did the layout and typing there for the *Bragg Briefs*, a monthly newspaper we put out. Our first issue was mimeographed; the others were printed, with pictures. The blacks put out their own paper for awhile, but it only lasted a couple of issues.

We would print the paper; then, when we were off-duty, we'd go into Fayetteville with stacks to distribute. We'd find other off-duty GIs, give it to them and try to solicit twenty-five cent donations. We raised money from GIs and donated some of our own; at the time I was contributing about a hundred bucks a month to the paper. We were also getting money from some left political group, but they didn't try to control what we did or said. We did what we wanted to do.

We decided not to work underground, even though people were being harassed and shipped off to other bases. Our idea was to print our names on the paper's masthead as the editorial board. This made it easier to show that people were being harassed because they were involved with the paper. Civilian lawyers advised us against doing this, but I think it worked out better that way. We weren't sneaking around. We were more visible and we became an example to others. We could say to people, "Hey, they can't do anything to you. This is a free country, you can say whatever you want." Everything we did was out in the open. We had public meetings, we didn't have any secret programs or anything. It kind of took the heat off in a way.

Of course, we knew we were being watched by military security. They had their people attend our meetings and so on. Once I went to a gas station that I frequented, and the guy there said to me, "You know, watch out. There are people around here who are keeping an eye on you." Mostly, they just kind of watched, but some of our guys were threatened, and the Quaker House was burnt down, almost certainly on purpose.

We had two antiwar rallies in Fayetteville. About 500 to 1,000 people came to the first one, with a good collection of GIs. The second one had like, 5,000 people, and a lot of GIs were there. Jane Fonda spoke at the rally, so a lot of people turned out to see her.

There were also a number of other demonstrations organized by GIs and civilians. Like, once the civilians called for a GI strike and we went along with it. It wasn't a strike where people went AWOL; rather, guys went on sick call, filed for a discharge as COs, turned in their war bonds or made antiwar organizations the beneficiaries of their military life insurance policies, stuff like that.

We were real psyched about being in GIs United. We suffered a lot of attrition due to transfer and discharge, but other guys would replace them. Guys would come to meetings and maybe write an article once in awhile. Lots of other guys were sympathetic, but were too afraid to get involved.

Meanwhile, I had really good rapport with my first sergeant. I didn't fuck with him. He tolerated me and sort of protected me. He was a lifer, but I got along with the guy. He kind of liked me, but thought I had it all wrong and that eventually, I would straighten out. We were totally different, but I did a good job in the orderly room. I kept the records, filed reports and kept things in order. So, we got along. Once, he even gave me a pass to New York City, knowing that I was going to attend an antiwar demonstration.

When I had about ten months left I came down on orders for Germany. So, I applied for a CO discharge. I wanted out, but I also knew that by filing the papers I would be able to stay there and to keep doing antiwar work. So, basically, I put this application in to slow things down. I didn't care whether or not it was approved, and they knew that too.

The application for discharge was much more political than the one I submitted for noncombatant status. At the time, they wanted you to tie your objection to a belief system that was strictly religious. I stated that this was ridiculous; the government viewed religion as being compartmentalized, as totally separate from other aspects of life. My opposition was no longer strictly due to my religious beliefs; I was opposed to the war in Vietnam and how it was being waged.

Two months later this master sergeant asked me where the application was. I said, "I gave it to the company clerk." He couldn't figure out why it hadn't been processed. He'd ask questions and I'd answer, "Look, I gave it to the company clerk." Finally, he said, "Well, who is the clerk down there." I said, "I am." He started screaming for me to get the application moving. So, I sent it to him and he kept his eye on it from then on. When Washington sent it back disapproved, I didn't care. It ate up a lot of time and kept me at Fort Bragg.

My entire military experience was very compelling. I was very tight with the guys in GIs United. It was kind of fun, exciting in a way. It was very stimulating to be there and to do this as a member of the military. To be a GI marching in a demonstration with other GIs was just incredible. We were saying, "This sucks, it's terrible, it's a bad idea, and it's immoral." I think we had an impact in ending the war, because we helped to change public opinion and that was really significant.

Personally, I like how I dealt with the war and how I behaved. It was the right thing to do at that particular time. I was aghast at what I saw, so I told those people to fuck off. I knew I could play or not play their silly games, but I also knew I could fuck them back. That was fun.

Getting out was bizarre. Being involved in GIs United had been so consuming that I got out and couldn't figure out what the hell I was going to do. It was like, what now? I have been involved in other social or political things, but it's so different when you are the one who is being oppressed. Like, with civil rights, I join a picket line, so what? After that I go home; I'm not black, I don't have to worry about a job. Being under the gun makes all the difference in the world.

Jim Kraus

During the winter of 1969, huge peace marches were held all over the country. My wife and I, and at least four other sailors—all of us in civilian clothes—marched and went to a rally in Idaho Falls, Idaho. The next day there was an article in the local paper that quoted one of us. Within hours it got back to our chief. We were in deep trouble. The chief called us traitors and assholes; he cut loose swearing at us for fifteen minutes or so. Then he told us that our punishment for marching was to cut our moustaches off. He handed us a razor and we had to shave our moustaches off dry, in front of him. I can vaguely recall saying to him that we had a right to free speech, and him saying something like, "Not when you're in the military you don't."

Shortly afterward, I got sent to New London, Connecticut, to attend Submarine School. A lot of colleges were on strike about this time, including Connecticut College near where we lived. We went to a couple of rallies on campus, and at one rally, I got handed a leaflet about CO discharges. This was the first time I knew this type of discharge procedure existed. The leaflet was put in my hand by someone from the New England Committee for Nonviolent Action (CNVA), one of the oldest antiwar, antinuclear groups in the United States.

I started making regular trips to a commune where the CNVA had a farm. A fellow there alerted me to the Central Committee for Conscientious Objectors in Philadelphia, Pennsylvania. I sent letters to them and got back lots of information. It was just incredible, I went from knowing nothing about Navy regulations to suddenly being well informed. I recognized that the existence of regulations on conscientious objection was a huge act of humanity inside a system that seemed, almost categorically, antihuman and insane. And I decided that it was time for me to take action myself.

This was at the time of the National Guard's murder of the Kent State students, and I felt that the responsibility for their deaths was in a direct way tied to the military establishment I was a part of.

The guys in the civilian community told me about a base legal officer who was anxious to help. He worked in the Judge Advocate General's office. This guy was a full commander, and he was powerful. When Kent State happened, he sent a letter resigning his commission, though it had not been acted on when I knew him. Through him, I met three other COs. These guys were doing counseling on the base, but I don't know how extensive or how active they were. It was like an underground support network.

One of these guys lived right across the street from me, and he turned out to be a big help. Not only had he filed CO papers of his own, but he was a journalist. My writing skills weren't too bad, but he edited my work and was able to steer me clear of any number of pitfalls.

When I met my division officer and handed him a letter stating I was applying for a discharge as a conscientious objector, he didn't know what to say. He had never heard of the regulations and I think he didn't even know what "conscientious objector" meant. It was funny, because he was expecting to meet a new second-class petty officer who was going to work for him, and I threw him this curveball. It ruined his day.

The interviews I had with the captain of my boat were memorable. He was a pretty thoughtful man, and I came away with a measure of respect for him. His position was that submarines and the threat of nuclear war provided an umbrella under which the planet would educate and lift itself to a higher level of civilization. At some point, he felt, nuclear weapons would be done away with. I kept saying to him, "Well, you know, there's a big fallacy in this kind of thinking, because for the umbrella to exist, one has to have made a commitment to fire the missiles, right? Doesn't that undermine the moral aspects of this?" He said, "It's a paradox, but we have to live with it." I asked him, any number of times, "Would you fire the missiles?" He steadfastly refused to answer. But that forced him to think about

who was going to push the button when the time came to
do so. I kept saying, "Hey, the time comes every time you
ask that question." So, at a pretty deep level, I believe he
thought nobody would push it. I also think this captain
didn't want to push the button, either. He was just on a
career merry-go-round of some sort. As far as he was concerned the nuclear issue didn't have to do with the justice
of the Vietnam war or with his own moral responsibility.

He recommended against my discharge, in part because
he was awfully concerned about what would happen if I got
the discharge. Would ten other crew members then want to
file for discharge? Nevertheless, the discussions I had with
him were really important events in terms of the politics of
what I was doing, the way I was communicating what I was
doing, and why I was doing it. I was more and more convinced that I was really onto something. I mean, "the enemy," so to speak, began telling me I was right; my captain
was saying, "Hey, you do have the power you claim to have
as a single, individual human being." And the power was to
simply say, "no."

For the next two months, my life was radically transformed. I was flown to Spain and was, in fact, if not on
paper, transformed from a nuclear reactor operator to what
amounted to a boatswain's mate. I scraped algae from the
fins of the boat while I teetered on a fifty-foot scaffolding; I
peeled potatoes and scrubbed pots; I spent days on end
hanging onto a pneumatic hammer inside the dive tanks.
And I argued and fought with most of the chiefs who didn't
like me any more than I liked them.

There was one really nasty guy from Arkansas who had
been in for twenty years and was still an E–6 or something.
He slept right across from me, two-and-a-half feet away. He
made these constant comments and veiled threats. I finally
got something to nail him on, though. I'd been told to stand
watch by the gangplank where people come on the boat.
You're supposed to carry a .45 and I said, "I'm not going to
carry the pistol, I'll stand there if you want me to, but I'm
not going to carry a weapon." Well, this guy got irate, he
flipped out and threatened to shoot me. He said, "If you

won't carry it, I'm going to shoot you with it." Other people heard him—and he could have done it—I was more than a little worried about it. This guy was in bad shape psychologically, so it was a real threat. I thought, "Now I've got this asshole," and I wrote a letter to my Congressman. I also sent a copy to my commanding officer. After that, they moved this guy's bunk; and from then on, they watched what they said and did very carefully. Everything became very legal and tight.

By this time I was so fervent and so absolute in my convictions that I was ready to go to jail. I had it imaged out; I was going to go to jail. Then, I pictured that I was in jail. In fact, I wasn't even worried about it; I wasn't exactly looking forward to it, but I had really reconciled myself to doing it.

Two days before my ship was to set out on patrol someone came up to me and said that I had a long-distance telephone call at the rickety little telephone booth at the end of the dock. Nobody got long-distance calls that way. It was my wife. She told me Senator Ribacoff's office had called to say my CO discharge had been approved. I marched into my commanding officer's office; I mean, there was no formality at all to my knocking on his door and telling him that the discharge had come through. Somehow, he didn't seem surprised. I was just ecstatic!

I should say that despite some of the older enlisted men on the ship who were really, really angry with me, most of the people I worked with were supportive. More than one came up to me and said, "Listen, if I didn't have just three months left in my enlistment, I'd be doing this too." At that stage, people were really upset, everywhere, at every level of the military.

David Brown

The first time I went to the stockade nobody understood why I was there. They asked, "How long were you gone?" I told them I wasn't AWOL, that I disobeyed orders. They said, "You did what? What is this?" And, when I told them about it they sort of nodded and said, "Okay, that's your bit." I wasn't who they were, in terms of why I was there, but it was sort of the same thing; you know, they didn't like the Army either. So, we got along; it was okay.

Looking at it in cultural terms, basic training was a blue collar atmosphere; the stockade was the street. This was my first exposure to street life and it boggled my mind. The games those guys played with the guards were amazing. It scared me to death. They were disrespectful, they broke the rules, and I thought we were all going to get in trouble. But, I didn't understand it was all a game; the guards played these games, too.

Also, it was now far enough into the Sixties to meet some kindred spirits. There were some semi-hippies who landed in the Army somehow and were doing their AWOL bit. I realized that in the stockade, more than anyplace else, I was with people who were most like myself.

I had been put on CCCO's list of imprisoned conscientious objectors, and during Christmas 1966, I started getting Christmas cards. One day my pile of Christmas cards was bigger than everyone else's combined. For awhile, during mail call, they were calling out names individually. But, they realized that my name was coming up an awful lot; so, they started bundling them separately. I was getting embarrassed, and I thought it was time to share; so, I passed out my Christmas cards to the others.

We petitioned federal court for a habeas corpus, on the grounds that I was a conscientious objector and the Army, by refusing to recognize my status, was holding me illegally. On the day of the hearing, which was held in Trenton, New Jersey, I had to pack all my stuff and leave the stockade barracks. I spent the day in a holding cell. The Army thought the judge might rule in my favor; so, they

were preparing me for release. Finally, at four or five
o'clock in the afternoon, the order came that I wasn't being
released after all. The petition was denied and I was returned to the cellblock. That was worse than being put in
the stockade in the first place. It was a real low point, I was
frustrated as hell.

I did the rest of my time, and was released from the stockade in January 1967. Whereupon, wonder of wonders, the
Army expected me to continue with basic training! This
time they took me to the supply section, and again I
refused to draw my gear. They threatened to give me another direct order and to send me back to the stockade. I
simply said, "Send me back." It was getting tiresome.

I went back to the barracks to pack for the stockade. But,
lo and behold, I got called back to the orderly room. They
said, "We suggest that you apply for a CO discharge again
and we'll recommend that it be approved. We think you're
sincere."

This time I was able to put together a good package. But,
it took forever for a decision to come back. I applied in
January and I didn't hear anything until the end of May
1967. It was a long, long winter and I was getting real
antsy about it. I was still in the Army; I was very aware
that, even where I was, I was doing a job for the Army. I
was explicitly not willing to do that, it was not where I
belonged. I became especially aware of wearing the uniform and what that symbolized. By wearing it I felt I was
expressing my support for war; it became very odious. I was
seriously considering refusing to wear the uniform; but the
ACLU advised me to wait until a decision was reached on
my CO application. So, I waited.

During this time I was reading and becoming more antiwar. For example, around this time the "Fort Hood Three"
surfaced. These were the first three guys to publicly refuse
orders to go to Vietnam. A journalist from the *Philadelphia
Inquirer* came to Fort Dix and interviewed some guys about
the Fort Hood Three situation. After the article appeared I
wrote the reporter a long letter. I told him some GIs supported the Fort Hood Three and thought they were doing

something that was very important. My letter was printed, not as an editorial, but as a feature article in the *Inquirer.* Shortly after that, I was called into the orderly room; the brass was absolutely furious. What really galled them was I had typed the article on their own typewriter, in their own orderly room, and on their own paper.

Eventually, my CO application came back denied. Prior to this, I had prepared a statement saying that if my discharge was denied I was not going to wear the uniform, I was not going to do any work and I was not going to eat. I gave it to the company commander, he looked at it and said, "Go home, I haven't seen this; go home and think about it." So, I went home, called the lawyers and made my plans.

Originally, I was going to take sanctuary in the chapel. But, that didn't happen. Instead, I wore civilian clothes, the suit I got married in, and appeared before the company commander. He gave me an order to put on a uniform and to report to my usual place of work. I refused. He got his .45 and drove me over to the stockade.

I was not going to do any work, so at workcall, I stayed in the cellblock. An hour or so later the sergeant came through rousting out whoever was there. I refused to go to work. All of a sudden, I found myself face down on the floor with my arms behind my back. It was very quickly and cleanly done; I didn't offer any physical resistance. Then, two or three of them hauled me over to the orderly room.

Then, the stockade commander gave me an order to fall out for workcall. I refused and explained why. So, they took me down to solitary confinement and put me in a cell. Later they called me up, put me in a room with two sergeants and told me I was going to put on a uniform. Again, I said, "No." Well, they got on either side of me, pulled my shirt and ripped it off. They grabbed my waistband and ripped my pants off. Then they got me on the floor and pushed a pair of fatigues and boots on me. I was physically not cooperating; I just went limp on them. So, they just kind of shoved me into the uniform. They cuffed my hands behind my back and took me to the control area to wait for an escort back to solitary. I was determined not to wear that uniform and I managed to wiggle my pants off. There I was standing in the orderly room with my shirt on and my pants around my ankles.

They led me back to solitary, took the cuffs off and told me to keep the uniform on. They threatened me saying, "If you take that uniform off we'll break your arm." I reached up to unbutton it and again found myself face down. They took my glasses off and put restraining straps on me, leg cuffs, wrist cuffs and a strap to hog-tie me. They picked me up, carried me along the hall, got to my cell and began to swing me, "one—two." Then they stopped, took the mattress off the bunk and swung me again, "one—two," and Lord have mercy, I landed on the bunk. They left me that way for a bunch of hours, until they brought me supper. They said they would untie me if I would agree not to take the uniform off. I told them that was hopeless; so, they said, "Okay, stay the way you are." Sometime that evening they untied me, I guess they figured I didn't have to wear my uniform to sleep. They untied me, I took off my uniform and that was that.

Since I wasn't following their routine they said I couldn't have any of the benefits. They took the mattress, they took my pillow and they took my blankets. I was there with nothing but the metal plate that hung down from the wall for a bunk. That and a New Testament, one of those little pocket deals, which became my pillow. I kept the uniform off for a whole week in spite of the fact that all I had was my briefs. My lawyers were calling, so there was some pressure on them to stop abusing me; they also finally got the message that they had to give me back my blankets.

During this time I was also fasting, water and plain tea, no nourishing liquids; so, they took me up to the medical station every day, in my briefs, to weigh me and to check my vital signs. That was the routine, me hanging out in solitary confinement, doing what reading I could, meditating and getting letters from people I didn't even know. The letters were wonderful. Somebody wrote and asked if she could send curtains for my cell! I felt strong and very, very together.

Finally, after twenty-five days, they decided I was beginning to dehydrate and they put me in the hospital. I was under threat of being force-fed; but before that happened, on the twenty-eighth day, I agreed to eat. I rationalized that I did not want to force them to use violence on me. Also, I knew feeding tubes were a wretched experience. I made it clear that if they sent me back to the stockade I was going to stop eating again. As a prisoner, in solitary confinement, I was in a resistance situation, because being there was unjust. They had no right to have me there and I wasn't going to cooperate. In the hospital I was getting medical treatment, because my fasting had dehydrated me; that was okay, I could cooperate.

I spent the summer at the hospital while the Army conducted an investigation that led to my general court-martial. I was charged with refusing an order to put on the uniform, refusing an order to report to work, and for possession of civilian clothes while in trainee status. I was looking at a maximum sentence of fifteen-and-a-half years. However, the ACLU raised a stink about my being assaulted and tied up, and people had organized a demonstration, on my behalf, outside the gates of the base; so, the charges were reduced to a single five year charge of disobeying a direct order.

I had four lawyers at my court-martial, three from ACLU and a JAG officer. I stated my case and had a jousting session with the prosecuting attorney. The court-martial panel, of course, found me guilty. There wasn't much to dispute, the orders were given and I didn't follow them. Then they got into sentencing. My parents came in from Chicago and testified, my wife testified, my chaplain testified, and apparently the panel was impressed. They retired to their deliberations and sent back a question; they wanted to know if they could sentence me to a general discharge. Well, the answer was no; so, they gave me eighteen months and a bad conduct discharge.

David Brown

Being convicted and sentenced made a difference in what I was willing to do. Before this I hadn't been convicted of a crime, I hadn't even gone AWOL. So, I felt it was an injustice for me to be in the stockade. Once I was convicted I agreed to be put to work. I was returned to the stockade and a few months later was transported to Fort Leavenworth, Kansas.

Finally, at Fort Leavenworth, I ran into other COs. There were also political prisoners there, people who had refused orders because of opposition to the war in Vietnam. The COs tended to be religious individualists; so, there were fundamental differences and a self-conscious division between the two groups. The COs were putting in their time, the political prisoners were into gaming the system. There wasn't much organizing going on; but, a Unitarian minister came in each Sunday for discussion groups. A lot of the political people attended this.

For me, Leavenworth was a pretty low-key place. The majority of the prisoners were there for AWOL and desertion. It wasn't a heavy scene, but you knew you had to be careful. Everyone, especially if you were not real big, went through a sort of testing to see if you were going to allow yourself to be used sexually. I had to do some fending off and did. But, that soon stopped.

My initial assignment was KP. That lasted for a couple of weeks until they got enough new guys to completely replace our shift. After that, I worked in the mental hygiene section doing screening tests. But, prison time is blank, dead, nothing happening time. The routine is set and things sort of happen to you; you don't make them happen. I read a lot. Before going to prison, I loved to read, but I came to hate it.

I actually got out of prison early; every general court-martial conviction of a year or more automatically got heard by some review board; they reduced my sentence to one year. By the time these machinations were over I had already served more than that. So, I was called in one day and told I was getting out; I left Fort Leavenworth three days later.

Abraham R. Byrd, III

**In-service, imprisoned CO
U.S. Army 1967–1970
Veteran U.S. Disciplinary Barracks,
Fort Leavenworth**

*I oppose the war on moral grounds . . . on political grounds,
historical grounds, practical grounds, and ethical grounds.*

[AUTHOR'S NOTE]

During the time I was in the military I attended three
court-martials, including the one you are about to relive.
Each time, the accused was charged with disobeying orders
related to opposition to the war in Vietnam. These courts
were convened to try disobedient soldiers, but it was the
Vietnam war that was really on trial. In each case, men
were imprisoned for their beliefs, and each imprisonment, I
believe, helped to hasten the end of the war.

These court-martials were noteworthy for a number of
reasons. Most importantly, they exposed the class nature of
military justice which pitted officers against the rest of the
hierarchy; they also projected a model of resistance that
encouraged individual responsibility and action.

At a general court-martial, the accused is not tried by a
jury of his peers, that is, by other servicemen or even by
noncommissioned officers, but by his superiors. These latter, trained in military academies, or college educated and
then commissioned, exercise power over the accused. They
are people he has to salute and to obey. Obviously, it is in
the best interest of the officer class that all orders be
obeyed. The reasons men disobey orders, be they legitimate
or illegitimate, become secondary considerations, relevant
only in determining the penalty to be applied.

In the case at hand, the law officer who was holding court
attempted to make the Vietnam war irrelevant to the case,
a perspective wholeheartedly endorsed by the other officers

Abraham R. Byrd, III (Record of Trial)

of the court. However, in an incredible display of class divisions, two noncommissioned officers supported Byrd, and even his commanding officer, a lowly lieutenant, testified on his behalf.

The personal witness made by Byrd and other court-martialed COs did not go unnoticed. Other GIs, numbers of whom were also beginning to question the legality and morality of the war, saw men who were much like themselves standing up to the system. They saw that it was possible to refuse to cooperate, and that some would prefer to accept jail rather than to compromise their beliefs. This had a powerful impact in an organization that attempted to maintain strict adherence to rules and procedures. Thus, the position that men like Rudy Byrd were espousing served as a model for the more generalized resistance that was developing within the ranks.

Abraham R. Byrd's story is presented to you through the vehicle of his record of trial. This device is used to allow readers to more completely experience the self-serving arrogance of the military courtroom, and to allow you to savor the eloquent and moving testimony that was presented on that day. Enjoy.

* * * *

Abraham R. Byrd, III (Record of Trial)

VERBATIM

RECORD OF TRIAL
(and accompanying papers)

OF

BYRD, ABRAHAM R. III	SP4 E4
(Name)	(Rank)
COMPANY B, USAG, U.S. ARMY	FT. LEWIS, Washington
(Organization)	(Station)

By

GENERAL   **COURT-MARTIAL**

Appointed by   THE COMMANDING GENERAL
                            (Title of convening authority)

HEADQUARTERS, UNITED STATES ARMY TRAINING
CENTER, INFANTRY AND FORT LEWIS
(Command of convening authority)

Tried at

FORT LEWIS, WASHINGTON	27 FEBRUARY 1969
(Place of trial)	(Date of trial)

LAW OFFICER: Colonel John G. Lee.
PROSECUTION COUNSEL: Captain Matthew N. Lees
DEFENSE COUNSEL: Captain Kenneth B. Kramer

MEMBERS OF THE COURT:

Colonel Kenneth H. Davidson
Lieutenant Col. Stonewall J. Myrick
Major Ernest S. Williams
Major Jimmy L. Jackson
Major Jack D. Duval

Captain Lawrence S. Janof
Captain Robert G. Cartwright
Captain Laurence J. Andrus
Captain William D. Prior

DD form **490**   PREVIOUS EDITIONS OF THIS FORM ARE OBSOLETE.
1 June 64

DEPARTMENT OF THE ARMY
HEADQUARTERS, U.S. ARMY TRAINING CENTER,
INFANTRY FORT LEWIS
FORT LEWIS, WASHINGTON 98433

GENERAL COURT-MARTIAL ORDER   9 April 1969

Before a general court-martial which convened at Fort Lewis, Washington, pursuant to General Court-Martial Convening Order Number 23, this headquarters, 18 February 1969, as amended by General Court-Martial Convening Order Number 34, this headquarters, 26 February 1969, was arraigned and tried:

SPECIALIST FOUR (E4) ABRAHAM R. BYRD III, U.S. Army, Company B, U.S. Army Garrison, Fort Lewis, Washington.

CHARGE: Violation of the Uniform Code of Military Justice, Article 90

SPECIFICATION: In that Specialist Four (E–4) Abraham R Byrd III, U.S. Army, Company B, U.S. Army Garrison, having received a lawful command from First Lieutenant Donald R. Stauffer, his superior Commissioned Officer, to properly clear this unit and report to the United States Army Overseas Replacement Station, Fort Lewis, Washington, prior to 2400 hours 9 December 1968, in compliance with Special Orders Number 340, Paragraph 52, issued by headquarters, U.S. Army Training Center, Infantry and Fort Lewis dated 6 December 1968, an order which it was his duty to obey, did, at Fort Lewis, Washington at 2400 hours 9 December 1968, willfully disobey the same.

PLEAS

To the Specification and the Charge: Guilty

FINDINGS

Of the Specification and the Charge: Guilty

The sentence was adjudged on 27 February 1969.

LAW OFFICER (LO): This court is now convened. Does the accused desire to challenge any member of the court or the law officer for cause?

DEFENSE COUNSEL (DC): The accused would exercise his right at this time.

DC: Members of the Court. The purpose of this is not to challenge your integrity, of course, but for me to ask you questions, from which I can gather certain information, which may or may not be prejudicial to the accused. Captain Prior, what are your feelings about conscientious objectors in general?

PRIOR: No feelings really, whatsoever. That's his opinion.

DC: Captain Cartwright?

CARTWRIGHT: Well, I don't really have any strong feelings one way or the other as long as the individual is, in fact, sincere in his belief.

DC: Major Jackson, how do you feel?

JACKSON: I feel that they can be sincere.

WILLIAMS, DAVIDSON, MYRICK, DUVAL, JANOF, ANDRUS: The same.

DC: Do you feel that a person who refused to go over to Vietnam would necessarily be a shirker, a hippie, a coward, a communist, or something of that sort?

PRIOR: Well, a man that refused could be anything. He could be a Seventh Day Adventist.

DC: Do you feel that a person could still be a good American and not go to Vietnam?

PRIOR: Yes.

CARTWRIGHT: Well, to answer the first part of your question, I feel that this could be any individual and whether he can be a good American, this is solely in his own conscience.

DAVIDSON: Let's put it this way. I don't believe a man has to go to Vietnam to be a good American; however, I believe that as long as a man is wearing a uniform and has not been declared in an exceptional category, then he's obligated by the military law and the rules of the service to comply with his orders.

MYRICK: Those are my feelings precisely.

DUVAL, JANOF, ANDRUS: I agree.

DC: Could you state your feelings about the Vietnamese conflict?

LO: Now, counsel, that's going too far. That's not a proper question. What does that have to do with whether this man disobeys an order or not? I consider that question to be entirely immaterial to what we're considering here today.

DC: Sir, I'm trying to find out whether the personal feelings and opinions of the individual court members would affect the sentence they would give in this case.

LO: Well, you might ask in that manner. We're not going into the merits of the Vietnam war here, so let's go to something else.

DC: Gentlemen, in the event you found the accused guilty, would your own personal feelings about the Vietnam war adversely affect the sentence that you may give the accused?

JACKSON: Well, I would view it the same as his being told to report to another station in the United States. An order that he disobeyed.

DAVIDSON: Not in the slightest.

MYRICK: Nothing that would adversely affect the individual.

PRIOR, CARTWRIGHT, DUVAL, JANOF,
ANDRUS: No.

DC: Could you briefly state what you feel the purpose of a jail sentence is?

LO: That's an immaterial question. We won't answer that question.

DC: . . . [Are] . . . there any circumstances or situations in which you would be obligated to follow the dictates of your conscience, although you knew that what your conscience told you was in opposition with the law?

LO: I don't understand that question. I just don't think that question is proper either.

DC: Why's that sir?

LO: Well, I don't need to tell you why. I just don't think it's a proper . . . question. See if you can rephrase it.

DC: Can you envision any situation [where] your conscience would make you disobey . . . a lawful order?

PRIOR: Would I, as a career soldier, think of disobeying a lawful order? Not offhand.

CARTWRIGHT: There is a particular situation where this could occur, yes.

JACKSON: As long as it was a lawful order.

DC: If you were given what you feel is an unlawful order would you disobey it?

JACKSON: Well, I would question it.

LO: Well, I just don't know how anybody can answer that question unless you are confronted with it.

DC: Have you ever heard of the term "God's law"? Or "natural law" or "higher law"?

PROSECUTION COUNSEL(PC): I would fail, sir, to see the relevancy of that question.

LO: Well, I don't know. I think they could answer it.

PRIOR: There is a God's Law.

DC: If there was a direct conflict between man-made law and God's Law...

JACKSON: Well, I've never known a lawful order that went against God's law.

WILLIAMS: I've never experienced the conflict.

DAVIDSON: I feel generally the same way. I personally never encountered a conflict between the two. God's law is a personal thing... the laws of society or the laws of the military... are laid down very specifically.

MYRICK: I've heard of God's law. I've never experienced the conflict. I cannot answer how I would treat it without that experience.

DC: Thank you very much gentlemen.

LO: Very well, gentlemen... in this case the accused has entered a plea of guilty to the specification and to the charge and [during the out of court hearing] I accepted it. Therefore, no further issue as to his guilt or innocence remains to be resolved. Defense Counsel, you may proceed.

DC: I'd like to present Exhibit C... which gives the accused's conduct and efficiency ratings in the service. All of them are excellent except two... which were unknown.

DC: At this time the defense calls Specialist Byrd to the stand for a sworn statement.

DC: ... How old are you?

BYRD: I'm 25, sir.

DC: How much education do you have?

BYRD: I have a Bachelor's Degree... and I went to a school of medicine [for] three years after that. I was a member of two honorary fraternities, Phi Beta Kappa and Phi Kappa Phi.

DC: Would you state... the type of family you come from?

BYRD: I come from a conservative family who regards obligation, duty, and loyalty very strongly and very seriously.

DC: Would you state . . . your political, philosophical, and theological beliefs in relation to military service?

BYRD: . . . I have been a member of the Christian or Disciples of Christ Church from the time I was very tiny. I am still a member of that church and I was brought up in the beliefs of that church. . . They believe very strongly in an individual's right to conscience; that is, he must decide himself, before God, what his obligations are. Naturally, as with all Christian beliefs, we hold human life in reverence. I subscribe to that.

I have been watching, with interest, our involvement in Vietnam. I became very strongly opposed to that involvement on the feeling that there was no necessity for the war and that the wasting of human life was unnecessary. I had to decide how strongly I held these beliefs, whether it was something that was just off the top of my mind or something that I held deeply enough . . . to act on. I finally decided that I could not participate in the war in Vietnam in any way.

This raised another very strong question . . . what to do about the draft. The choices were: I could refuse induction or I could participate in the military and refuse only when I was called to participate directly in the war in Vietnam. I decided that the moral thing to do, the thing which made the most sense, was not to refuse induction, because I did not have an objection to military service, per se. I therefore decided to go into the military and serve until I was ordered to participate directly in the war. Knowing that this was a likelihood, I determined I should do everything in my power to avoid this confrontation, if I could. Therefore, I did talk with Army recruiters and told them about my beliefs [and] my very strong medical background.

I was persuaded by the recruiter to enlist for the infantry Officer Candidate School plan. His feeling [was] that I had a virtual certainty of a branch transfer to the Medical Service Corps. I talked to the recruiter and to the OCS people before coming into the service, and a number of people afterwards. Their feelings were that some arrangement would be made. Also, before I came into the service I made a notarized statement, on my Personal History Form, that I could not participate in the war in Vietnam. This was later added to my 201 file. It read:

> I, Abraham Ruddell Byrd III, do hereby state that although I have full intention to enter military service, I cannot, for reasons of conscience, participate in the war in Vietnam in any way. I make this statement fully realizing that this does not exempt me from being ordered to a position of participation in this war; and I am under no misconceptions regarding the consequences of my actions, were I to receive such orders and refuse to obey them.

Things really did not come to a crisis until I got to OCS. They became aware of the statement in my Personal History Form, [and] I was placed in holding status; they were unsure whether I would qualify for OCS. I tried to determine what chance there would be for a branch transfer [because] I knew an infantry commission was tantamount to going to Vietnam—and for me, that would be a straight sentence to jail; I knew that would lead me right into the conflict I was trying to avoid.

I found out there was no chance, whatsoever, for a branch transfer and realized I would have to drop OCS. I did, and shortly thereafter I requested a deferment from Vietnam based on my personal beliefs. This was returned without action, because it did not fit any Army regulation which would allow such a deferment. Very shortly thereafter, I was placed on orders for Vietnam.

Prior to this, I had talked to company commanders and chaplains, none of them could see anything I could do. Their advice, of course, was that I should obey orders. According to the principles I believed in, and had to follow, I could not obey orders. Finally, when I was placed on orders, [and] feeling that all recourse had been exhausted in the military, I wrote to my Congressman. On the basis of a letter that he wrote to the Secretary of the Army, I was placed on hold [at Fort Lewis] and a directive came down that I was to be counseled to apply for conscientious objector status.

I did make this application on 25 June [1968] and on the 25th of October, it was denied. On the 9th of December, I was on orders for Vietnam and I respectfully refused to follow those orders.

DC: What are your feelings about service in the military, generally speaking?

BYRD: The feelings I have [are] based upon what I have been brought up with. The social contract says that when one has the benefits of citizenship, the responsibilities go with it . . . you can't really take one without the other. Basically, you must go along with the law because this is what society is. I do very strongly hold to this position. The only situation under which I will consider violating a law is if there is, for me, conflict where I have to obey a higher law. In other words, if the law which I consider the law of God states one thing, and the law of the land states another, I must in good conscience, obey the law of God, even though it means disobeying the law of the land.

Still, the social contract operates; and that means once you have violated the law you don't try to get out of it. When you violate the law because of conscience, you have to accept the punishment for it. This is the position that Martin Luther King took. He violated the law because [he felt] he had to violate the law. He was [also] willing to accept punishment for violating the law.

DC: Why are you opposed to the war in Vietnam?

BYRD: It would be most simply stated that I regard it as needless. Now, this gets into a matter of religion. I hold human life in reverence and the most morally questionable act that a human being can commit is the killing of another human being. I regard war this way also; therefore, unless I was absolutely convinced that it was necessary, this is something I could never participate in. In the case of Vietnam, I am absolutely convinced that it is not necessary, and my actions stem from that.

QUESTIONS BY THE PROSECUTION:

PC: At the time [you enlisted] did you submit an application as a conscientious objector?

BYRD: No, sir, I did not. May I have the opportunity of explaining to the court the reasons for that?

PC: That's not the answer I asked for. When you submitted your conscientious objector application, did you know why it was turned down?

BYRD: Yes, sir. It was turned down because objection to participation in a particular war is not grounds for discharge.

PC: I assume there is no mandate in your religion that prohibits you or all members of that Church from participating [in Vietnam].

BYRD: Sir, the mandate of the Church is to obey the demands of conscience.

PC: Is it not in your conscience that the war in Vietnam, as you stated, is a waste?

DC: Sir, I'm going to object to that.

PC: He testified to that on direct examination.

DC: I don't like the use of the word "waste." It has. . .

PC: That's the witness's own word.

LO: Let's don't argue, counsel. The objection is overruled. Please answer the question.

BYRD: I did state that it was a waste; if counsel would prefer I can explain the meaning of that word.

PC: You stated also . . . is this true . . . that you would not participate in the war in any way?

BYRD: Yes, sir.

PC: You also stated in your [CO] application that the interests of the United States . . . were not served by engaging in that war. Would you care to explain that?

BYRD: Yes, sir. When one is faced with the position of having to decide what constitutes a just war, he makes the decision upon his own abilities, his own mind, and every scrap of evidence he can find. I oppose the war in Vietnam on moral grounds. I also oppose it on political grounds, historical grounds, practical grounds, and ethical grounds. Yes, I definitely do feel that it is not in the interest of the United States to be there.

PC: I notice with all the grounds that you stated you left out the word "religious."

BYRD: I stated moral grounds, sir. My morality stems from my religion.

PC: Do you feel that you have the right to decide for yourself the involvements this country is engaged in and whether you will participate or not?

BYRD: Sir, when human life [is] involved I feel that I not only have the right, but I have the obligation to decide for myself. This was the very basis of the judgments of Nuremberg, that the individual is responsible for his own actions before God, before history, and the rest of mankind.

PC: In other words . . . although this country be involved in a war . . . if you are not convinced, you will not participate.

BYRD: Sir, if I am convinced that the destruction of human life which would take place [when] I would be involved, directly or indirectly, is not necessary—I cannot participate.

PC: Could there possibly . . . be a war that you would feel justified to participate in?

BYRD: There might be. I don't know.

PC: I have no further questions.

LO: Do you have any redirect [questions]?

DC: One question. Specialist Byrd, would you comment on your answer "there might be."

BYRD: Yes, sir. The problem of conscientious objection and [who] is recognized as a conscientious objector is [that] a person [must have] absolute objection to war. [But,] a conscientious objector makes the determination that war is wrong based upon the circumstances that he knows. A conscientious objector, in this country, at this time, would be basing that opinion mostly upon the Vietnam war. An absolute objector then generalizes from that position. He says, "On the basis of my understanding of this war, and what I know of the past, I cannot participate in any war." I do not honestly feel I could make that strong a statement, because I just don't know. I know that I cannot participate in this one.

LO: Does any member of the court want to ask this witness any questions?

JANOF: Since you've had medical training, why would you object to being a medical corpsman?

BYRD: Sir, that is the hardest question I had to answer when I was deciding to what extent I would refuse participation. I decided that even though I would be serving in a life-saving capacity, I would still be participating in the war. It is the war itself, not just the killing, but the whole war itself I was opposed to. I felt if I participated as a corpsman I would have been doing a small good and a greater evil. In the sense that I am . . . now refusing participation, I feel I am doing a greater good and a smaller evil.

LO: Any other questions? If not you may be excused. Go back to your seat.

DC: I have here the accused's application for conscientious objection . . . I'd like you to notice that Lieutenant Donald Stauffer recommended approval of his application. Colonel Gilbert, the Adjutant General at Fort Lewis, also recommended approval. The Assistant Post Chaplain . . . stated that he felt the accused was sincere.

DC: I would like to read a statement . . . from the accused's first sergeant who could not be here today:

I have been in the Army for a total of nineteen years, which includes combat in Germany and Korea. When a man refuses to fight for his country my first reaction is to hate and distrust him. However SP4 Byrd's outstanding conduct and efficiency have led me to believe that he is very sincere in what he is doing. He is a man of unquestioned honesty and has the respect of the men in the unit. I would rather see him discharged for the good of the service than court-martialed, because although he committed a very serious offense, he did so because of strong personal conviction and without criminal intent. He refused orders in a very tactful and unbelligerent manner. SP4 Byrd is a man of outstanding character.

DC: At this time the defense calls Lieutenant Swick, the accused's commanding officer.

Lieutenant Swick, would you state your opinion of the accused?

SWICK: He is a very conscientious individual, very hard working. He takes the initiative [and] has done a very good job. His appearance has always been of the highest standard on and off duty. His military bearing, his manner, his courtesy have been of the highest caliber. I'm not in agreement with his views, but at the same time I respect his right to have them.

DC: Do you feel that confinement in this case would serve any useful purpose?

PC: Sir, I'd object. . .

LO: Overruled,

SWICK: No, I do not feel that a period of confinement would be serving justice in this case. He did disobey orders and the Army cannot accept this, but at the same time his crime has been the things that he believes. In my opinion. . .

LO: You've answered the question enough now. Let's not go into any philosophical reasoning for it.

DC: That's all.

DC: The defense calls Sergeant Screws . . . detachment sergeant at Company B, Garrison.

DC: Sergeant Screws, tell the court of the jobs [Byrd] has worked on and the manner of his performance.

SCREWS: Well, when he first came into the company I realized by looking at his records and his appearance that he'd make a good clerk in the orderly room. But, at that time, it was against our policy to use conscientious objectors due to past unpleasant experiences. Somebody in the Supply Division needed a clerk, so he went out there to work. He was there for two or three months when we had to pull him back. Our first sergeant wanted to have all the conscientious objectors right there, under his thumb. When he left Supply, [Byrd] received a letter of appreciation, because he was doing an outstanding job.

Byrd then took over the duty roster for the Inspector General. We had a perfect roster. Every task I ever gave him took a minimum of supervision. He's one of the most reliable individuals I've ever had work for me.

DC: What is your opinion of conscientious objectors.

PC: I object to that as being irrelevant.

LO: Sustained.

DC: Sir, could I be heard on this for a moment?

LO: No. You don't need to be heard. We don't need his opinion of conscientious objectors. It has nothing to do with this trial.

DC: No further questions.

PC: Sergeant Screws, . . . if a conscientious objector has been disapproved and he disobeyed an order, do you feel that man should go into confinement?

SCREWS: It would depend on his other actions . . . the character of the individual, his criminal intent, whether or not he had a belligerent attitude, and so forth.

PC: What you're testifying is that if a man politely denied an order. . .

SCREWS: Without believing it, yes sir.

PC: Despite the fact that he disobeys an order?

SCREWS: Yes, sir.

PC: No further questions.

LO: You may argue on the sentence, counsel.

DC: Gentlemen of the court. This is an exceptional case. This is, perhaps, the most exceptional case I have seen since I have been at Fort Lewis.

Specialist Byrd has a moral, religious code which he feels he must obey, regardless of the consequences. That consequence happened here, today. He refused to go to Vietnam. It is not a question of cowardice. I don't think that possibility can be raised in your minds based on the evidence and what you have heard. We may not feel he is right, but we must respect his beliefs. He has a right to those beliefs and he must be respected, because he is willing to take those beliefs to the extreme, to the ultimate end a man is capable of taking his beliefs. He is willing to undergo punishment and the disgrace of a general court-martial for them.

He is fully cognizant of what he has done. He knew he would follow this course of action long before he came into the service. He made his beliefs known before he came into the service and he has consistently stated his position. He never had any doubt from the beginning, when he donned that military uniform, as to what course of conduct he must take. I emphasize the word "must," not "like," but "must" take, in view of his philosophy and moral, religious training. He has done everything in his power to try to avoid being here today . . . believe me, a man of his intelligence could have avoided the service if he really wanted to, but he is not that type of individual.

He has come before this court-martial because there are no other ways open to him. His fate lies solely in your hands and in the hands of no other. Administrative means have been exhausted. I am asking that he be judged on the basis of the validity of the circumstances here, on his whole life, what he has done in the Army, his performance as a soldier, the testimony of the character witnesses, and the pure strength of his own personal convictions.

Specialist Byrd has made a contribution to the Army. He has served approximately a year-and-a-half. I would say, unpresumptuously, that he has probably contributed more to the service already than many of his counterparts that serve two or three years. He has tried to do the best he possibly can in the military and still obey the law he feels is higher.

Certainly, all these things should be taken into consideration. Gentlemen of the court I ask that confinement not be given to this man. No one would benefit by it, there is no necessity for confinement in this case.

I ask you to consider what you would do if you were placed in a situation where your conscience was diametrically opposed to the law as it exists. This question has existed throughout the ages. Is man ever justified in disobeying the law of his state when his conscience dictates that he cannot obey? The question has never been resolved and never will be. I submit to you that Specialist Byrd, with the beliefs he has, is taking the only course that he can, ethically and honestly. Thank you, very much.

PC: Members of the court. The defense counsel has presented the accused in an excellent light. There is no question about his character, background and that he could be a good soldier.

He enlisted into the Army . . . on his qualifications. Everything in this trial, everything that I've heard, everything every witness testified to is to what this boy wants. Everything revolves around the accused.

The accused did not want to go to Vietnam. He did not want to go, even under a noncombatant status. He sat on the stand and testified that he had religious reasons. Intermixed and comingled with that were political reasons, ethical reasons, and moral reasons. Moral reasons can be religious.

He doesn't want to go to Vietnam and he asks you to say there is a higher law. Well, for 192 years this country has been engaged in wars of one sort or another, [and] has called upon its citizens. I don't mean to wave the American flag, but the defense counsel stated this was an exceptional case. I'm raising the American flag for one reason, it is this man who defies it. He's a man that says, "I do not want to participate. I'll participate in the Army, sure, but not in Vietnam." He'll participate in the service, but the Army isn't built for show, but brought forth to engage in combat or to secure peace. I ask you, does it make a difference whether a man comes before you dressed in white robes, comes forth with an excellent background, fine character, fine conduct, and disobeys the law? Do we say we've looked at your case and you are a fine boy? I ask you, is this what we're building to?

Look at the violation. Many men have violated orders. Did we base what was done to them on their backgrounds, and not the purpose of the law? What is the more important fact? Is this discipline? Can the Army get along without discipline? Can the Army stand the chance of saying we don't punish people with a fine background?

Ask yourselves a question. If a man comes from a golden white background and commits a crime, is he not to be punished for that crime? Should we say that confinement serves the sole purpose of rehabilitation? This man can't be rehabilitated, but I ask you, is not the purpose of confinement also for punishment? Look at this case. Look where the facts lie in this case—there was an order disobeyed.

Is not the single factor of disobeying an order what's really in question here? You must decide the future course to be dealt to this man, and I submit to you that this court should come forth with a punishment that best serves the order he disobeyed and not his background. I'm sure you'll reach that decision. Thank you.

LO: Gentlemen, you are about to deliberate and vote on the sentence in this case. The maximum penalty is a dishonorable discharge, total forfeiture, [of pay and allowances], confinement at hard labor for five years and reduction to the lowest pay grade of E1. Sentencing is purely a matter of discretion, the maximum ceiling is nothing more than a ceiling, you are at perfect liberty to arrive at any lesser sentence that you deem appropriate.

You should have, in your closed session, full and free discussion; the influence of rank may not be employed in any manner in an effort to control the independence of the members of the court. To adopt a legal sentence, six of you have to agree.

Mitigation and extenuation has been presented to you today which you should take into consideration. You have documentary evidence which has been presented to you. Certainly, these are all matters you should consider during your deliberations.

And finally, in arriving at your determination, you should select based upon all the facts and circumstances of the case, the kind and amount of punishment which will best serve the ends of good order and military discipline within the Army, the needs of the accused, and the welfare of society. Do either of you object to the instructions I have given the court?

PC: No objection by the government, sir.

DC: We have no objections, sir.

Whereupon at 11:53 hours, 27 February 1969, the court was adjourned.

The court reconvened at 12:20 hours, at which point the sentence was read:

Confinement at hard labor for two years, forfeiture of all pay and allowances and dishonorable discharge from the service.

[AUTHOR'S NOTE]

After the sentence was read Abraham Ruddell Byrd, III, reflecting a high degree of military bearing, issued a snappy salute to those who had just condemned him to prison. He then executed a perfect about-face, clicked his heels and marched, with dignity and pride, off to jail. Jaws dropped in amazement. One could sense the gentlemen of the court questioning what they had just seen and done. Rudy had beaten them at their own game. I remember I wanted to start singing *We Shall Overcome*, but was afraid that somehow, they'd punish Rudy even more; it wasn't his style anyway, though I now know it would have soothed and pleased him. On that day, he taught me two things: that one could truly respect one's enemies, and perhaps even love them; and, by saying "no" and meaning it, one most assuredly could overcome.

Abraham R. Byrd, III (Record of Trial)

[POSTSCRIPT]

Following a review of the record of trial made by the Staff Judge Advocate General, Abraham Byrd's sentence was reduced to a bad conduct discharge and confinement for one year. He spent a total of nine-and-half months in the Fort Lewis stockade and the United States Disciplinary Barracks at Fort Leavenworth, Kansas.

CHAPTER 5

Later: The Past as Prologue

. . . if the Vietnam war demonstrated anything, it was that individuals and governments are quite distinct propositions.

Daniel Lang

Jeffrey Porteous

When I got out of the Army's prison I was as tight as a drum. I'd been run through the drill and it would take years before I would be able to say that I finally walked out of prison. I was on the edge for years. I was an angry man. That rage also traded over to people in suits and ties, to the establishment and to my country. That experience split my life apart in a way that made me feel like I had a life before the Army and a life afterwards—like I was two different people.

I don't know what it means to people when they see the flag go by, but I have a hunch it doesn't mean the same thing to me. I am a veteran of the Army's bootcamps, its infantry schools, stockades and Leavenworth penitentiary. I am a United States veteran who invested a little over three years of my young life in their institutions. But I cannot forget those other veterans, for I'll always remember I was not seeing the worst the military had to offer. They were putting that little show on ten thousand miles away, on the other side of the world.

People sometimes ask me if I was ever in the Army, and I sometimes tell them, all that I can. But there are times when I'll just say, "yeah," and let it go at that. You learn to pick and chose, you don't owe everyone the price of admission—except, perhaps, the young—because an assessment is made each time the story is told. And I already paid mine.

But, of course, you never stop paying. We live in a warrior society. This is such a matter of course, we don't even see it anymore. If you don't believe me, take in the nearest toy store, see what our country is manufacturing for its children's play. This is the horror, right under our noses.

In some situations I tell people I was someone who refused to go to Vietnam. For the most part, they're intrigued. They've never met a CO before and they want to get to know me. They'll say, "Sit down and tell me about it." That's nice, because there's not a lot of us out here—but there may be more than people know.

Jeffrey Porteous

To be an American, and to declare yourself a conscientious objector, is to enter into a life-long meditation upon good and evil; upon what is strength, and what is weakness; what is cowardice, and what is heroism? Each has to answer for himself, and then live with the answer.

Did I do the honorable thing by refusing to fight in Vietnam? There have been times I thought suicide the only honorable act left me. At times I've been hugely proud of what I was able to do as a very young man. Let me put it this way, given the same circumstances would I do it again? Yes, I would, over and over and over again. And my dreams have never told me I am wrong. Not once.

Ultimately, conscientious objectors are as common as dirt, and as old as time. Conscientious objectors are the young men who have simply said, "no," to the old men's wars. No to the sterile blandishments of: *Dulce et decorum est pro patria mori.* [It is sweet and seemly to die for one's country.] And yes to love, yes and yes and yes again to love. Hell, I think we are all conscientious objectors—until we are swindled out of it.

John Lawrence

I was an observer to a crime, a national crime. I'm still feeling guilty about participating—that I didn't do more to try to stop it. But, I had always heard love America or leave it. Well, maybe I do love America, much more than people realize. I would like America to be an upstanding nation with good morals and values, and an overriding principle of good will toward all. I mean, that's loving your country as much as going to a war and killing people indiscriminately.

Okay, if you were to sit down for an evening and try to chalk up something good about Vietnam, what would you say? Did we save anybody? Did we create good order? Did we rebuild Vietnam like we did Europe after the war? Was there a healthy reconciliation like we had with Germany and Japan? Let's face it, the Vietnamese people had a stronger will than we did, in terms of what their goals and objectives were, and they expressed it through their determination to stay with it.

My Vietnam experiences really hit me hard. When I got back I started drinking and getting into drugs. I had these night terrors where I would sweat through my bedding, mattress and everything. I'd wake up exhausted the next day, and I'd do it night, after night, after night. These were horrific, awful, black dreams—a lot of them about dismembered bodies. I'd wake up, stark awake, at night. I'd shoot up out of bed, at any sound, and I'd just be drenched with sweat.

My mind tended to exaggerate, distort or abstract these experience into—a feeling kind of situation—so, in addition to the grotesqueness, the dream created a feeling. This carried on for quite a few years; it was my penalty for going, I think.

I went to the VA in 1971 to get help. They gave me the Minnesota Multiphasic Personality Inventory. The counselor was listening to the World Series on the radio. He had his feet propped up on the desk and he said, "Have a seat." Then he listened to the baseball game for fifteen minutes or so. Finally, I broke in and said, "What do I do about these nightmares?" He said, "Don't worry about it, in time they'll take care of themselves, they'll go away. Your test shows that you're pretty well in the normal bracket, except for a bit of paranoia, we're going to send you home with some valium."

I went home. I didn't know that ten years could be forever. I waited for it to go away, but those nights were awful, it was night, after night, after night, after night and yes, in time, it began to diminish. But also, in time it began to take on other forms. I began to lose interest in everything, I didn't care about anything. I didn't care about a career, I didn't care about making money. I was just surviving. I did manage a job, somehow. But, for a year-and-a-half I dropped out and collected unemployment, that was my reprieve; if the government wasn't going to give it to me, I was going to give myself a chance to reconstruct myself. I've spent two-to-three thousand dollars of my own money for therapy, dealing with this Vietnam issue. The government gave me the GI Bill and a lower percentage rate on my mortgage, but the things that really counted—therapy, getting help when I needed it, I've had to pay for on my own. I've asked the government to compensate me, but it's not there. And I don't really expect the government to compensate me for it, because I'm a conscientious objector. I'm still "the enemy."

Stopping the war was also important to me when I got back, so I joined the street marchers; but that wasn't enough. Internally there was something missing. I needed to compensate for what I had experienced; so, a group of Vietnam vets got together and we started shouting on the street corners about Vietnam, showing movies like *Hearts and Minds,* handing out fliers announcing rallies speaking out against the draft. This was a catharsis, it was therapeutic. It was important for us to get all that gunk out in the open and try to get people to see where we were coming from.

We were depicted in the press as drug-addicted, crazed killers and it was a stereotype that stuck. The naive public bought the press hype about Vietnam vets. But we weren't

that way; we were just Joe-Blow citizen-soldiers that went
over, did what we thought was supposed to be done, came
back and found out that it was the wrong thing! So, in a
sense, because people bought the press hype about the ster-
eotypical Vietnam vet they were also buying themselves.
The gods have cursed us to believe our own propaganda and
so the reflection that Americans buy into is our own image.
As a nation we are all crazed, drug-addicted killers. Because, if Joe-Blow, working-class American can go over to
Vietnam and come back that way, then we must all be that
way. But nobody ever sits down to think this through. It's
scary when you think about it, because that was the whole
idea of the Nuremburg Trials. Who was doing all that mass
murdering anyway? Hitler? No way, the people did it.

It's hard to justify going to Vietnam. You know, war is
bad enough when it's given approval. It's Milton's *Paradise
Lost* when you come back and you find out folks back home
aren't really supporting it, at any level. The prowar people
were down on the Vietnam vet for losing the war and the
antiwar people were down on the Vietnam vet for having
gone. I'll never forget the contradictory position I was in
because I went over as a conscientious objector and came
back as a Vietnam veteran. I had people refer to me as a
"woman-raper" and a "baby-burner" because I was a Vietnam veteran; and yet, I was the one espousing principles of
pacifism!

There were mixed feelings, naturally. Some antiwar people were going, "Yea, the Vietnam vets have joined our
ranks!" The prowar people were going, "Those drug-
addicted, crazed killers, look what they're doing now!" I
know my family had a hard time with Vietnam. It was
kind of like a death in the family, something you didn't
talk about, and we still don't talk about it. Vietnam is a
very embarrassing subject. It's difficult. You just don't talk
about Vietnam over a meal. But, you know, even the Vietnam veterans were split over this. Half of them for it and
half of them against it, a Hatfield-McCoy kind of thing.
Some of the combat vets were very sympathetic, a lot of
them did feel like the whole thing was a waste—nothing

worse than to come away from the Alamo and realize you didn't need to be there in the first place.

I identified with the Vietnam vet in terms of the catastrophic quality of the war, and I knew then that I was split. I was in neither camp. If I were ever on the outside, it was when I came back. I was a fish totally out of water, because I couldn't be accepted by either side. It wasn't until ten years later that the antiwar people accepted me over the prowar people. I feel a great deal of camaraderie with the Vietnam veteran because we shared a common experience; but, I have to reject the Vietnam experience as being evil, dark, malicious, nefarious, however you want to describe it—the blackness. So, you see how those two operate at the same time. Not only am I a walking war memorial, I am a walking contradiction.

I think America really lost its identity over Vietnam. We are still trying to recover it through these remakes of the Vietnam war, you know, *Rambo* and *An Officer and a Gentleman.* Those movies are trying to reconstruct our identity, they suggest we're not such bad dudes after all, that we still have some masculinity left in us. You can almost look at this with a little bit of humor and say, "Give America points, they keep trying, they never give up. We'll go back and do it again."

We look for anything we can to fortify our image of ourselves. No one likes to think of himself as bad or evil or dark; and the Vietnam soldier doesn't want to think of himself as bad, evil or dark; and the American civilian that sent him over there doesn't want to think of himself as bad, evil or dark. But, I think if most Americans were honest with themselves they'd also be struggling with who they are, the good guys of World War II or the bad guys of Vietnam. Learning our lessons from Vietnam means accepting our darker side. Now, do people who see *Rambo* also see *Apocalypse Now?* I'd say watch *Apocalypse Now* if you want to see what Vietnam really was.

I had an insight about America. America never goes to war. It merely sends to war, a big difference. If the American population went to war, they would know what war is about, they wouldn't have to play around with it in the movies and write books about what it's like. They would know, just like the Europeans, and there wouldn't be any of this, "Well, these bad GIs, or these bad Vietnam veterans." We have to look at ourselves, everyone needs to pay the price. That was the unfortunate thing that happened to the Vietnam vet, he came back to owe up to everybody's guilt and to the "mistake." I'll never forget the feeling I got when one President referred to Vietnam as a "mistake." I mean, you can't believe how that felt. A mistake.

My CO experience has been the ultimate experience in my life. It's like taking a fork in a road and continuing down that road. I'm trying to rediscover who I am. You know, here I am forty years old and I have the dual identity of being a Vietnam veteran and a conscientious objector; I'm trying to reconcile those two. I feel that Vietnam was my failure and my conscientious objection was my success. I came back a little wiser, and I'm going to salvage something out of this.

I tell as many people as will listen about my CO experiences. About six-to-eight years ago I went to the high schools around here on a lecture binge. I would go classroom to classroom and tell them as much as I could. At first I was self-conscious, later I got used to speaking out and talking about it. I know that I have an unpopular view, but I don't know why it's so unpopular. I'd emphasize the casualty aspect, that war is a gruesome, awful thing and there's nothing glorious about it. There's absolutely no glory at all in war, just a lot of young men and civilians dying. Just a lot of death. You max-out on death in a war. I'd tell them that I never saw anything approaching the heroism portrayed in the movies. Rather, most people operate out of a great, intense fear and the ones that have the greatest adrenaline are the ones who do these dynamic things, but they're afraid, probably more than anyone else, yet they're classified as heroes.

One time, I was talking to a high school class and a kid asked me if I was patriotic. And I said, "I am the patriot." I am not going to back down, my experiences were too traumatic, too caustic for me to abandon them and say, "You're right kid, I wasn't patriotic, I was a coward." No way! Give me any male in this country who is willing to go through a combat zone without a weapon and see how much cowardice there is. Our definitions get all screwed up. The guy who is armed to the teeth with bandoliers and bazookas and antipersonnel gear, now he's a hero. The guy walking around with nothing but a soft cap and fatigues is a coward. We've got to start changing definitions. We have to look at masculinity. What is masculine? The big, rough, tough guy who is armed to the teeth, but inside is really stone afraid, just like me? What's he afraid of?

I'm sure I'm looked upon as a traitor, by some, for my belief system. But never did I say I would not serve my country. I just wanted to serve it in a way that was compatible to my belief system. You see, patriotism is an interesting thing. People somehow think that patriotism just is; but, patriotism isn't a given. It's a quality of feeling. Nobody can make me feel patriotic, nobody can make me feel unpatriotic. So, when the government asks you to be patriotic, they better hope there is a feeling behind that. They won't get much in return if there isn't any feeling. The greater the alienation, the more difficult it is to respond to the nation.

War is no longer an option. We can't afford to experiment with nuclear holocaust to find out if we can be pacifists or not. We have to be pacifists. That's the irony of this whole thing, we have evolved militarily to the point where we can no longer use our weapons. We can create more Vietnams, but all that does is undermine the moral fiber, the ethical values of our system. We truly want to believe that we are better than others, but when we experiment with these Vietnams we find out we are not.

I think conscientious objection is an intense belief system and its origin is based on a higher ideal. The fact that conscientious objectors exist implies a spiritual quality about human beings that can't go unnoticed. Metaphysically, there's a lot that I don't understand; but I know there's more out there than the physical realm. If I had nothing more than animal instincts, I would not be a CO. But, we are beyond animal instincts, and I think conscientious objection is a tribute to our desire to achieve the higher ideal. The reason it's a threat to those who buy into the destructive element is because it is more difficult. It's not an easy concept.

As a society I think we still perceive the world as a hostile environment, so when somebody comes along talking pacifism, that's a real threat to their survival mechanism. And so, for us to go beyond survival and accept the possibility that we can negotiate our differences, primarily our economic differences, well, that's too much for people. When your whole life is being spent in front of the TV set, drinking beer and watching football, you are not going to accept some yahoo who is standing out there saying let's not carry weapons anymore. It's just not going to happen.

Mike Ferner

While I was in the Navy I worked with the American Friends Service Committee, the Quaker peace organization. I went to their San Francisco office and learned how to write press releases, how to leaflet, and how to talk to reporters.

I also stuck with the ACLU case brought against the Navy for not allowing me to petition on the *USS Hancock.* The case was called "Allan versus Monger." Monger was the captain of the ship. The case had to be brought by another serviceman since I was no longer in the military. So, my friend who helped me petition had the nerve to allow his name to be put on it. We beat them at the first level of federal court. They appealed, and we won again.

There were a couple of other First Amendment cases that became part of this case. There was another petition case from the *USS Ranger,* and one from an Air Force captain raising the issue of hair length as a matter of personal expression. So, the ACLU combined these cases. We went through all the appeal processes, and eventually it went to the Supreme Court. But, the case was not heard on my issue, nor the *USS Ranger* petition case—it was heard on the haircut issue. The petition cases would win or lose on that issue. By this time, there had been enough reactionary appointments to the Supreme Court that we lost. We went that far, but we didn't make it.

I got discharged at the end of March 1973 and my boat sailed back to Vietnam in May. I joined the protest that was held as the boat sailed out of San Francisco Bay. It was kind of an emotional moment for me, because of the guys I knew who were going back to Vietnam.

I continued working with the American Friends Service Committee until I left California in September 1973. The peace treaty had been signed and things were beginning to wind down. So, even though I really wanted to stay in California, I packed up my wife and daughter and went back to Ohio.

I wasn't in Ohio a week when I felt all this fervor and interest that made me want to do something. But, there was nothing going on, there was no peace movement that I knew of. Well, I saw an environmentalist on the nightly news who was trying to do something about water pollution. So, I hooked-up with him, asked him if he wanted some help, and worked on that particular issue for a little while.

Then I started reading about nuclear power and nuclear waste, and I realized something was drastically wrong. Normally, I would not have questioned it, but I knew the public was being lied to about Vietnam; so, I had a very jaundiced view about other things that came from official channels.

The more I looked into nuclear power, the screwier it seemed. In 1975, I helped form an organization called the Toledo Coalition for Safe Energy. The process of working on safe energy issues and reading about other social issues brought me in contact with a guy who worked with the American Federation of State, County and Municipal Employees. I asked him about the union and what they were working on. He told me they were trying to organize a hospital in Toledo. So, I offered to give him a hand. Before I knew it, I was in there talking to the employees trying to get them to join the union. That campaign didn't work, but I began to look into unions more.

I slowly began to see connections between safe energy, environmentalism, jobs, and labor issues. After I'd been in the safe energy movement for several years it became clear to me that job issues, and the kinds of energy policies we pursued, were very much related. What turned out to be good for the environment, also turned out to be the best way to create jobs.

More and more, I had trouble fitting into the normal scheme of things. I didn't think my CO experience caused me difficulties adjusting, in fact I kind of wrote the experience off as an interesting chapter that was behind me. But when I got out of the Navy, I fit the "angry young man" picture pretty well. The things that were supposed to be important—like a job and family responsibilities—seemed to pale next to what I felt were burning social issues that demanded attention.

Before long my marriage hit the rocks. My wife told me she'd try and stick by me, even though it was becoming clearer that I wasn't going to be able to balance staying married and being a traditional breadwinner. It might sound odd to some people that there could be something more important than your family, but after my experience in the Navy, there were things I felt I needed to do, things that, more and more, were not related to my family.

A society that was ruining the environment seemed pretty screwed up to me, especially when such a thing was accepted without people fighting back. So, I fought for the things I believed were important; and I felt more at peace when I spoke out on things that were too important to ignore.

I've faced many frustrations in the safe energy and the labor movements, but it's good work, because it's doing something for other people. A lot of times it seems like I'm banging my head against a wall, but there are lots of good reasons not to despair. Things still get crazy and hectic, but these days I feel much better.

I see myself as part of a long line of activists that fight for social justice. I'll probably never see the things come about that we are working for, but to simply work towards them is a worthwhile goal. I might live to be fifty or sixty or eighty and I'll keep doing this. Along the way, I'll try to have as much fun as I can with the people I'm doing it with, and that'll be my reward.

On another level, I have signed the Pledge of Resistance as a way of protesting U.S. involvement in Central America. I saw Ron Kovic [author of *Born On The Fourth Of July*] speak at a peace rally a couple of years ago, and I was in tears. He compared what's going on in Central America with Vietnam. I could never say what he said, as well as he did, but in my heart I feel the same.

Mike Ferner

I joined Veterans For Peace (VFP) because the group made sense to me. Unlike the Veterans of Foreign Wars and the American Legion, which tend to support the administration and the Pentagon, VFP is interested in trying to change U.S. policies to be less militaristic. VFP members are doing this as vets, claiming a right to speak out, because we have served in the military, and we know there is a better way.

VFP members speak at local high schools about the military, Vietnam and U.S. foreign policy. This is something that is very important and very rewarding. It gives me a chance to talk about the real causes of social unrest in places like Central America, what happens when we take our government's say at face value, and what alternatives exist.

I also went to Guatemala, Honduras and Nicaragua with VFP. We saw the conditions there, and we listened to the U.S. embassy officials. They gave us the same rationale for U.S. involvement in Central America that I heard before and during the Vietnam war. I saw VFP members, combat veterans from Vietnam, stand up to these embassy officials. We told them they were lying to the American public, and that we would do our damnedest to see that they didn't get away with it. These veterans for peace were the truest patriots I've ever seen.

So, this government isn't going to do it again, not without discovering that people won't stand for it. You see, I've never forgotten that people in power are vulnerable, it was a sweet day when I learned this. Whether it's standing up to the Navy, trying to organize employees, going up against the officials of some utility company, or whatever, those kinds of people can't scare me.

David E. Wilson

There's no way I'd ever lay down my life, or the lives of my children for something stupid like Central America or any other conflict that vaguely resembles Vietnam. That is ridiculous. I would not go back and fight for this country unless it was directly under attack. In fact, I don't think I could go back into combat at all. I don't think I could do that again.

If I got into a war again, knowing what I know now, I'd probably be crazy, kill anything that moved. There's no way I could do what I did when I was nineteen years old. Emotionally, I don't think that I could cope with being totally defenseless; I don't think I could handle it. To be honest, I'm not real sure how I did it the first time.

In Vietnam I learned how to cover up my emotions, to repress everything. So, when I got back to the States, I didn't recognize my emotions anymore. It was like I didn't have any. Like, I got married for the first time about a year after I got back, but I'm not sure I felt anything even close to love at that time. I don't even know why I got married. In Vietnam I learned not to get too close to anyone, because they could be dead in a split second and I would have to deal with the loss.

I just felt numb for a long time; then, about seven or eight years down the road I started feeling things again. But, I didn't understand what I was feeling, my emotions were all jumbled up and inappropriate. I was confused and didn't know where to turn for help.

I talked with priests, ministers, and clergy from my parents' church, but I couldn't get any answers. Things just didn't make any sense. So, I got some psychiatric help; I'd sit there talking about Vietnam and crying. The stuff that I put under wraps in Vietnam started to come out, but I didn't know how to deal with it. I got to the point where I actively contemplated suicide, I even planned the method. I just felt like I couldn't take it anymore. I felt like I was being tortured and I didn't know what I had done to deserve it.

David E. Wilson

My second wife was getting upset, so she gave me an ultimatum to force me to go down to the Vet Center to talk with a psychologist. He asked a lot of questions and then showed me a list of symptoms for delayed stress syndrome. He said, "You know, there are thirty items on this list and you have given me concrete evidence that you suffer from twenty-eight of them."

I finally knew what was going on, so I joined the vets group there. Initially, that made things worse for me. I was so fucked up by the time I got through with that group that I wound up at the VA hospital. I took a leave of absence from work and spent two-and-a-half months with a group at the hospital.

I couldn't relate to a lot of the things other guys were there for. Some of them came because they killed children, or just due to the fact that they had killed someone. I was more into a guilt sort of thing, because of the guys in my unit who died. I felt guilty because I wasn't able to keep them alive. I finally came to realize that it wasn't reasonable for me to feel this way, that I had turned myself into some sort of superhuman, expecting things of myself that were totally unrealistic.

Luckily, I had a counselor who literally dragged me through my experiences in Vietnam. He wouldn't let me overlook any little detail and this is what finally straightened me out. I was an emotional wreck for several years, but I finally came out of it about four years ago.

Now, I'm much more in touch with my emotions than I used to be. I still have a lot of grief and anger about what happened, but it doesn't affect me as much anymore. My experience has left me with a deep feeling of mistrust for authority figures and human nature. I was also left with many unanswered questions about religion. Many decisions I make are based on an acute sense of my own mortality which Vietnam gave me. I feel like I went from being a child to looking at life like an old man, without the benefit of experiences gradually happening over my adult life.

Tom Cox

Becoming a conscientious objector got me involved in other social causes. What I faced not only taught me about Vietnam, but how our government and the economy works, how class systems come into play in war, and how the rich and the educated get draft deferments. I grew up politically, and learned there were causes everywhere that I could be a part of. I didn't have to go out and look for them, they were there when I got discharged and they're still there. I mean, there are social causes in my own neighborhood—people are sleeping in the streets. Once you are exposed to injustice, and you try to do something about it, you just can't turn that off. It doesn't end there, it's not going to end now.

My role is to do as much as I can to make people aware of what's going on. I try to make it easier for young people to get information so they can make informed choices. I tell people of my experiences, and compare what happened to me then, with what is happening now. I tell them about alternatives, that there are other ways, that it's not just a one-way street. And, if people choose to resist, I support them as much as I can. I talk about peace, weapons spending and nuclear power. I think I'm effective in informal, one-on-one situations, just by talking and bringing these things into casual conversation. My role, these days, is just to share what I've learned.

Tom Fischer

When I got out of the Air Force I felt really good about myself. I felt like I had won a big victory. But, there weren't any parades and nobody really wanted to hear about it. No one was there to pat me on the back and say, "You fought for your rights, good fight." So, it was a personal victory, but also an isolating one.

When I first came back I wanted to work for peace. I didn't know where I could fit in, because I didn't know anything about the antiwar movement. So, I came back looking for hippies, but this was 1972 and things had changed. I got trained as a draft counselor, but nobody was interested anymore. The draft was dead and high school kids weren't interested.

Then, I started to have a real hard time adjusting. I was always feeling pressure and would literally go for days without saying anything to anybody. I couldn't talk to anybody, I felt so bad I just didn't know what to say. Also, my mind was always going real fast, just spinning. I couldn't put things together, I couldn't make things fit and nothing made any sense. People didn't make sense, events didn't make sense and I was questioning everything—myself, people, the world.

I moved around a lot. In terms of visiting places, I'll match my record with any hard-core transient. I never stayed in one place very long, because I kind of wanted to hide. There were years where I was just a lost soul. Things just came apart for me. I was real, real isolated.

During those first few years I lived in a beat-up apartment in Toledo, Ohio. I didn't have any friends. I was scared, walking the streets at night, living on VA checks I got for school, but I had dropped out. I was in no shape, socially or intellectually, to go back to school. I was giving blood downtown—it's hard to talk about it—giving blood to make money, walking the streets at night, hanging out at bus stations, shit like that.

God damn it! Nobody tells you! Nobody tells you when you come back that maybe you'll have a hard time; and if you do, nobody tells you who you can call. They just dump you back. It doesn't matter if you were a guy in the field or a CO; you get on a plane and you come back by yourself, and you're dumped down in an airport. And that's it.

When I moved to the South, I kind of hid. I lived in the woods; shoot man, that was my life. I had a little house out there that I was living in rent-free, because I was fixing it up. I stayed there with my dog and my cat. There were deer and wild turkey all around. I had it made, I was away from the world.

You know, up until about a year ago, I didn't know what was going on in the world. I just stopped reading papers and watching the news, I couldn't handle it. It didn't concern me; I just had to take care of myself. It has taken me a long time; I've only started to surface in the last year.

I guess things just started to catch up with me. I started to meet some people, including the woman I'm living with now; she's been working in the peace movement since she was fourteen years old. And she has a little girl who I love, so all of a sudden, things are important. The future looks good.

I still got a lot of stuff to take care of. There's still a lot of pain involved. Like, for a long time I kind of justified being in Vietnam. I thought I was okay because I did the CO thing, and I never pulled a trigger. But, it recently occurred to me that what I was really doing in Vietnam was guarding planes. Those planes were flying 'round the clock dropping bombs and napalm on people. So, I had to face up to that; I couldn't avoid it any longer. The fact is, I did play a part in that. But, these days, I think, "What do I do with it?" I can let it destroy me, or I can do something about it. Now, I'm trying to do something about it.

I've become politically active in the last year, doing real good, powerful stuff. I helped organize a workshop for veterans to talk about Central America. We held it the same night the state's Vietnam Veteran's Memorial was dedicated. It was a real good workshop. Also, we had an all-night veteran's vigil to protest aid to the contras; we got all kinds of press coverage. We had Vietnam veterans staying up all night and saying to the government, "You are doing the same fuckin' thing you did in Vietnam and we are not going to let you do it."

I'm trying to get more veterans involved, because people need to hear about war, about choice and about conscience. Like, we go to the off-base housing at Fort Walton Beach, Florida. We say to the military people there, "We're vets, we'd like to talk to you about what's going on in Central America." We tell them about civilians being bombed and napalmed in El Salvador, and we make comparisons to what happened in Vietnam. We give them things to think about; stuff that I didn't think about before I went over.

I'm also hoping to make presentations in the local high schools. I'll talk about Central America and about registering for the draft. I want to help kids make the connection between registration, the draft and war. The recruiters are hitting the high schools real heavily now, especially the minority kids; I'm really angry about what they are doing with these kids.

So, I'm feeling real good about being a veteran these days. I feel good about being out there telling people not to rewrite history, not to forget, not to let people say that Vietnam was a noble and just cause. I tell people we can't put Vietnam behind us, we have to put it in front of us. We have to realize what we did to that country, what we did to those people, and realize that it's not our right to go into a country and level it for the sake of profit, security or whatever. And, people respond to me real well. People are listening. I'm exercising the power I didn't feel for such a long time, doing just what I need to do.

Lou Judson

That one year in the military undermined my respect for authority. I have no respect whatsoever for the United States government; it's dishonest, very inhumane and not democratic. Even if it is the least of all evils on this planet, I'm still bitter and distrustful. I have faith in the process, but very little faith in the people who have come through that process, even those I have supported in elections for Congress.

The Vietnam era is not necessarily something people are proud of, but I am proud of having been discharged as a conscientious objector. I stood up for myself, declared what I valued, what I wanted, and I got my way. That experience also made me more inclined to speak out against things I don't think are fair, and to support things I think should be done.

These days I would like to help prevent war in Central America, but I feel a sense of powerlessness. I'm a volunteer for National Public Radio and I'm really interested in making accurate information available. But, it's hard to counter the flat-out lies the White House puts out. I think it's important to raise consciousness. Education and providing information about what people can do is an answer. I'd also be interested in counseling people about the military and conscientious objection. It's important for people to know that conscientious objection to war is an option, especially since the draft registration law doesn't even state that this option is available.

Harold O.

I came back with stress caused by the intensity of Vietnam. I was like a lot of the guys who became known as "trip wire GIs," I went back to the woods. I lived alone and backpacked for two-and-a-half years. I outfitted myself with the money I accrued over there; I got a nice shelter, a good sleeping bag and good equipment. I backpacked across the Rockies, I lived in the Florida Keys in the winter, I fished the salmon in Oregon and the trout in Montana, and I watched the leaves change from Vermont to Georgia, driving down slowly in my car, and I just—got better.

But still, I can barely watch things on TV about Vietnam. It kills me. I'm in tears through the whole fuckin' thing. It was such an intense period of my life that I go through this cleansing crying, but when I cry I feel better.

Before I got drafted I had been on the verge of radicalism; but a year after I came back from Vietnam I realized that the American system was not so bad, that it does work. It just takes time; you can get thousands—millions—of people out there yelling and shouting to Congress and the President about the things we won't stand for anymore.

I couldn't understand what took the unions so long to become opposed to the war. Thank goodness they saw the light. Finally, when everybody had a "kid come home in a box," professional people also started speaking up against the war. Our movement never had validity until those people stood up. Before this, these people acquiesced, they kept their mouths shut. But, with the unions and the professional people involved we were able to bring the troops home. It just can't be the rabble of people, because the power structure won't listen.

In spite of everything said against COs, it is the way to be. But, it's tough, it's a tough row to hoe. I was lost when I said "no" to my draft board and to my country, because everybody else was marching around like lemmings. It was so much easier to join the bandwagon and get swept up into war.

Harold O.

Conscientious objection pushed me to the point of seeking until I found, and to focus on love. It's hard for anyone to understand that unless they've experienced it. But, when I'm around people who understand conscientious objection, I wear the fact that I was a CO as a badge of pride. So, if I can be known for anything in my life, this is it. I stood up. I said, "No, this is wrong, I don't want to do it, and I'm not going to do it." It changed my life and caused me all sorts of hardship, but I did it. I did it.

Michael Rosenfield

Before I went into the military I would say I was a liberal Democrat; but life in the military led me to adopt a radical lifestyle and radical political ideas. I came out, did a lot of reading on anarchism, and became a hippie of sorts—all because I knew what it was like to lose my freedom. I was very resentful at the way I was treated by the government. I had such a bitter taste in my mouth that I realized I could never go back to being the middle-class lawyer I once thought I was going to be. The military experience changed the rest of my life.

If it hadn't been for my military experiences, I don't think I ever would have adopted the politics I have now. I decided I never wanted to be part of the bourgeois world. I didn't want to be part of a society that allows the military to do what they do to wreak havoc on the rest of the world.

So, after I got out of the military, I joined a group of radicals and in 1970, formed the Pittsburgh Law Collective. We were interested in alternative lifestyles and alternative ways of practicing law. I learned military and draft law and did counseling for the Friends Meeting House in Pittsburgh and for the Central Committee for Conscientious Objectors. I was always available whenever they had someone who needed counseling. I even spent some time in New Mexico counseling military people who were referred to me. I felt very strongly that nobody should have to remain in the military if they didn't want to be there. I also felt that people shouldn't be forced to go in against their will. I realized I made a mistake by going in and I wanted to help other people not make the same mistake.

We founded the law collective on the radical principles of providing good legal services for not very much money. So, I've had a rough time professionally. Of the people who originally founded the collective, I'm the only one that's not making big bucks. All of my friends have joined the middle-class and have become bourgeois in their lifestyles. They no longer understand where I'm coming from; so, in a sense I feel isolated. They've all been bought off and they think I'm nuts because I'm not making sixty to seventy grand a year.

So, one of the reasons I am the way I am has to do with my experiences in the military. Having gone through that hell made me a much stronger person. And yet, I wouldn't want anybody else to go through that experience against their will. It made me appreciate things more and it taught me humility. I think I've maintained my radical principles, in part, because of how I got through the military; you know, I didn't breeze through with a physical deferment or something. I went through a very bad, traumatic experience that made me stronger and made it easier for me to adhere to my principles. I learned what can happen if you get co-opted; it's just so easy to say "don't make waves," it's so inviting. But, it was wrong for me not to make waves. Making waves made me realize you can overcome adversity and you don't have to knuckle under to the powers that be. So, being in the military was like having a character building course—not the character they wanted to build, not the "good soldier," but rather, the character of the rebel.

Stephan Gubar

When I came back, I was malnourished—I am 6′ 2″—I weighed 135 pounds. I couldn't walk, I'd walk twenty feet and had to sit down. I hadn't slept, effectively, in a year. I'd wake up with nightmares. My wife never woke me up, because she was afraid of what would happen. I was essentially unemployable. I would do things in extremes—it was a horrendous time, absolutely horrendous. Because of this, it was much easier to bury these things and not discuss them. Some seventeen years later those images are still painful.

I went to school, I stayed home and became a househusband. I got a job as a stockboy, even though I had a college education. People I worked with everyday had no idea I had been to Vietnam. Later, I got a job as a psychologist in Paterson. Again, people I worked with for eight years had no idea. My extremely close friend was one of the first people I spoke to about the experience. It was very disjointed, it was pure emotion, there was no logic or sense to it. Then, as I began to talk about the experience with my wife and my friends, I began to organize those thoughts to the point where I've spoken to a couple of classes about Vietnam.

I was really pleased when I did those classes, because these were young people who, at least, were confronting the issue of possibly being drafted. I hoped that in some way my experience was enlightening to them. I think it was valuable for them to find out what it was like to go through this. The only thing I can do is educational in nature; although, if my son were faced with the same situation that I was faced with, I would have no difficulty expatriating. I would never want him to go through those kinds of things.

Some of the questions you get from kids today are amazing. There's a lack of understanding and knowledge of what went on during that period. I don't mean this as a putdown, they just don't have contacts and we all buried it. I'm afraid of what kids are learning about Vietnam. They're learning this idea of welcoming home the Vietnam veteran, which I see as a lot of garbage. I have a sense that what's happening in the country now is that the war is being made "better," it's no longer this horrendous thing everybody participated in; now it's becoming a jingoistic kind of situation. And, people are going to forget. People are going to rewrite the history of Vietnam and it's going to happen again.

My concern is that it is going to happen in Central America. That's why the recognition of Vietnam veterans is now an important thing for the government. I think that's why the Rambo kind of shit is a big thing. I think that's why the Vietnam War Memorial in Washington has been changed. Changing the wall by putting in the statue was a horrendous mistake—but certainly planned by the government. I think it's a part of the way the propaganda is being spread, that Vietnam was really an honorable war, as if there ever was an honorable war. So, when eighteen year olds are sent to invade Nicaragua, or sent to support El Salvador, it will be another "righteous cause." That scares me.

I have trouble considering myself a veteran. I guess it's my image of what veterans consider themselves to be. I was like an indentured servant, forced to go and do these things against my will. Perhaps I was a willing indentured servant because obviously, there were other options—which I rejected. Also, I wouldn't like to think of myself as a soldier without a gun because that puts me a little bit too close to the people who were over there doing it, and at the time, at least, were glad they were doing it.

I'm a member of the Montclair Committee on Central America and the Rainbow Coalition. We organized a demonstration when Reagan came to Bloomfield, New Jersey this year. It was actually three demonstrations: we had a demonstration the day before, an all-night vigil the night before, and the demonstration the day he arrived. We were instrumental in getting hundreds of people to sign the Pledge of Resistance. We've done a lot of educational work, and we raised thousands of dollars for Medical Aid for El Salvador.

Also, each year there is a street fair in Montclair complete with jugglers and musicians. The merchants come out to sell their goods cheaply and so on. The Montclair Committee on Central America was also there this year. I was dressed as a waiter and the person I was with was dressed as a waitress. I carried a domed tray around; on the tray was pasted a large map of Central America with little army figures on it. I would walk up to people and uncover this tray and say, "Did you order this war?" We'd get numerous reactions but most people said, "no!" I would close the domed tray and the person I was with would hand them a bill and say, "Well, you're paying for it anyway." We got a lot of good reactions.

We were confronted only once by a storekeeper who talked about his military service and asked how I could do these things. My response was that I was in the Army, too. He said, "Well, I was in the Army during Vietnam." And I said, "I was *in* Vietnam. I have to do these things, because I don't want it to happen again."

I got old fast, I think that was one thing the war did for everybody. I've certainly developed more resolve. I don't think I'm as afraid as I used to be, not because I faced anything, but simply because I know I have to follow my convictions. I can't give in to my fears anymore. I can't let my fears stop me from being involved in civil disobedience on issues like South Africa or Central America.

There's still a lot of unsettled business, still a lot of things I haven't taken care of. One of the things I control all the time is the rage, because I know it's there. But, right now, I don't think I would like to lose that rage. I don't think I'd like to lose the anger. Because if I do, I might become very passive, not a pacifist, but very passive.

Another thing I have not yet come to grips with is my own regret for having served, for not following my convictions originally, for not maintaining my convictions and for being afraid of what those circumstances would lead to. I just want to make sure I don't allow that to happen again. I want to make sure my resolve is stronger this time.

I know the feelings and emotions I had were not just the feelings of a conscientious objector, of someone who was opposed to war, to killing, or to that particular war. I think these were emotions shared by everybody there who was sensitive to what was going on, by everyone who was human. I don't think conscientious objectors were necessarily any more sensitive. I don't think we were any more frightened and I don't think we were any more brave. I think we were just like everybody else.

Dave Billingsley

There were things about Vietnam that come into your person and are with you for the rest of your life. Smells, sounds. To this day, I'll be certain places and I'll hear something or I'll get a certain smell, and man, I flash. I'm back in Vietnam. Click, just like that. I'm back in a different world, in a different place and a different time. These are things you do not forget.

There's not a day that goes by that I don't think about the war. Not a day. Maybe it's because I don't want to let go, I don't know. It's with me. But, I adjusted really well to mainstream society. I feel pretty normal; there's nothing really the matter with me. And, I don't think about the war in an unpleasant way. I enjoyed the experience. I really enjoyed the friendships I made.

Vietnam taught me that there probably isn't a situation that I can't deal with. Vietnam taught me my limitations and capabilities. Under the right circumstances I could kill somebody and not feel bad about it—under the right circumstances. But, I don't have a hard time thinking of myself as a CO. The bottom line is I didn't have to shoot anybody. But, Vietnam did teach me that I have the capability to blow somebody away. I know I have that potential or instinct, whatever it is, a killer instinct, a survival instinct, it's within me. The other side of the coin is I also know I don't have the heart for it.

I have real mixed feelings about the war. Vietnam, if nothing else, was a conflict of emotions. You live for the day you go home, then it comes and you don't want to go home. You develop bonds with people, a rapport. I remember guys going home and just standing there, crying, tears running out of our eyes, hugging each other. I mean, I was closer to certain people at certain times over there than I'll ever possibly be with my wife. As corny as it sounds, it was almost the true, clear meaning of what brotherhood is about. It's hard to describe, because it's something you never experienced before, and you know you'll never experience it again.

Dave Billingsley

I have profound respect for the Vietnamese people. What they were saying was this, "We are a country that is centuries old and we've always been dominated by the Chinese, the French, and the Americans. All we want is the right to govern ourselves, however that may be, communism, democracy, nationalism. We just want the right to self-government." That's the whole basis of what America was founded on. I had no qualms about that. But, the problem with this country is we always paint ourselves as wearing the white hats. This is bullshit. We do as much black hat shit as any other country.

I'm glad I am an American, I'm proud I am an American, and I'm proud I served in Vietnam. I wear a Vietnam Veterans of America shirt because I get pleasure shoving it down peoples' throats; it's like, "You'd all like to forget, but I won't let you." Also, I feel bad for the guys who need help. The guys in the VA hospitals, and the guys getting disability checks slashed. I don't want these guys to be forgotten.

I kind of romanticize my experiences in Vietnam. I had some very intense, exciting and pleasurable experiences that make me different from my peers. But, there was no doubt in my mind that I was opposed to the war. I had no doubt that Vietnam was wrong, I don't think we should have been there to begin with. Vietnam was a bad thing, and I'm glad I was able to experience it from the point of view of a noncombatant.

Steve Akers

When I got out I thought I'd get a job, get married, get a house, but none of that really meant anything. So, since then, I have tried to find ways to translate the philosophical elements of going through the process of pacifism and the process of being a soldier into day-to-day experiences and challenges. Some I have worked out and some I haven't.

For seven years I worked with young people in a neighborhood center in Pasadena. I have also been involved in private efforts to generate creative learning opportunities for young people in a not-for-profit setting. We get kids to think about themselves by considering the potential within one seed. Our motto is, "You can count the seeds in an apple, but you can never count the apples in one seed." We work with kids who have been branded as "incorrigible." These are low-income kids and peripheral gang members who tend to fight one another. We try to get the kids to consider their common denominators, like their culture. For example, Puerto Ricans and Mexicans are all Latinos, so we explore some of their common history and culture. We have a youth club with kids from all races; we get them to shake hands symbolically at their first meeting. We try to make them imagine getting along with kids from the other side of town. That's as much of a challenge to them as is beating the other kids up. We try to get them to believe that they are just as much a man if they are able to shake hands.

We also try to teach them how to act, individually and collectively, to have an impact on what's going on in their worlds. The idea is to try to seek bridges between people, even though sometimes the government gets in the way. Politically, I'm trying to build more local self-reliance, and through that to help people realize that they do have an impact on society and can choose what they wish to do.

I think people are in process and for that reason I think it is good to allow an option like conscientious objection. The government sees things as either day or night, either you are a pacifist or not. I'm not sure things are like that; where people grow and learn, things are not so black and white. For example, back then, it was appropriate for me to be a 1–A–O noncombatant. Now, given my experiences, I am more of a 1–O type conscientious objector; I've moved more toward that end of the spectrum. I would rather do alternative service than be a noncombatant in the military. My own form of patriotism is working with kids. Now, I see defending our country as being able to respond with compassion, as trying to understand everybody else in the world.

I see everybody as a participant in the peace process, and personally, I've been in touch with peace groups doing work on El Salvador, Guatemala and Nicaragua. I'm also involved with "Operation California," which sends medical supplies to Vietnam. I've been in touch with the nuns who run an orphanage there.

For me, the whole process of the CO expression is ingrained within a person's heart. It's a primal scream, like, "War is an absurdity, it's an affront!" Conscientious objection is deeply held, but it can be learned, because intuitively everybody knows war is wrong. In our heart of hearts we know we are all one.

Jim Kraus

When I got back home I started doing antiwar work. I would always be the one who would go over and talk to the cops or the GIs. Somehow, I've always felt that this is where the real battles had to be fought.

During one antiwar rally someone got up and said, "You know, everything we are doing is totally futile here. We're not going to stop the war, but we have to do this. And we have to reconcile the futility of what we are doing with the necessity for doing it." I thought a lot about what he was saying. Now, twenty years later, it doesn't seem as futile as it did then.

It was of the same fabric as the power of a collection of individuals, of people, to make change on a local scale—to inevitably change things for the better. And what can be done locally, maybe even privately, can have altogether un-anticipated long-range consequences. We kids who didn't want to insult blacks back in St. Augustine squirmed and did nothing. A year later, in the same town, a little crowd of individuals set out to change forever—and for the better— the whole structure of American government, to make it, after hundreds of years of oppression, a government of all the people. I came out of the CO experience optimistic about the ability of the individual to have that kind of re-silience and strength. I think it's there, empowering the individual spirit.

To me, a conscientious objector is someone who puts the power of the individual above everything else, above insti-tutions, above even the institutionalization of war. A con-scientious objector is a kind of anarchist, you know—one who's saying "I have absolute power to determine my life and my relationship to the world, and to the society around me"; one who's saying, "I have more political power than any state, or any constitution." It seems a biological fact that the individual has this kind of power, yet I know social structures preempt this power at every step along the way. The conscientious objector is someone who recognizes this power at one point in life and validates it by taking a stand. By doing that, the conscientious objector is also taking one of the most profound political actions that any human being can.

David Brown

I got out of prison in July 1968, and I had trouble getting back on track. I was in a real drift for awhile. I drove a taxi part-time and worked half-time for the group called Clergy and Laity Concerned. They just loved having an ex-GI prisoner doing organizing for them. We held demonstrations against the war, did draft counselor training and we worked with draft resistance groups. I also did some speaking.

Once, I spoke at a draft resistance meeting at Yale University. I got up there and at some point departed from my notes and started telling my story. I just told what had happened to me. When I was done, I went to sit down and they applauded. Then, they stood up and applauded. They applauded for five minutes! I was amazed, I was just floored by this. After that, I became a little self-conscious and it was harder to tell my story.

I went back to school in spring 1969. But, the mobilization marches were going on, lots of antiwar things were happening and I decided to leave school. Stopping the war was all that counted. So, I spent three years with the New England Committee for Nonviolent Action in Connecticut. I did antiwar organizing and draft and military counselor training. I also got involved with the Black Panther Party in New Haven and did prison resistance support work at Danbury prison. After this, I went to Philadelphia to work with the Central Committee for Conscientious Objectors in a federal prison visiting program.

I'm a Methodist minister now, and I pointed to my military experience in my writings for ordination. I consider what happened to me to be a conversion experience. My life was simply turned around, both spiritually and politically. And, since that experience, my life has continued along that "need for justice" type of situation.

Jeff Engel

Vietnam wounded me, my beliefs, and my metaphysical relationship with reality. My involvement in the issue was so in-depth, broad and personal that I was wounded by it. The Vietnam experiences were exciting, perhaps the most exciting period of my life. Vietnam was a trip. Gosh, it was a vibrant, exciting time! But, I really think it takes second place to the healing event that is ongoing now.

Upon coming home, I got into a real abusive situation with myself and with substances. This was a response, not just to going to Vietnam, but to my family's, and my country's response to going to Vietnam, and to my being a conscientious objector. I can't remember what I felt like. But within four or five months, I knew something was wrong. I felt unable—I felt disabled. I felt unable, powerless, worthless, very bad when I came back.

The years 1971 to 1974 were a real disconnected time. I was having this vision of, "Okay, I have an experience that has impacted on millions of lives; I gotta' share this." I still had the missionary zeal, I was still on a spiritual quest, but I was not able to put it together. I was angry; angry, depressed, two sides of the same coin. I was ineffective and having failure experiences, being fired from jobs and getting into some real disconnected situations.

The Veterans Administration, of course, didn't recognize any problems at this point. So, as part of my healing process, I joined the University Veterans Organization, located in Eugene, Oregon. I was a leader among those veterans, the "sane" one, the "organized" one in the group. I was one of three founders who were "together," compared to others in the group.

The University Veterans Organization met for months, we talked, told war stories and helped one another. I testify that I still do not completely understand what those who actually did have to kill are going through. See, I was a combat veteran and I didn't kill anybody. I can't imagine what young men who actually did kill have to go through. I can imagine it intellectually, but I can't emotionally imagine what they go through. But, I empathize, I feel for them.

Other veterans in the group could not imagine being in Vietnam without a weapon. They often said, "You must have been a crazy dude." I heard that a lot. The experience of the unarmed conscientious objector highlighted the storytelling process because of the disbelief, the incredulousness of anyone being in that situation without a weapon.

I would hope that veterans, of whatever war, understand conscientious objection better than the average man or woman on the street, and would seek to search because of it. I also hope that legislators and lawyers who design civil systems would continue, on a national or global level, to design options for belief systems like this; but, I don't see that being the pattern in this country or in a lot of others.

It's extremely difficult to explain conscientious objection, just as it is difficult to characterize the Vietnam experience. Conscientious objection is a metaphysical experience; essentially, that is what questions of conscience are all about. It has to do with the division of mind and spirit that has characterized human history. The same is true with two veterans, one regular army, and one a conscientious objector. They can't totally understand one another's experience. No book, no life-long relationship can enable anyone to totally understand the experience. But, at the same time, the dialogue must continue. This question of conscience is part of the working-out of human history, part of the evolution of mankind.

Now, I am a teacher. We have a good social studies department which has a segment on Vietnam toward the end of the year. A fellow my age teaches it. He wanted to bring a symposium of Vietnam veterans in to talk. They had been very effective in other school districts. We talked about this with the entire department; they all felt good about it, so we took it to the principal. He said, "Whoa. I don't know if we better do that. You get a bunch of crazy Vietnam veterans in here and God knows, no telling what might happen. The community will get all upset. What if they use bad language or something? You know, what if they have a psychotic break or something?" And, he continually referred to using the resources we had here in the district, and on and on and on.

In his last comment to me, he reached across the desk, touched me and said, "Jeff, I want you to remember as long as you are here with us, I'll never let any of those 'conscientious objectors' talk in our school." I looked at my colleague and I said, "I guess we'll just have to use in-house resources for this." So, for the last four years I have been going up to this class doing "one man's point of view," as I indicate to the kids. I've been giving them an oral history when they could have had several points of view, if this principal had his head screwed on right. But no, we didn't want to shake the boat.

So, I feel like I am doing good things and I will continue. I feel like I can up the ante too. But, I need to define problems and intervene in them in the most effective manner that I can, as an instructor, as a teacher, because that's how I view myself. That's what I do the best. It is very cathartic and fulfilling to find a young man or woman listening and possibly understanding my experience, and changing their lives on the basis of that experience.

Now, I feel really strong. I know I do good work and I'm getting stronger and stronger. I feel more competent now, at age forty. I know that I won't lose the passion and compassion that puts me in conflict with people who are blind consumers of nationally advertised ideas. More, I see a great need to work on a number of things, beyond antiwar issues, that will improve the quality of life—spiritual and physical—for any number of people in need. That's my avocation perhaps, that's my mission. It's not to be a football coach anymore, it's to be a human being.

Richard Lovett

When I first got out of the military I was shell-shocked by having gone through that experience. I felt a tremendous amount of disorientation, and I was thrown into sort of a void. I had been called on to do something extraordinary, something that was beyond my powers to do. And having done it, I was left mentally exhausted and physically debilitated. I had felt a tremendous sense of power and self-respect going through the CO event itself, but once I came out of it, I was sort of catapulted back into my own private void. I was not functioning again. I didn't feel any of the resiliency that I had when I was dealing with the Army. None of that carried over, and I fell into a state of depression. Life after the military was sort of anticlimactic.

I retreated back into a private world. I lived alone, I went back to reading, and I was drinking much more than I should. I had no sense of planning, and no sense of the future. I found myself cultivating a very internal world, a world of sorting out very abstract sorts of things. It took me two or three years to work my way out of that.

If you are called on to do something extraordinary, things that violate a certain sense of boundary, you exceed the possibility of having the resources to do that. And that's overwhelming. We were just kids who had to do something extraordinary. It is like being terrorized, but at the time you can't admit the terror, because you have to function, perform and get yourself through that situation. All that stuff hits you after the fact, and I think that's where a lot of the anger Vietnam veterans feel comes from. We had to do something that was involuntarily thrust upon us. People were coerced to go through this, and it was a terrifying thing to go through.

The recovery process involves being able to integrate the power of your experience with its maturation over the years. Who we have become may be who we would have become anyway, I don't know; but that event sort of pushed the mark up ten, fifteen, maybe twenty years.

It's hard for people to sort out the fact that I am a veteran and a CO. It's too mind boggling and complex for them. I think that's because this country has all sorts of difficulty dealing with dissent. They can't understand how you can live and function in normal society and also be a dissident. You are not seen as a healthy member of the society. But, I have come to accept that you can be a dissident and get along in society. It doesn't mean you're ambivalent, it means you are clear about your responsibilities and actions.

Becoming a CO enabled me to clearly speak my convictions and to state them very powerfully, without any sort of equivocation. It has allowed me to overcome fear. I came to realize that to be alive means being able to overcome fears. To overcome fears means to overcome the fear to say "no." That's been the story of my life, to see and to speak to causes, concerns and values, and to speak right on the mark, as to what those things are in the world.

I'm very upset that history dies so quickly; in fifteen or twenty years people forget, and you have to be attuned to that. The Vietnam war is not part of the upcoming generation's history. But, it is part of the legacy, and hopefully the young have met people who were involved in that era, people who can translate what happened then to what is happening now in Central America. As appalled as I am, it is typical of the flow of history. People forget about wars very quickly. We have to be vigilant. There is a realistic prospect that given the opportunity, Reagan would go into Central America. People can't get caught up with thinking this is an ephemeral or innocuous thing that is going on. It's a real threat and we should treat war in Central America as an imminent, concrete possibility.

I would tell the younger generation to be aware that they have options, and they have to think of the options in advance of events that may occur. One of those options is conscientious objection, a conviction that stands for the principles of nonviolence. People arrive at conscientious objection on two levels, the instinctual and the political. The instinctual level is a disavowal of physically abusing another person, an understanding that doing so is a violation of human dignity. Level two is the political, a realization that violence on the level of mass terror is not a justifiable or a humanly dignified way of achieving certain ends. Conscientious objection is not just a subjective experience, there is a world out there, and through conscientious objection we give credence to those who would assert a commitment to peace and human dignity.

I also want to stress that we shouldn't have the burden of special qualifications to assert our political rights to conscientious objection. Until the day comes that conscientious objection is as acceptable—I mean as a belief that opposes wars, whether specific or generic—as other political belief positions, then we are not free nor dignified as a people. Our legacy, as I see it, is to advance both that freedom and dignity.

Finally, for myself, I can now approximate clarity when I speak about the war experience. Yet it has taken some twenty years to feel the clarity, to begin to say goodbye to the original pain. In fairness to others, such clarity may remain mired in more struggle, more time for healing. Others may have reached their peace much earlier than I did. Whether clear or pained in expression, the experience changed our lives, converted our personal lives to a testimony of history—a burden we carry for a country unprepared to witness such values of human dignity and peace.

CHAPTER 6

Two others: different folks

... I believe that the concept of the antiwar warrior
has relevance for everyone on this earth.

Robert Jay Lifton

CHAPTER 6
Two Others: different folks.

There were two other men interviewed for this book, Kendall Johnson and James H. Burdge, Sr., both Vietnam veterans. Because they did not fit the "operational definition" of a conscientious objector that guided this work, they were not included in the above chapters. And yet, after long and painful meditations, I decided I could not leave them out of this book. While these men were not COs in the formal meaning of the term, they *were* opposed to the war, they *did* seriously consider or proclaim their objection, and they *tried* to distance themselves from the killing. Their stories are powerful testimonies of what can happen physically and psychologically to men who get involved in wars they do not support.

Both defenders and detractors of the concept of conscientious objection might argue that these stories do not belong here, that they would be more appropriately placed in a generalized volume on resistance to the war. This may be true. Nevertheless, I realized that the Burdge story, a classic case of the average individual being railroaded by the Selective Service System and the military, had to be told.

Then, after consulting every other man whose story appears here, I decided Ken Johnson's story should also appear. This is not to imply that there was uniform agreement among the COs. Some felt the inclusion would detract from the book. Others, like Jeff Porteous wrote the following, "We cannot judge our troops by the military's rules. I recognize him as an ally. Glad to have him." Tom

Two Others: Different Folks

Fisher spoke most supportively saying, "His story points to the tormenting ambivalence, doubt and pain that many GIs felt while contributing to the military effort. The decision to participate in the military effort, to play the cruel game of the warmakers was not by any means, for most, a clear cut, black and white decision."

Except for the fact that Burdge and Johnson were in the military, their attitudes reflect those of a substantial part of the male population of that era. We must remember that the significant unrest in the military was merely the tip of the iceberg. Millions of other civilian males successfully manipulated the Selective Service System, others expatriated or went to jail. Fully two-thirds of all draft age males at that time (some 20 million men) did not don a military uniform. These stories, then, are about all young men who struggled with questions of morality and patriotism. They are about all who felt compelled to find any possible way to remove themselves, and others, from the evil they perceived as occurring in Vietnam. The Burdge and Johnson interviews, at the very least, depict the depth of that struggle and the consequences suffered from the choices they made.

Ken Johnson found an out. Jim Burdge participated minimally. Initially, they both tried to play by the nation's rules governing conscientious objection, but quickly found out they were not eligible to play the game. That is, Johnson could not express opposition to all wars, and Burdge was a victim of class bias—the draft board and the military simply ignored his claims for CO status.

Johnson, and untold numbers of other soldiers, sailors and airmen, became antimilitary and antiwar, but felt trapped by a system that used them in a cause they did not support. Although not formally or legally recognized as conscientious objectors, these men objected to and resisted the war in ways they considered appropriate. They resorted to a variety of legal and illegal actions to escape the moral dilemma they found themselves in. Ken Johnson was one of these war resisters.

Two Others: Different Folks

As a younger man, Ken could not honestly state that he was opposed to all wars. He believed in maintaining a military force and in defensive, as opposed to aggressive, wars. Ken anguished over the question of conscientious objection, and eventually decided that he did not qualify for CO status. He then joined the Navy Reserves, in part, to give him time to ponder the issue.

Within a few months of joining the Navy Reserves Ken became appalled by what he saw; first, during medic's training (which he then refused to continue) and later, as a seaman on tour off the coast of Vietnam. Three critical incidents turned him against the military and the war. Ken explained them this way:

> Japan was the home port for my ship; from there we dispatched to Vietnam. One time, one of the ships, the *Enterprise,* came into port. It carried nuclear weapons, and the Japanese decided to protest. I knew nothing about it. Suddenly, the MPs locked all the gates. There was a peace march going on outside. The MPs had their rifles out, and I realized they didn't want us to get to them. I watched the Japanese people walk by the post in a candlelight parade, and here I was in this welter of enlisted men who were screaming, cursing and spitting at them. At that point, I realized I was on the wrong side.

Later, off the coast of Vietnam, Ken reported the following incidents:

> First, we intercepted two coastal craft and—and just blew them up—just went over and blew 'em up. I'm not a fighter, but *this* was not a good fight. It was just unmitigated hostility.

> Another time, I was given a crew and told to paint a stack. The stack was real high off the water, the highest point on the ship. I had done some mountaineering, so the height didn't bother me. I got the paint, the

brushes and the crew. I made sure their life vests were on and said, "Okay guys, over the side onto the scaffolding." Well, this new guy, just on the ship, was afraid of heights. So, I said, "C'mon just go on over, you'll be fine." The guy wouldn't go over. Pretty soon, the Bo's'ns Mate, a real hard-ass, started yelling at me to "Get that son-of-a-bitch over the side!" The new guy was just a wreck, he was so scared he started to cry. The Bo's'ns Mate was still screaming, "Get that motherfucker over the side!" It was just awful, so I tied on the rope, and over the side I went. That was it, I had had it with the service and decided to get out. I could not live with this anymore. I was totally against it.

Ken began speaking out against the war, but found few antiwar sailors on the ship. He said, "This was real early in the war, a time when most people were prowar. I got a lot of threats, but I didn't get jumped."

After six months off the coast of Vietnam, Ken was desperate to find a way out of a war he considered intolerable. He discovered an underground network of sailors who used their training and positions to get others reassigned or discharged. He then enlisted the help of some sympathetic psychiatric aides, feigned illness, and was discharged for administrative reasons.

For years following his discharge, like large numbers of other Vietnam veterans, Ken suffered from the effects of Post Traumatic Stress Disorder. He reported feeling "massively at odds with my society." He said:

The main problem, for me, was accepting the fact that I allowed myself to be part of Vietnam. I never triggered anybody's death, or shot anybody with small arms, but I helped pass shells, and helped to keep the boat out. I'm reconciling that. Part of me gets things all settled and the rest of me is still digesting it. In some ways I'm pretty settled about it; it's just what happened. Other parts of me are more perfectionist. But, I accept the way I handled Vietnam. The way I ended that situation was appropriate; I can live with that. Well, perhaps I could have done it more honorably, by expressing my beliefs. I sort of wish I had taken a stance. Now, I know I am a conscientious objector; but then I couldn't take that step.

I went through a long period in which I was living a sort of a marred existence, dwelling on this horrible fact about myself. On the one hand, I had this set of noxious experiences and on the other, this failure to meet the challenge. I had a feeling of inadequacy that added up to a deficit mind-set. But, in the last three or four years I started to let go of it. I became more and more aware that I had a backlog of stuff left over from the war. Until that time, I wasn't too certain about this at all, and then it started surfacing.

It's sort of funny, and this may sound esoteric, but I think we sometimes take on negative identities; we do some things, that if all things were equal, could be seen as positive. The part of me that hasn't resolved all this satisfactorily wants nice, clear responses. It wants perfect, clear, simple, unequivocal answers, and I don't get 'em. The bottom line is I think I do more good now than I did back then.

Those who would pass judgement on Ken Johnson and other similar resisters should first consider how the nation's laws and military regulations were stacked against young men who came to oppose the war. One could not simply quit, as if it were a job, and go home. Reassignments were unlikely and discharges, for men of conscience or other antiwar veterans, were extremely difficult to get. Therefore, those not attracted to active resistance and those who could not fight back in other ways did what they could to gain a sense of personal control over their lives and actions. More, given the lie that was Vietnam, one must ask which actions were more untoward, the planning and conduct of the war by politicians and the military hierarchy or misrepresentations carried out by individuals in an effort to distance themselves from the lie? The answer to that question explains why Ken Johnson's story had to appear in this book.

* * * *

Jim Burdge naively believed that simply proclaiming CO status would keep him from being sent to Vietnam. He said, "I was a dumb kid off the street. I figured whatever the system told me must be right." He trusted them. Jim simply told his draft board that Vietnam was "no good," and he "didn't want no part of it." He did formally apply for CO status from both his local draft board and from the military, but they took one look at this gruff, working-class man of few words and simply ignored his claims; violations of the law in both cases.

Burdge knew instinctively that he did not belong in Vietnam. He went AWOL prior to shipment to Vietnam, and upon arrival in-country, was escorted through processing by an MP. He also never got R&R, because the military knew he would not return to Vietnam from leave.

Burdge was upset about performing duties in Vietnam, but he felt trapped and never took a stand against it. He said, "It bothered me, but I figured I had no choice. Either I did what they told me, or I'd be put in prison. I did what I was told." Although he wanted no part of Vietnam, he got more than his share. Assigned to an artillery unit he had fairly heavy combat experiences in Vietnam. At one point, his fire base was overrun and he found himself face-to-face with a sapper. Burdge shot him. He said, "It was either him or me. I felt like shit. My mind was all screwed up. It's still screwed up. I felt sorry for the guy's family."

At the time of our interview Jim was labeled as suffering from Post Traumatic Stress Disorder, and is also seriously Agent Orange afflicted. He told me:

> I can no longer work due to my skin condition. I have a rash growin' on my arms, my legs, and my feet. It's in my hair and it's growin' on both my eardrums. I get headaches, blurred vision, trouble hearing, severe chest

pains and stomach pains. I've been diagnosed as having ulcers, I get numbness in my feet and legs—probably nerve damage.

Sadly, his three children are also Agent Orange afflicted. He has a daughter labeled "perceptually impaired" with blurred vision, severe headaches and stomach cramps. One son, born with a double hernia and asthma, is neurologically impaired. His second son was born with no vital signs. The boy was revived and suffers from chronic asthma. According to Burdge, his son "takes enough medication for five adults." The child's lungs occasionally stop working, so he must be hooked up to a bronchial dilator three times a day. All this has made Jim Burdge a bitter man. He told me:

> As far as I'm concerned, my life was ruined the minute I was inducted into the service. I blame the United States government for what's happening to my kids, and I blame my draft board, too. Because, if they gave me the CO status I never would have gone to Vietnam and been exposed to herbicides and other illnesses that were transferred to my children. This country screwed up my life and my family's life; not just mine, but the rest of the Vietnam veterans. And I want something done; I want answers and I want them *yesterday*. Not today or tomorrow.

Jim Burdge is serious about getting those answers, and will. The government may have ignored the younger Jim Burdge, and his requests for conscientious objector status, but they are taking notice of him now. Since 1978, he has been active in Vietnam veteran affairs. For example, he works very closely with the New Jersey Agent Orange Commission. He has testified before Congress, the Veterans Administration and in federal court as a member of Chapter 12 of the Vietnam Veterans of America and the New Jersey State Council of the VVA. "Every time I go there," he said, "they get nervous, 'cause I don't shut up and I point fingers at them."

Jim also works with six different veterans organizations helping other veterans file disability claims. According to Jim:

Seein' what happened to the Vietnam veteran got me heavily involved. I figured somebody's got to be out there doin' something for them. I think the United States government sucks. I want somethin' done for Vietnam veterans. I want this country to know what the Vietnam veteran had to put up with. And, I don't want to see it happen again to anybody. It's not right.

As I shook Jim's blistered, salve-covered hand he told me, "I'm available twenty-four hours a day, seven days a week, to help the Vietnam veteran." As a 19 year old, Jim may not have had the strength to stand up and defend his beliefs, but he chooses to speak up now. He is a powerful advocate for Vietnam veterans and a forceful critic of imperial wars. He is a selective objector to war, and is educating others, while actively fighting for his beliefs. All major reasons why Jim Burdge appears in this book. Welcome home, brother.

AFTERWORD

The Choice, The Promise.

So, for the record, here is what conscientious objectors object to: We object to killing. We object to killing in the name of capitalism, we object to killing in the name of Communism, and we object to killing in the name of religion. We object to being forced to register for war and killing, and we object to being forced to participate in the preparations for war and killing. We object to killing innocent civilians, and we object to killing soldiers. We object to nuclear weapons, and we object to conventional weapons. When war comes, many of us will perform peaceful alternative service. Many of us will go to jail rather than compromise deeply held beliefs. But we will not fight. We will not kill.

Charles A. Maresca, Jr.

AFTERWORD

The initial plan for this book was to let the narratives stand on their own, leaving readers with their thoughts fixed on the men whose stories they had come to know. This focus on narration is, after all, the sum and substance of oral history. But the controversial stand taken by conscientious objectors is often misunderstood and disparaged by many Americans. Thus, it seemed important to supplement the narratives with a short discussion of conscientious objection and the more generalized resistance that occurred in the military at the time. This discussion is not meant to be a definitive statement on in-service conscientious objection or resistance in the military; rather it is a way to summarize some of the general themes that surfaced from the narratives and to consider the role COs played in that part of the antiwar movement.

As Jeff Porteous explained, "I was made in America." A revealing insight, and one that is significant in understanding conscientious objection in the Vietnam era. For, resistance to the war in Vietnam can, in part, be viewed as a natural product of the political, cultural, and moral socialization of the young in American society.

Weaned on the coattails of the nation's success in World War II, baby boomers learned that America could do no wrong; more, it would do no wrong. We were the good guys. Part of that legacy involved sitting tall in the saddle, perched and ready to join the fray, wherever our notions of freedom, justice and democracy were threatened. Every baby boomer's high school history book advanced the same scenario: America had become the greatest nation on earth, and as always, it was every young man's responsibility to perform military service to keep it that way.

Nationalistic bravado aside, the young also learned that one reason America had become great was due to the array of individual and political freedoms enjoyed by its citizens. The popular culture supported this ideology by providing baby boomers with entertainment promoting larger-than-life characters who dreamed those impossible dreams and fought those unbeatable foes. For example, as Lifton (1973) pointed out, it is not surprising that many Vietnam era veterans reference John Wayne as an important role model, not just for his patriotic swagger and hypermasculinity, but also for his portrayal of the honest person's quest for truth and justice. Larger than life, John Wayne always wore a white hat. And a gun.

Raised to believe in individual rights and freedoms, an entire generation moved, during the 1960s, to put that into practice. But, as Jim Kraus pointed out, there was "tension between conformity" and "breaking away to be very different." Unfortunately, at the exact point in life where the word freedom began to take on real meaning, the demands of the nation's war machine conspired to take much of that freedom away. Ultimately, belief systems came smack up against the reality of the Vietnam war, the result being that masses of young men could not jibe what they were taught with what they were being asked to do. As Jeff Porteous suggested, "Each had to decide for himself, and live with the decision."

Some decided to register their conscientious objection to the war, or to become resisters within the military. Despite the popular view, these types of actions did not reflect a lack of patriotism. Nor were these war resisters an unfortunate aberration that grew out of a tragic national "mistake." Rather, those who opposed the war, like those who supported it, were attempting to put into practice the very same values of truth, justice and honesty learned from the major socializing institutions that shaped their lives. These acts of defiance were rooted in the American spirit, and in a patriotism that demands resistance to intolerable laws or behavior on the part of the government.

Yet, in our increasingly militaristic society COs are often seen as slackers, cowards or traitors. However, resistance to conscription and conscientious objection to war have a rich and spirited history in our nation. Indeed, in 1789 James Madison attempted to include a conscientious objector clause as part of what ultimately became the second amendment to the Constitution. (Friedman, 1982). Madison's proposal to make conscientious objection a constitutionally protected guarantee did not succeed, and the struggle between the government's desire to raise troops by force of law, and the right of the individual to refuse to participate in the military, began. During the Vietnam era this struggle between state power and individual conscience rose to a fever pitch. The resistance to military service and warmaking was unparalleled in our history; it took on a variety of forms and complexions in both civilian and military life. Conscientious objection was just one form of that resistance.

The following statistics provide a general outline of personal resistance and antiwar activity that occurred in the military at the time. During the Vietnam era there were approximately 10 million men in uniform (about one-third of all males who reached draft age). Among those in uniform, 563,000 men received less-than-honorable discharges (including 34,000 who were imprisoned following court-martial). There were 1,500,000 AWOL and 550,000 desertion incidents (Baskir & Strauss, p. 115). The rate of AWOL offenses increased as the war dragged on, ranging from a low of 38.2 per 1000 men in 1968 to 84.0 in 1971. The desertion rate ranged from 8.4 per 1000 men in 1966 to 33.9 per 1000 in 1971. Nonjudicial punishment meted out by officers to enlisted men (Article 15 of the Uniform Code of Military Justice) ranged from 137 per 1000 men in 1968 to 183 per 1000 in 1972 (Cortright, pp. 12–13, 23). Added to this were escalating problems associated with substance abuse, petty and serious acts of sabotage, and assaults on officers and other cadre.

Afterword

This unprecedented display of disaffection and resistance within the ranks is neatly summarized by the following breakdown of disciplinary actions that occurred in 1971. Among a random group of 100 members of the Army, one could expect: 7 desertions, 17 AWOLs, 2 disciplinary discharges, 18 lesser punishments, 12 Congressional complaints, 20 marijuana users, and 10 regular narcotics users (Baskir & Strauss, p. 110).

Note the emphasis on escape revealed in these statistics, literal exodus through AWOL and desertion, or vicarious escape through substance abuse. Consider also, that for the most part, these were the types of actions taken by individuals, by those seeking some way to assert themselves in the face of a horrific reality that seemed beyond their control. Whether or not these actions are considered acts against the military or the war, this activity did demonstrate a high degree of discord among the troops. At the very least, these unfocused, mostly apolitical actions can be viewed as personal acts of indignation and resistance. However motivated, this activity threw a wrench in the military's well-oiled machine, a contribution to ending the war that should not be ignored.

Much more obvious antiwar activity also occurred on a fairly large scale. In a 1980 study conducted for the Veterans Administration, Louis Harris found that 9% of all Vietnam era veterans admitted taking one or more of the following actions: attending an antiwar rally, participating in an antiwar demonstration, writing letters critical of the war to an elected official or to a newspaper, or helping someone to avoid the draft (Committee on Veterans' Affairs, pp. xxviii, 346).

It is important to note that the categories used by Harris to define antiwar veterans were rather narrow, especially given the array of antiwar activity fomented by Vietnam era servicemen. Actually, while the sorts of activities posed by Harris could be, and obviously were, carried out by large numbers of GIs, they were the types of actions that are geared more toward the civilian experience. Note, for example, the absence of categories like applying for a CO discharge. Also, there is no mention of exposure to, or involvement with, a GI "underground" newspaper or a GI coffeehouse. Yet, these were perhaps the two most visible manifestations of the GI movement during the war.

Approximately 300 GI newspapers were published at some point during that time. Some lasted only a few issues, but others published for years (Cortright, pp. 54–58, 286). Relatedly, GI coffeehouses sprang up outside several major military installations, and despite ongoing attempts by local governments and the military to disrupt their operations, they served as a cultural and political hub for Vietnam era servicemen. In addition, there was an active attempt to organize GIs into a trade union, the American Servicemen's Union. Stapp (1970) reported that over 6,500 servicemen joined this organization by 1969, and their newspaper, *The Bond*, was widely distributed to tens of thousands of GIs worldwide.

Additional categories that are more reflective of inservice antiwar activity include: refusing to cooperate with superiors, disobeying orders, and resigning commissions due to personal beliefs. Other possibilities involve: counseling or helping fellow GIs get discharged or reassigned due to one's position on the war, or publicly speaking out against the war to one's peers or to superiors. Questions on sabotage, fragging and the disruption of standard operating procedures, as an expression of antiwar feelings, would also have been appropriate.

Even without this relevant information, the findings presented by Harris are significant. The 9% figure multiplies out to approximately 900,000 veterans who took part in one or more of the antiwar activities posed in that study, almost 1 in 10 men who wore a uniform at that time. One can only imagine how many Vietnam era servicemen would have been identified as antiwar veterans if more GI-specific categories were included in the Harris study.

It should be noted that participating in demonstrations was an activity taken with some risk, especially if the serviceman marched in uniform. For here, the resistance changed from individual acts of dissatisfaction to collective activity, and the military did not appreciate such public displays of discord. Several of the COs presented in this book were disciplined because they participated in antiwar marches or rallies. Most notably, Jeff Engel was escorted back to his base by armed plainclothesmen, and Mike Ferner was brought up on charges. The author was among a group of COs who were denied passes to Seattle, Washington one holiday weekend. An antiwar rally was scheduled to be held there; but while the rest of Fort Lewis was operating on a skeleton crew, COs from the holding company were ordered to perform spring cleanup details. The brass knew we intended to go to Seattle; I suspect they also knew that two of us planned to speak at the rally.

It is important to note that the tactics used by many of the COs were rooted in the classic techniques of nonviolent resistance. Its American tradition, espoused most notable by Henry David Thoreau and Martin Luther King, recognizes the primacy of conscience in breaking laws that the individual determines to be unjust; but at the same time, one has to be prepared to accept the penalty for such behavior. The adoption of these principles, combined with the extensive use of fundamental rights of free speech and association, was a trademark of the in-service CO, especially those seeking discharge. Indeed, these tenets were also a critical element in the larger GI movement against the war.

Virtually all of the COs knew their actions could lead them to prison, and many prepared themselves psychologically for that possibility. For them, jail became a viable alternative to further cooperation with the military system. As several COs pointed out, coming to such a position was no easy task. Desertion and expatriation were considered by some; but for these men, such thoughts seemed to be part of the process they had to go through in order to arrive at the decision to be jailed.

For the most part, the COs in this book stood their ground. If they were medics, they did their jobs, and almost to a man they resisted ongoing attempts to get them to pick up a weapon. As far as Jeff Engel was concerned, "It

was medicine I was preparing for, not war that I was training for." If they opted for a CO discharge they refused to
compromise by accepting noncombatant status. Tom Fischer summed it up well saying, "No matter what job I did, I
was still supporting and affirming what we were doing
there." If they were harassed or their requests for discharges were turned down, they either kept fighting or
went to jail. Said Richard Lovett, "Once the adrenaline
started flowing, everything seemed to fall into place."

As we have seen, some COs had few formal or informal
supports. On the other hand, many had civilian and peer
support, learning from and contributing to the ever-
deepening resistance to the war. But, if the experience of
the COs in this book is indicative of the general experience
of antiwar GIs, then few resisters had formal training in
the effective use of these techniques.

It should be pointed out that many of the COs came from
rather conservative backgrounds, and most had parents or
close relatives who had been in the military. Also, most of
these COs reported that as young men, they only had a
vague idea of what conscientious objection was all about.
However, probably due to knowledge of the civil rights
movement, many seemed to be aware of nonviolent resistance. Then again, among the men featured above, only
Stephan Gubar, Harold O. and John Vail had more than a
passing exposure to the use of these techniques. It appears
that the COs came to utilize these tactics by translating
their knowledge of nonviolent action and the Bill of Rights
into personal, and sometimes collective, action. In effect,
they acquired "on the job training" in resistance and organizing. For many, this was triggered by their military experiences and it snowballed as they fought to maintain their
convictions, and to stop the killing of Americans and
Southeast Asians.

Many COs functioned as sounding boards for their peers
who were having problems coming to grips with military
life or the war. The COs affected a model of personal resistance that helped make it possible for others to question
and to look for alternatives to what they were being asked

to do. Jeff Porteous and others pointed out that GIs often approached them to find out about conscientious objection. Relationships developed from there, and some men began to look to them for support and help with a variety of problems. John Vail and I actually had drill instructors and other noncommissioned officers refer men to us who were interested in conscientious objection, or who needed assistance with other military related problems.

Of course, those COs who functioned as medics were actively sought out as both healers and confidants. They enjoyed the acceptance of their peers, and received a goodly measure of respect from the brass. Thus, consciously or unconsciously, the COs became helpers and organizers. Their message may have been unusual, but it was often accepted as a voice of reason during a confusing time and in an atmosphere that often reeked of meanness and violence.

The COs demonstrated how the individual could stand up to what was going on. Their very presence made it possible for others to begin to question the validity of the war and their role in it. The COs were able to suggest to others that they may be feeling bad about participating in the war because the war was bad; and that under those historical conditions, activities like disrupting the military and working for peace were expressions of patriotism. Said John Lawrence, "I am the patriot."

But, like Vietnam combat soldiers who felt they were fighting their own individual war for survival, COs and other antiwar GIs also often struggled on their own. Mike Ferner expressed this sense of being isolated most eloquently. Among the thousands of men on his ship, he knew only a handful of others who were taking direct action to resist the war. As you may recall, at one point these feelings of isolation and self-doubt caused him to question his actions and his sanity.

A similar phenomenon is noted by Lifton (1973). He reported on a handful of men who did not participate in the massacre of civilians at the village of My Lai, Vietnam. One particular young man thought he must be crazy because he did not participate in the slaughter. Lifton re-

Afterword

ported that this man, and the few others who had not killed, felt uneasy, were ostracized and spoke cautiously to others about that event. They thought there was something wrong with them for refusing to participate in the massacre. Thus, Vietnam era veterans who chose to separate themselves from the military program, either by becoming antiwar GIs or by drawing the line at participating in certain actions, often suffered as much self-doubt and guilt as those combat veterans who later came to question what they had been forced to do.

To underscore this point, note the experiences of Post Traumatic Stress Disorder reported by those COs who were combat medics. Many of the classic symptoms are there: night terrors, guilt, escapism and rage. As Dave Billingsley expressed it, "There's not a day that goes by that I don't think about the war."

This generation of warriors and war resisters remains uncertain about the "correctness" of their actions. The warriors report rejection, remorse and uncertainty. Many antiwar veterans feel the same, and some also struggle with the contradiction of being both a GI and a resister. Some think they did not do enough to distance themselves from the war. Others, purposefully, are still "outsiders on the inside"; radicalized, they channel their rage over what happened to them in the military into progressive political activity. It is suggested that whether one opposed the war or actively participated in it, whether one served as a healer, or got caught up in unnecessary killing, the moral and ethical dilemmas raised by the very fact of America's presence in Vietnam were often overwhelming. Vietnam was Vietnam, and being caught up in it, on any level, hurt. It hurt bad.

As we have seen, resistance to the war was often personally motivated, and for the most part, diffused and decentralized. Then again, there were many who were politically motivated to end the war. Some of these were also conscientious objectors, and vice versa. But as a group, I consider the politically motivated young men who joined to organize their peers as the heart of the resistance; and although

Afterword

many conscientious objectors would take a more reserved position on this, I see the COs as its spirit, the moral center of the in-service resistance to the war.

As more and more GIs came to oppose the war, this generation of citizen-soldiers seized history. As servicemen slowly rising up in resistance, they not only helped to put an end to conscription, they hastened the end of the war. They may have also set the stage for similar revolts by citizen-soldiers elsewhere.

I say this because in theory, the Nuremberg Principles make every citizen and soldier accountable for their actions, and for the actions of their governments. Now, following the Vietnam experience, new generations of servicemen and servicewomen have the actions and example of American antiwar veterans to study, emulate or adapt. They know that through their acts of resistance they can have an effect on military and political decision making.

There are indications that this blending of theory and action is occurring, both here and abroad. Continuing to spearhead the resistance, American GIs have come forward to object to aggression in Central America, and to expose violations of law in that conflict. Also, in the last few years, Philippine troops have refused to fire on citizens who massed in opposition to the Marcos regime; in addition, there have been reports of discontent among Soviet troops in Afghanistan; and Israeli Army reservists, "the Yesh G'vul," (meaning "there is a Limit-Border") have made it known they will not submit to a call to fight in Israeli occupied territories (Catholic Peace Fellowship, 1988). These are bold actions of personal witness and solidarity, encouraging signs in a world continually threatened by mass terror and organized mass violence. And this is just the beginning; in the quest for liberation from war, it is a very good start.

And yet, there is a long way to go. Many nations still do not recognize conscientious objection to war; in most, neither civilians nor members of the military can apply. Indeed, according to a United Nations study on conscription, only 35% of those nations reporting provide for conscientious objection (United Nations, 1982). This must be changed. The right to refuse to kill another human being, or to serve in an organization whose main purpose is to do so, must be recognized as a basic human right. More, the hoary notion that conscientious objection can only truly be expressed, and be legally recognized, solely when it stems from spiritual beliefs, must be abandoned. This has long been an age of science, a secular age; and yet, governments apply medieval standards in dealing with the thinking of their citizens on issues of war and peace. To deny a claim of conscientious objection because it is grounded in a political belief, or grows from heartfelt philosophical or sociological perspectives, runs against the grain of knowledge and modern day thought.

This struggle will continue. Those antiwar veterans, like myself, who have become lifers in the peace movement will not let it end. We have seen the solutions the politicians and their military servants have proposed, and we know there is a better way.

We know the average American citizen comes to the military with a frame of reference and a sense of morality and justice that does not jibe with the military message. We are in solidarity with those servicemen and women who transcend socialization and stand up to their leaders, when they know those leaders are wrong; for, we know that by doing so they serve their country and the people of the world well.

We will counsel those who refuse to participate, those who refuse to be pawns in the gross historical scripts written by politicians, because we know these resisters are on the cutting edge of history. We will teach the children about the sheer force of conscience and will, because we know those powers transcend politics and military might.

We know we can have a nation that is not a permanent warfare state, and that we can have a world at peace. We know we can make our own way in the world, a world that for too long has wallowed in a deeply rooted spiritual crisis centered on economic exploitation and military power.

We know, and during the Vietnam era the American peo-

Afterword

ple demonstrated, that we can bring a sense of justice, integrity and morality to what the government does in our name. We know how to fight, and we know how to win. That is the legacy of the Vietnam era in-service conscientious objector and other antiwar veterans. And this is the promise: we will continue to work hard to assure that there will be no more Vietnams. None, ever again.

REFERENCES

Baskir, L., & Strauss, W. (1978). *Chance and Circumstance: The draft, the war and the Vietnam generation.* New York: Alfred A. Knopf.

Catholic Peace Fellowship Bulletin. (Spring, 1988). Ofenloch, B. (Ed.) (Available from the Catholic Peace Fellowship, 339 Lafayette Street, New York, NY 10012).

Committee on Veterans' Affairs, U. S. Senate. (1980). *Myths and realities: A study of attitudes toward Vietnam era veterans.* Washington, DC: U. S. Government Printing Office.

Cortright, D. (1975). *Soldiers in revolt.* New York: Anchor Press.

Friedman, L. (1982). Conscription and the Constitution: The original understanding. In M. Anderson (Ed.), *The military draft: Selected readings on conscription.* (pp. 231–296). Stanford, CA: Hoover Institution Press, Stanford University.

Lifton, R. J. (1973). *Home from the war, Vietnam veterans: Neither victims nor executioners.* New York: Basic Books.

MacPherson, M. (1985). *Long time passing: Vietnam and the haunted generation.* New York: New American Library.

Rohr, J. (1971). *Prophets without honor: Public policy and the selective conscientious objector.* New York: Abingdon Press.

References

Stapp, A. (1970). *Up against the brass.* New York: Simon and Schuster.

Tatum, A., & Tuchinsky, J. (1969). *Guide to the draft.* Boston: Beacon Press.

United Nations Commission on Human Rights. Subcommittee on Prevention of Discrimination and Protection of Minorities. Thirty Fifth Session. (June 15, 1982). *Preliminary report: The question of conscientious objection to military service.* Mr. Eide & Mr. Mubanga-Chipoya. (pp. 1–10, 12–17). New York: United Nations.

GLOSSARY

1–A–0: a conscientious objector certified by the Selective Service System or the military to perform noncombatant military service.

1–0: a conscientious objector assigned alternative civilian service by the Selective Service System; a person to be discharged from the military for reasons of conscientious objection.

201 file: the military personnel file containing every action taken by or for the individual.

Agent Orange: a toxic defoliant used extensively in Vietnam.

AIT: Advanced Infantry Training.

Article 15: part of the Uniform Code of Military Justice allowing commanders to impose discipline without trial by court-martial.

ARVN: Army of the Republic of Vietnam.

AWOL: unauthorized absence without leave for less than 30 days.

B–40: small rocket-type ordinance used by the North Vietnamese and the Viet Cong.

beans and motherfuckers: C-rations composed of lima beans and ham; not a favorite among the soldiers.

C–4: plastic explosive.

Glossary

Charlie: nickname for the Viet Cong.

CID: Criminal Investigation Division in the Army.

CO: for the purposes of this book, conscientious objection, or a conscientious objector; in the traditional military context it is often used to refer to a Commanding Officer.

connex: a corrugated metal crate.

company: an infantry unit of about 100 men organized into three or more platoons.

DD: Department of Defense.

desertion: AWOL for more than 30 days.

DI: a drill instructor in basic training.

dink: a derogatory term for the Vietnamese people.

dress greens: dress uniform usually worn off-base.

dust off: evacuation by helicopter.

fire fight: an armed encounter with Viet Cong or North Vietnamese forces.

flack jacket: heavy vest-type garment used for protection from shrapnel.

FNG: abbreviation for "Fucking New Guy," a recent arrival in-country.

fragging: actions taken to harass, injure or kill an officer or noncommissioned officer of one's own troops.

grunt: an infantry soldier.

hooch: a small hut.

hump: to be on a patrol in battle gear.

in-country: being in Vietnam.

immersion foot: cracking and bleeding feet caused by continued exposure to water.

JAG: Judge Advocate General, or a lawyer from that unit.

Glossary

KP: kitchen police, usually a 12–14 hour assignment in the mess hall.

lifer: a career officer or noncommissioned officer.

LZ: a landing zone, usually for helicopters to deliver troops, supplies or to evacuate the wounded or ill.

Long Binh Jail: an infamous military stockade in Vietnam.

M–16: the lightweight combat assault rifle used in Vietnam.

M–60: a portable machine gun.

mama san: an older Vietnamese woman.

medevac: helicopters used in medical evacuations of troops from the field.

MOS: a military occupational speciality such as infantryman or medic.

NCO: noncommissioned officers, usually sergeants, E–5 and above.

NVA: North Vietnamese Army.

OCS: Officer Candidate School.

papa san: an older Vietnamese man.

platoon: an infantry unit of about thirty men.

point man: the forward position in a column of troops.

Post Traumatic Stress Disorder: emotional reexperience of a psychologically traumatic event outside the range of usual experience. PTSD is often characterized by a numbing of responsiveness to, or reduced involvement with, the external world.

Pledge of Resistance: a statement signed by tens of thousands of American citizens pledging to actively resist U.S. military intervention in Central America.

punji sticks: sharpened sticks or poles, often coated with human waste, concealed on the ground or in traps.

Glossary

RA: regular army, someone who enlisted as opposed to being drafted.

R&R: "rest and relaxation" a short leave given approximately halfway through a one-year tour of Vietnam.

sapper: a Viet Cong or NVA soldier, usually armed with explosives, who attempted to infiltrate secured areas.

shake and bake: a derogatory term used for inexperienced officers and noncommissioned officers who were fresh out of leadership training schools.

strack: precision in following military rules and decorum, "a strack troop."

TDY: temporary duty or assignment.

the world: slang for the United States.

to the max: for maximum effect; doing things as best as one possibly can.

tracks: Armored Personnel Carriers.

VC: the Viet Cong, members of the South Vietnamese communist guerilla forces.

APPENDIX

PEACE GROUPS-INFORMATION ON CONSCIENTIOUS OBJECTION.

American Friends Service Committee
1501 Cherry Street,
Philadelphia, PA 19102

Catholic Peace Fellowship
339 Lafayette Street,
New York, NY 10012

Central Committee for
Conscientious Objectors (CCCO)
2208 South Street,
Philadelphia, PA 19146

CCCO-Western Region
PO Box 42249,
San Francisco, CA 94142

Committee Against Registration
and the Draft (CARD)
201 Massachusetts Ave., NE
Washington, DC 20001

Fellowship of Reconciliation
Box 271,
Nyack, NY 10960

National Campaign for
a Peace Tax Fund
2121 Decatur Place, NW
Washington, DC 20008

National Interreligious Service
Board for Conscientious Objectors
800 Eighteenth St. NW Suite 600
Washington, DC 20006–3599

Midwest Committee on
Military Counseling
343 So. Dearborn, Room 1113,
Chicago, IL 60604

Mobilization for Survival
853 Broadway, Room 416,
New York, NY 10003

Pax Christi USA
348 East 10 Street
Erie, PA 16503

War Resisters League
339 Lafayette Street
New York, NY 10012

Women's International League
for Peace & Freedom
1213 Race Street
Philadelphia, PA 19107

VETERANS ORGANIZATIONS.

Citizen Soldier
175 Fifth Avenue
New York, NY 10010

Vietnam Veterans of America
2001 S St. NW Suite 700
Washington, DC 20009

Vietnam Veterans Against the War
PO Box 408594
Chicago, Il 60640

Veterans for Peace
PO Box 3881
Portland, ME 04104

APPENDIX

SELECTED QUESTIONS FROM THE SELECTIVE SER-VICE SYSTEM'S SPECIAL FORM FOR CONSCIENTIOUS OBJECTORS, SSS Form 150, revised February 10, 1966.

RELIGIOUS TRAINING AND BELIEF.

1. Do you believe in a Supreme Being? Yes No.

2. Describe the nature of your belief which is the basis of your claim . . . and state whether or not your belief in a Supreme Being involves duties which to you are superior to those arising from any human relation.

3. Explain how, when, and from whom or from what source you received the training and acquired the belief which is the basis of your claim.

4. Give the name and present address of the individual upon whom you rely most for religious guidance.

5. Under what circumstances, if any do you believe in the use of force?

6. Describe the actions and behavior in your life which in your opinion most conspicuously demonstrate the consistency and depth of your religious convictions.

7. Have you ever given public expression, written or oral, to the views herein expressed as the basis for your claim? If so, specify when and where.

Appendix

PARTICIPATION IN ORGANIZATIONS

1. Have you ever been a member of any military organization or establishment? If so, state the name and address of same and give reasons why you became a member.

2. Are you a member of a religious sect or organization? Yes No.

2a. State the name of the sect, and the name and location of its governing body or head if known to you.

2b. When, where and how did you become a member of said sect or organization?

2c. State the name and location of the church, congregation or meeting where you customarily attend.

2d. Give the name, title and present address of the pastor or leader of such church, congregation, or meeting.

2e. Describe carefully the creed or official statements of said religious sector organization in relation to participation in war.

3. Describe your relationships with and activities in all organizations with which you are or have been affiliated, other than military, political or labor organizations.

ABOUT THE AUTHOR

* * * *

Gerald R. Gioglio was discharged from the Army in 1969 for reasons of conscientious objection. Upon discharge he trained as a draft counselor and became actively involved in the peace movement. He is a member of Vietnam Veterans of America and Veterans for Peace. Mr. Gioglio is a graduate of Livingston College, and holds a Masters degree from the Graduate School of Arts and Sciences at Rutgers University. He has also done considerable postgraduate study in sociology.

Mr. Gioglio works as a researcher for the State of New Jersey. He has conducted several studies and has published many papers on a variety of issues that include: homelessness, adult protective services and child welfare. Mr. Gioglio is also an Adjunct Assistant Professor of sociology at Rider College and an Adjunct Instructor of sociology at Trenton State College.

* * * *

The Broken Rifle Press publishes on issues of war, peace, aggression and nonviolence. Future volumes will consider military training and war from the perspective of those whose voices are rarely heard—noncombatants, resisters and the families of military personnel.

Additional copies of *Days of Decision* can be obtained from:

THE BROKEN RIFLE PRESS, PO BOX 749, Trenton, NJ 08607. $14.95, softcover. $1.50 shipping and handling. NJ residents add $.90 tax.

* * * *

QUANTITY PURCHASES.

Nonprofit groups, churches, clubs and other organizations can qualify for special discounts when ordering quantities of this title. For more information contact THE BROKEN RIFLE PRESS.

2238

338